Military Spouses
with Graduate Degrees

Military Spouses with Graduate Degrees

Interdisciplinary Approaches to Thriving amidst Uncertainty

Edited by
Leandra Hinojosa Hernández
and Jennifer Belding

LEXINGTON BOOKS
Lanham • Boulder • New York • London

Published by Lexington Books
An imprint of The Rowman & Littlefield Publishing Group, Inc.
4501 Forbes Boulevard, Suite 200, Lanham, Maryland 20706
www.rowman.com

6 Tinworth Street, London SE11 5AL

Copyright © 2019 by The Rowman & Littlefield Publishing Group, Inc.

All rights reserved. No part of this book may be reproduced in any form or by any electronic or mechanical means, including information storage and retrieval systems, without written permission from the publisher, except by a reviewer who may quote passages in a review.

British Library Cataloguing in Publication Information Available

Library of Congress Cataloging-in-Publication Data

Names: Hernández, Leandra Hinojosa, editor. | Belding, Jennifer, editor.
Title: Military spouses with graduate degrees : interdisciplinary approaches to thriving amidst uncertainty / edited by Leandra Hinojosa Hernández and Jennifer Belding.
Description: Lanham, MD : Lexington Books, [2019] | Includes bibliographical references and index.
Identifiers: LCCN 2018054931 (print) | LCCN 2018056256 (ebook) | ISBN 9781498582094 (Electronic) | ISBN 9781498582087 (cloth : alk. paper)
Subjects: LCSH: Military spouses—United States—Education. | Military spouses—United States—Employment. | Graduate students—Family relationships—United States. | Graduate students—Employment—United States.
Classification: LCC UB403 (ebook) | LCC UB403 .M558 2019 (print) | DDC 355.1/2—dc23
LC record available at https://lccn.loc.gov/2018054931

∞™ The paper used in this publication meets the minimum requirements of American National Standard for Information Sciences—Permanence of Paper for Printed Library Materials, ANSI/NISO Z39.48-1992.

Printed in the United States of America

This book is dedicated to the military spouses holding down the fort, particularly those engaged in various educational and career pursuits.

Contents

Acknowledgments	ix
Introduction: Military Spouses with Advanced Degrees: Current Findings and Pathways Moving Forward *Leandra Hinojosa Hernández and Jennifer N. Belding*	1

PART I: A CHRONOLOGICAL APPROACH TO ACADEMIC AND MILITARY IDENTITIES

1	Navigating Academic and Military Life: A Personal Journey *Marcia M. Bouchard*	15
2	Military Spouse Strategies for Navigating Academic and Personal Life: A Collaborative Autoethnographic Review of Post Graduate Pursuits *Alissa E. Harrison, Annette Maldonado, Beth van Kan, and Henri Cooper*	37
3	Cultural Collision: A Review of Literature *Amy May and Victoria McDermott*	59
4	Exploring Identity, Professionalism, and Patriotism within a Multicultural Military Relationship: Intimacy Overseas *Precious Yamaguchi*	87

PART II: ACADEMIC, PROFESSIONAL, AND MILITARY CHALLENGES

5	Becoming Whole: Balancing Dual Identities as a Graduate Student Marine Wife *Elise Dixon*	109

6	Military Spouses' Uncertainty Management: Navigating Academic Goals and Military Needs *Michael Sollitto and Catherine Cole*	125
7	Military Spouses, Advanced Degrees, and the Myth of Keeping Busy *Abby E. Murray*	143
8	Counsel for the Military Spouse: Law School, the Bar Exam, and Beyond *Katherine Lee Goyette*	163

PART III: STRATEGIES FOR ENHANCING ACADEMIC, MILITARY, AND PROFESSIONAL LIFE

9	Joining the Ranks: Considering Military Spouse Life as a Lesbian Graduate Student *Karen Tannenbaum*	179
10	Overcoming Obstacles: A Practical Guide to Meaningful Employment as a Military Spouse *Georgia K. Jones and Lindsey Lee*	197
11	Military Spouses with Advanced Degrees: A Unique Subpopulation to Study for the Science of Motivation and Goal Pursuit *Jennifer N. Belding*	217
12	"We Get It Done Because We Have To": Military Spouses with Advanced Degrees, Career and Educational Experiences, and Grit amongst Uncertainty *Leandra Hinojosa Hernández*	239

Conclusion: Advice from the Trenches 259
Jennifer N. Belding and Leandra Hinojosa Hernández

Index 269

About the Editors 273

About the Contributors 275

Acknowledgments

As the age-old saying goes, it takes a village to raise a child. It also takes a village to write a book.

First, we would like to thank our contributors and research participants who graciously shared their experiences with us and poured their hearts and souls into this project. This book would not have been possible without you. We learned immensely from you all and feel honored that you entrusted us with your life stories and all that you have learned from your time as military spouses. Thank you for contributing to and uplifting the military spouse community, who will benefit immensely from your advice and encouragement.

JENN

I would like to take a moment to acknowledge and thank those who have served as my advisors in many capacities, including my family, graduate school mentors, and the wonderful military spouses who have guided me so far. Special thanks go to my husband, Chris, for being the reason I have had experiences that led directly to editing this book, and my father, Bill, for teaching me from a young age to always respect the service and sacrifices of our Armed Forces.

LEANDRA

I would like to thank my family members—Froilan, Ernestine, Alexandria, Pedro, Laura, and Jorge—for their ever-constant support of my research, academic interests, and educational and career goals. I am thankful that my parents and extended family members instilled in me the respect of those who serve our country, starting with my grandfathers, uncles, cousins, and now Pedro, my husband. Even through the tied migration challenges and experiences of being a military spouse, I wouldn't change it for the world. Pedro, it has been a wonderful adventure, and I am excited for the future!

Introduction

Military Spouses with Advanced Degrees: Current Findings and Pathways Moving Forward

Leandra Hinojosa Hernández and Jennifer N. Belding

Military families are an integral part of a country's national defense, workforce, and community makeup. As the Blue Star Families' annual Military Family Lifestyle Survey (2016) illustrates, military families "are central to the health and capability of the All-Volunteer Force and are good neighbors actively engaged in making their civilian communities great places to live" (p. 6). As a unique cultural sub-population with less than 1% of the U.S. population currently serving in our active-duty military (Blue Star Families, 2016), military families experience lifestyle and employment contexts that are different from the larger civilian population, including frequent relocation, deployments, and family separation. Moreover, given unique military employment experiences that differ from civilian employment, there is still a prevailing perception "that civilian understanding is especially low regarding the challenges and sacrifice associated with service" (Blue Star Families, 2016, p. 20). As such, this volume seeks to interrogate, unravel, and explore one aspect of the military lifestyle and culture: military spouses with advanced degrees. In this introduction, we will provide information about the current composition of American military families and discuss how a military spouse employment and education perspective can help bridge the civilian-military knowledge gap. We hope that this volume will assist not only scholars and students interested in learning more about military families, but also military organizations, professionals, and policymakers working directly with military families and advocating directly for military families at the policy level.

WHY STUDY MILITARY FAMILIES?

As of late 2018, there were 2.1 million military personnel in the U.S. military with nearly 2.8 million dependents (Defense Manpower Data Center, 2018). In 2015, 54.3% of active-duty service members were married (DoD, 2015). Of this population, 41.3% were married with no children, 34.9% are married with children, and 41.2% of all service members have children. Moreover, there were 641,639 spouses of active-duty service members and 374,621 spouses of service members in the reserves and National Guard. Age-wise, military spouses are equally distributed across age ranges (about 14–24% across 5 categories), and active-duty military families tend to marry and have children younger than their civilian counterparts (Clever & Segal, 2013).

Military families encounter and respond to many of the same issues as civilian families, with added challenges from military-specific experiences (Drummet, Coleman, & Cable, 2003). Scholars have emphasized the need to study the health and well-being of military families, with a particular emphasis on ensuring that these studies are updated to reflect the current nature of war and the differences in our Armed Forces over time (e.g., moving to an all volunteer force; see Ross, 2014). There is also an increasing interest in studying the importance of military families among the Military Health System as evidenced by the fact that there was a symposium with 10 speakers at the first Military Families session at the Military Health System Research Symposium.

Military service may affect family members in a number of ways because of unique stressors that families experience, including frequent relocations, frequent and prolonged separations, and challenges with employment, among other stressors. These stressors impact service members' and spouses' health and well-being in a myriad of ways. Studying the experiences of military spouses is important because, as Green, Nurius, and Lester (2013) note, military spouses are the "keystone" of the military family: "the central family member upon which the family and its well-being depend; the supporting element that locks the whole together" (p. 754). As a result, military spouses are critical to family wellness during a service member's deployment or separation and are an important buffer to the negative effects of military service and deployment on family members (Byng-Hall, 1995; Chandra et al., 2010; Flake, Davis, Johnson & Middleton, 2009; Green et al., 2013; Lester et al., 2010; Riggs & Riggs, 2011). Military service, particularly deployment and prolonged separations, is stressful for military spouses and families (e.g., Padden, Connors, & Agazio, 2011). Unsurprisingly, military spouses experience a number of stressors, which can increase psychological stress (Green, Nurius, & Lester, 2013), such as relocation, deployment, single parenting amidst relocation, juggling worklife balance, and more.

These stressors can lead to negative health outcomes (e.g., Padden & Posey, 2013). In a study of 346 Army spouses, researchers found that several elements of military service (e.g., physical separation from one's spouse, living overseas, and frequent relocations) were negatively associated with physical and psychological well-being (Burrell, Adams, Durand, & Castro, 2006). Military families respond to stressors differently, which can be complicated by poor mental health (e.g., PTSD; Marek & D'Aniello, 2014) and lack of mental health service. Thus, it is important to study military cultures, military families, and the effect of service on military spouses to more thoroughly understand the nuances of military life and also design programs to enhance military life, family mental health, and family educational and career experiences (Hall, 2011; Meyer, 2015).

Moreover, stressors associated with the military have important implications for social relationships. On the one hand, long separations within military families can hinder relationship satisfaction (Drummet et al., 2003). Military spouses may be less likely to share stressors during deployment, particularly if there is a threat of physical danger to the service member (Joseph & Afifi, 2010). On the other hand, when active-duty families are satisfied with the service member's work hours, they are likely to be more satisfied with a military career and perceive their work/family fit is well-balanced, resulting in less marital tension (Pittman, 1994). From a community social support perspective, people, including both active-duty service members and spouses, draw on and utilize connections within their community as sources of support, which can promote their well-being. For instance, those in the military community can draw on the military community within which they live and work, as well as the civilian community (O'Neal, Mancini, & De Graff, 2016). As a result, military spouses with advanced degrees may be particularly susceptible to challenges because they may feel even less connected to their military communities, though they could find solace and support in academic or employment communities. Overall, having a support system as a military spouse is helpful (Drummett et al., 2003; Eubanks, 2013; Huebner, Mancini, Bowen, & Orthner, 2009; Palmer, 2008; Skomorovsky, 2014). Social support systems, both formal and informal, can help minimize stressors and strains (Orthner & Rose, 2009), whereas spouses with limited support are more likely to struggle with psychological distress in isolation (Green, Nurius, & Lester, 2013).

Military Spouse Employment

The challenges associated with being a military spouse, particularly one who is employed, have received much attention and discussion (e.g., Castaneda & Harrell, 2008; Harrell, Lim, Castaneda, & Golinelli, 2004; Lim, Golinelli, &

Cho, 2007), due to factors including tied migration, relocation, and indefinite time with an employer or organization. As such, there are several different reasons why employers may be hesitant to hire military spouses, such as the perception of an upcoming move (see Drummet et al., 2003).

Tied migration, one factor that strongly shapes military spouse career experiences, occurs when one person follows another (e.g., a spouse) from one location to another, often for occupational or employment reasons. It implies that while one spouse may incur employment, career, and financial gains, the other spouse might incur job losses, underemployment, or unemployment as a result of the relocation, as Bouchard describes in Chapter 1. From a tied migration perspective, both men and women show negative effects of being a tied migrant on employment as a function of military spouse status (Hisnanick & Little, 2015). Military spouses, regardless of gender, are less likely to be employed as a result of tied migration. Specifically, trailing military spouses (regardless of gender) were significantly less likely to be employed and, when employed, worked on average 4–5 hours less per week than non-trailing spouses (Cooke & Speirs, 2005).

Although there are plenty of reasons to understand why military service has changed over the past 30 years, results from a 1985 study of employment among Army spouses showed similar findings to what we might expect today: military service can challenge family member labor force participation. However, more educated spouses were significantly more likely to participate in the labor force (Schwartz, Wood, & Griffith, 1991). As Whitby and Compton (2018) show, "Military wives are about half as likely to be in the labor force compared to non military wives . . . we show that the relationship between military wife status and LFP [labor force participation] is greater for those with higher education" (p. 515). These findings persist even after controlling for migration, and things seem to be improving over time for military spouses with advanced degrees.

However, this participation in the labor force is still met with wage loss and decline. As Whitby and Compton (2018) illustrate, "Between 1990 and 2010, the relative wages of military wives to non-military wives fell from 67 to 58%. Moreover, despite a slight increase in the labor force participation rate of prime aged women in the U.S. over this time period, the labor force participation rate of military wives fell steadily from 63 to 57%" (p. 514). Moreover, job mismatch is a concern as well. As Clever and Segal (2013) note, "While fewer than 10 percent of civilian married women work in a job that is mismatched with their education level, nearly 40 percent of military wives do so" (p. 28).

These findings are significant for the American labor force and more particularly for the Department of Defense (DoD), considering that spouses who rely solely on their active-duty spouses are less satisfied on average than their employed counterparts, particularly at lower ranks. In general, working is associated with positive mental health (for a review, see Clever & Segal, 2013). In a study of 5,505 Army Officers, researchers found that officers whose spouses were more supportive of their careers were significantly less likely to leave service four years later and that this effect was due in part to work interfering with family and job satisfaction. As a result, a spouse's satisfaction with the military lifestyle is important for retention (Huffman, Casper, & Payne, 2014). Thus, understanding military spouses' experiences in career contexts can help improve both military spouse satisfaction and also service member retention.

Military Spouses with Advanced Degrees and Employment

Although there is a large body of research that explores military spouse career barriers and experiences more generally, there is a paucity of research that explores the experiences of military spouses with advanced degrees. According to the 2012 Military Spouse Employment Report, 32% of military spouses have a master's degree or above (cited in Woodworth, 2015). Research from interviews with over 1,100 military spouses revealed that the majority of military spouses believe that military service negatively affected their employment; this effect is more prevalent among more senior spouses (Castaneda & Harrell, 2008). Furthermore, "the higher the spouse's level of education, the more likely she was to perceive a negative impact of moving" (Castaneda & Harrell, 2008, p. 395). Three-quarters of spouses with graduate degrees reported negative effects of moving on their career, and more educated spouses were less likely to mention a service member's absence as harmful to their career (Castaneda & Harrell, 2008). Spouses with college and graduate degrees were more likely to list stigma toward military spouse employment as a negative factor (Castaneda & Harrell, 2008). In spite of prevailing perceptions that military families are highly compensated, presuming a spouse's reduced need to work, many military spouses choose to work to be able to meet financial obligations (Castaneda & Harrell, 2008). Military spouses with advanced degrees were significantly less likely to list avoiding boredom and significantly more likely to list personal fulfillment as a reason for working than their college and high school educated comparisons. There were no differences in motivation to work to provide for financial obligations (Castaneda & Harrell, 2008).

Although there are many programs to support military spouse employment, as of the early 2010s, scientific assessment of the DoD's programs to improve military spouse employment were subpar (United States Government Accountability Office, 2012). Relatively little research focuses on the needs of the unique subpopulation of military spouses with advanced degrees. Thus, there is a need for continued research on the experiences of this important group of military spouses. While there is a significant amount of research in the communication discipline, for example, on military family communication, the relationship between the media and the military, and rhetoric surrounding the military (Knoblock, Theiss, & Wehrman, 2015; Maguire, 2015; Maguire, Heineman-LaFave, & Sahlstein, 2013; Maguire & Wilson, 2013; Parcell & Maguire, 2014; Parcell & Webb, 2015; Sahlstein, Maguire, & Timmerman, 2009), there is a dearth of research on military spouses with advanced degrees, which negatively impacts programs designed to help military families more generally and military spouses more specifically.

The Importance of a Multidisciplinary Perspective on Military Spouses with Advanced Degrees

This book utilizes an interdisciplinary perspective to explore the interpersonal, career, and educational experiences of military spouses with advanced degrees. An interdisciplinary perspective provides the richness of different theoretical and methodological approaches in tandem with the experiences and analyses of spouses from different branches. Moreover, a multidisciplinary perspective is important for several reasons. First, military service can affect education. Active-duty service members are less likely to be educated than their civilian counterparts, even after they separate from service (Teachman, 2007). Military spouses experience unique stressors that can influence their learning in the college classroom, though certain policy changes have been recommended to address these issues (e.g., Gleiman & Swearengen, 2012). In a survey of U.S. college students, military spouses and civilian spouses were equally likely to report depression and anxiety symptoms, but military spouses reported significantly higher perceptions of social support and marital discord (Asbury & Martin, 2012).

However, little research has examined how military service affects family members' abilities to pursue education beyond an undergraduate degree. Thus, a multidisciplinary approach is necessary because these issues—interpersonal issues, support issues, educational struggles, and career struggles—are inherently complex. Who better to speak on these issues than military spouses with advanced degrees? Their rigorous education and astute realizations surrounding military life are essential. Thus, to that end, the military spouse educators, academics, and researchers featured in this volume utilized their academic backgrounds to investigate and understand the elements critical to being a successful military spouse with an advanced degree in both educational and degree contexts.

Organization of the Book

This book is meant to provide a chronological approach of sorts that highlights the unique challenges military spouses with advanced degrees face when navigating educational and career pursuits in contexts where goals, identities, and expectations might not always line up with those of the military. However, these chapters highlight the resilience of military spouses in adapting to their unique situations and the strategies that can be utilized in permanent changes of station, deployment, relocation, and career contexts. As such, the book begins with a chronological approach to military, academic, and career identities and progresses with an exploration of struggles faced and strategies that can be utilized in academic, non-academic, and military contexts to help military spouses with advanced degrees thrive amidst uncertainty. One of the utmost strengths of the volume is that all chapters are written by military spouses, which adds a valuable experiential component to the research presented.

The first section of the book, chronological approaches to military, academic, and career identities, begins with Bouchard's chapter on tied migration for military spouses. As one of the most senior military spouse contributors, her chapter takes the reader on her life journey as a military spouse and illustrates how tied migration—being tied to a service member's relocation and duty stations—impacted her educational and career experiences and decision-making processes. Tied migration is one of the primary themes that impacts all of the contributors' chapters and experiences, and as such, Bouchard's chapter provides an effective platform that weaves the subsequent chapters' themes and topics together. In Chapter 2, Harrison, Maldonado, Van Kan and Cooper similarly explore strategies to assist with navigating personal and academic life, and they use a collaborative autoethnographic method to analyze their graduate career pursuits in tandem. In doing so, they explore how motivations and challenges based on achievement motivation factors could provide a platform to identify strategies for successfully achieving a graduate degree. Chapter 3 continues with the theme of military experiences in academia by analyzing how the potential clash of military cultures and academic cultures impact marital communication and relational outcomes. May and McDermott trace the cultural contours of academia and the military with the military spouse located in the center and ultimately conclude that military spouses with advanced degrees must precariously toe the line of both cultures constantly in order to function in both systems. In Chapter 4, Yamaguchi illustrates some of the cross-cultural communication processes and outcomes between herself and her spouse that are introduced in Chapter 3. Her narrative explores her experiences as a Japanese American Communication Studies professor with her husband, a Mexican American Staff Sergeant in the U.S.

Marines, and how her identity and academic interests became critically challenged upon the development of her relationship with her spouse. She concludes that an analysis of intercultural narratives—military cultures, historical cultures, and racial/ethnic cultures—can help illustrate our diverse roles and contributions to our country and also illuminate the unique cross-cultural communication challenges that interracial/interethnic military couples face.

With tied migration, academic pursuit motivations, and cross-cultural communication concepts as the platform, Part II of the book highlights and analyzes some of the military, academic, and professional challenges that military spouses with advanced degrees face while on academic and career paths. In Chapter 5, Dixon details and analyzes several of the gendered challenges faced by academic spouses with advanced degrees in certain military contexts. Her autoethnography explores how her experience as a military wife has been challenged by her role as a graduate student and describes how her perceptions of the military's heteronormative practices and construction and treatment of spouses have been changed by her time as a military spouse. Dixon's autoethnography illustrates how academic life and military life are more complementary than one might think and have much to offer one another. In Chapter 6, Sollitto and Cole also explore some of the uncertainties military spouses face while pursuing academic degrees. Using uncertainty management theory, they analyze how uncertainty occurs for military spouses, how they manage it, and the result of their uncertainty management in academic contexts. They conclude by providing practical strategies that can be utilized by military spouses and advisors, instructors, and administrators to make sense of their academic journeys. Continuing with the theme of the intersection of academic experiences and military life, in Chapter 7 Murray introduces the myth of keeping busy, the myth that military spouses' work is tangential to military life, that spouses are busy only when spouses are away, and that spouses would put academic and career work to the side when service members return from deployments and missions. Blending poetry and autoethnography, Murray analyzes some of the challenges she faced while navigating her academic life and military life and, reaching similar conclusions as Dixon, details how military life and academic life are intertwined in a mutually informative manner. In Chapter 8, Goyette also discusses the uncertainty and struggles associated with career and military life, but from a legal perspective. As a military spouse attorney, her chapter is an autoethnographic exploration of her experiences in the legal field, some of the regulations military spouse attorneys face while pursuing meaningful employment amidst relocation, and other issues military spouse attorneys currently face. She concludes by presenting recommendations for military spouses who are seeking to maintain their careers through multiple military relocations.

In Part III, the final section of the book is comprised of chapters that provide strategies for enhancing academic, military, and professional life. The section begins with Chapter 9, Tannenbaum's autoethnographic analysis of her experience as a queer military partner pursuing an advanced degree. She systematically explores the intersecting identities of military partner, gay woman, and PhD student, and she utilizes social psychological theories related to minority stress, love, and intersectionality to explore the context of romantic military relationships. She concludes her chapter by providing strategies to address three themes related to intersecting identities: considerations for military partners, considerations for lesbian military partners, and considerations for military partners with advanced degrees or who are in the process of pursuing advanced degrees. In Chapter 10, Jones & Lee similarly provide an overview of some of the challenges faced by military spouses in career contexts and provide strategies on how to overcome career barriers and gain meaningful employment while serving as a military spouse. Their chapter provides tangible tips and tangible resources that all military spouses can use in both academic and non-academic contexts. In Chapter 11, Belding reviews the social psychological science of motivation and goal pursuit that is applicable to military spouses with advanced degrees and discusses how unique elements of our service to our service member and our country may force us to overcome obstructions along this path. In other words, she considers the factors, such as grit, that help military spouses thrive in academic contexts, and she concludes with her personal recommendations based on scientific literature and empirical research related to goal pursuit and her experiences as a military spouse to assist other military spouses pursuing advanced degrees and careers. In Chapter 12, Hernández weaves the book's main themes together—military life and identity, academic motivations and pursuits, and career barriers and pursuits—by analyzing how 85 military spouses make sense of military, academia, and career life. Her chapter, similar to preceding chapters, highlights the joys and challenges associated with serving as a military spouse with an advanced degree, and it also illustrates the grit, perseverance, and resilience that military spouses embody when navigating academic and career contexts. The volume concludes with a revisiting of the book's main themes and advice from the trenches, where several of the volume's authors contribute their perceptions of military spouse life and advice for current and future military spouses. Belding and Hernández created a brief survey for military spouses about their experiences as military spouses with advanced degrees, and the conclusion highlights recommendations for service members (i.e., our spouses), military leaders and support specialists, faculty and staff at higher education institutions, and policy makers. If you're a military spouse pursuing meaningful employment, a military spouse in graduate school, a military spouse considering graduate school, or considering becoming a military spouse, we hope that this book gives you courage, faith, and reassurance that you can be successful in this life and that you are not alone.

REFERENCES

Asbury, E. T., & Martin, D. (2012). Military deployment and the spouse left behind. *The Family Journal, 20*(1), 45–50.

Blue Star Families (2016). Military Family Lifestyle Survey. Retrieved from https://bluestarfam.org/wp-content/uploads/2017/03/ComprehensiveReport-33.pdf.

Burrell, L. M., Adams, G. A., Durand, D. B., & Castro, C. A. (2006). The impact of military lifestyle demands on well-being, Army, and family outcomes. *Armed Forces & Society, 33*(1), 43–58.

Byng-Hall, J. (1995). Creating a secure family base: Some implications of attachment theory for family therapy. *Family Process, 34*(1), 45–58.

Castaneda, L. W., & Harrell, M. C. (2008). Military spouse employment: A grounded theory approach to experiences and perceptions. *Armed Forces & Society, 34*(3), 389–412.

Chandra, A., Lara-Cinisomo, S., Jaycox, L. H., Tanielian, T., Burns, R. M., Ruder, T., & Han, B. (2010). Children on the homefront: The experience of children from military families. *Pediatrics, 125*(1), 16–25.

Clever, M., & Segal, D. R. (2013). The demographics of military children and families. *The Future of Children*, 13–39.

Cooke, T. J., & Speirs, K. (2005). Migration and employment among the civilian spouses of military personnel. *Social Science Quarterly, 86*(2), 343–355.

Defense Manpower Data Center (2018). DoD personnel, workforce reports & publications. https://www.dmdc.osd.mil/appj/dwp/dwp_reports.jsp.

Department of Defense (DoD) (2015). 2015 demographics: Profile of the military community (Special Report).

Drummet, A. R., Coleman, M., & Cable, S. (2003). Military families under stress: Implications for family life education. *Family Relations, 52*(3), 279–287.

Eubanks, T. (2013). Life as a military spouse. *Urologic Nursing, 33*(2), 97–99.

Flake, E. M., Davis, B. E., Johnson, P. L., & Middleton, L. S. (2009). The psychosocial effects of deployment on military children. *Journal of Developmental & Behavioral Pediatrics, 30*(4), 271–278.

Gleiman, A., & Swearengen, S. (2012). Understanding the military spouse learner using theory and personal narratives. *New Directions for Adult and Continuing Education, 2012*(136), 77–88.

Green, S., Nurius, P. S., & Lester, P. (2013). Spouse psychological well-being: A keystone to military family health. *Journal of Human Behavior in the Social Environment, 23*(6), 753–768.

Hall, L. K. (2011). The importance of understanding military culture. *Social Work in Health Care, 50*(1), 4–18.

Harrell, M. C., Lim, N., Castaneda, L. W., & Golinelli, D. (2004). *Working Around the Military: Challenges to Military Spouse Employment and Education.* Santa Monica, CA: Rand National Defense Research Institute.

Hisnanick, J. J., & Little, R. D. (2015). Honey I love you, but . . . Investigating the causes of the earnings penalty of being a tied-migrant military spouse. *Armed Forces & Society, 41*(3), 413–439.

Huebner, A. J., Mancini, J. A., Bowen, G. L., & Orthner, D. K. (2009). Shadowed by war: Building community capacity to support military families. *Family Relations, 58*(2), 216–228.

Huffman, A. H., Casper, W. J., & Payne, S. C. (2014). How does spouse career support relate to employee turnover? Work interfering with family and job satisfaction as mediators. *Journal of Organizational Behavior, 35*(2), 194–212.

Joseph, A. L., & Afifi, T. D. (2010). Military wives' stressful disclosures to their deployed husbands: The role of protective buffering. *Journal of Applied Communication Research, 38*(4), 412–434.

Knoblock, L. K., Theiss J. A., & Wehrman, E. C. (2015). Communication of military couples during deployment: Topic avoidance and relational uncertainty. In E. S. Parcell & L. M. Webb (Eds.), *A Communication Perspective on the Military: Interactions, Messages, and Discourses* (pp. 39–58). New York: Peter Lang.

Lester, P., Peterson, K., Reeves, J., Knauss, L., Glover, D., Mogil, C., Duan, N. Saltzman, W., Pynoos, R., Wilt, K., & Beardslee, W. (2010). The long war and parental combat deployment: Effects on military children and at-home spouses. *Journal of the American Academy of Child & Adolescent Psychiatry, 49*(4), 310–320.

Lim, N., Golinelli, D., & Cho, M. (2007). *"Working Around the Military" Revisited: Spouse Employment in the 2000 Census Data* (Vol. 566). Santa Monica, CA: Rand Corporation.

Maguire, K. C. (2015). Military family communication: A review and synthesis of the research related to wartime deployment. In E. S. Parcell & L. M. Webb (Eds.), *A Communication Perspective on the Military: Interactions, Messages, and Discourses* (pp. 19–38). New York: Peter Lang.

Maguire, K. C., Heinemann-LaFave, D., & Sahlstein, E. (2013). "To be so connected, yet not at all": Relational presence, absence, and maintenance in the context of a wartime deployment. *Western Journal of Communication, 77*(3), 249–271.

Maguire, K. C., & Wilson, S. R. (2013). Introduction to the special section on communication and wartime deployment. *Health Communication, 28*(8), 749–753.

Marek, L. I., & D'Aniello, C. (2014). Reintegration stress and family mental health: Implications for therapists working with reintegrating military families. *Contemporary Family Therapy, 36*(4), 443–451.

Meyer, E. G. (2015). The importance of understanding military culture. *Academic Psychiatry, 39*(4), 416–418.

O' Neal, C. W., Mancini, J. A., & DeGraff, A. (2016). Contextualizing the psychosocial well-being of military members and their partners: The importance of community and relationship provisions. *American Journal of Community Psychology, 58*(3-4), 477–487.

Orthner, D. K., & Rose, R. (2009). Work separation demands and spouse psychological well-being. *Family Relations, 58*(4), 392–403.

Padden, D. L., Connors, R. A., & Agazio, J. G. (2011). Stress, coping, and well-being in military spouses during deployment separation. *Western Journal of Nursing Research, 33*(2), 247–267.

Padden, D., & Posey, S. M. (2013). Caring for military spouses in primary care. *Journal of the American Academy of Nurse Practitioners, 25*(3), 141–146.

Palmer, C. (2008). A theory of risk and resilience factors in military families. *Military Psychology, 20*(3), 205–217.

Parcell, E. S., & Maguire, K. C. (2014). Turning points and trajectories in military deployment. *Journal of Family Communication, 14*(2), 129–148.

Parcell, E. S., & Webb, L. M. (2015). *A Communication Perspective on the Military: Interactions, Messages, and Discourses* (Eds.). New York: Peter Lang.

Pittman, J. F. (1994). Work/family fit as a mediator of work factors on marital tension: Evidence from the interface of greedy institutions. *Human Relations, 47*(2), 183–209.

Riggs, S. A., & Riggs, D. S. (2011). Risk and resilience in military families experiencing deployment: The role of the family attachment network. *Journal of Family Psychology, 25*(5), 675.

Ross, S. M. (2014). 21st century American military families: A review in the context of the wars in Afghanistan and Iraq. *Sociology Compass, 8*(5), 888–902. doi: 10.1111/soc4.12168.

Sahlstein, E., Maguire, K. C., & Timmerman, L. (2009). Contradictions and praxis contextualized by wartime deployment: Wives' perspectives revealed through relational dialectics. *Communication Monographs, 76*(4), 421–442.

Schwartz, J. B., Wood, L. L., & Griffith, J. D. (1991). The impact of military life on spouse labor force outcomes. *Armed Forces & Society, 17*(3), 385–407.

Skomorovsky, A. (2014). Deployment stress and well-being among military spouses: The role of social support. *Military Psychology, 26*(1), 44–54.

Teachman, J. (2007). Race, military service, and marital timing: Evidence from the NLSY-79. *Demography, 44*(2), 389–404.

United States Government Accountability Office (December, 2012). Military spouse employment programs: DoD can improve guidance and performance monitoring. Report to Congressional Committees.

Whitby, B., & Compton, J. (2018). The labor supply of military wives in the US. *Review of Economics of the Household, 16*(2), 513–539.

Part I

A CHRONOLOGICAL APPROACH TO ACADEMIC AND MILITARY IDENTITIES

Chapter One

Navigating Academic and Military Life

A Personal Journey

Marcia M. Bouchard

For the U.S. Army, an institution steeped in deep tradition dating back to the Revolutionary War, the externals have remained the same—the crisp dress uniform, ceremonies, and beautiful historic posts. The frequent moves that characterize military life has also remained unchanged. However, underneath the steadfast military traditions the role of the Army spouse has shifted. The Army spouse's role has evolved from a nuisance or camp follower, to a dutiful and cheerful community volunteer who always put the needs of her husband and his career above her own. However, the push for the Equal Rights Amendment and the women's movement spurred Army spouses to look outside their traditional roles for fulfillment. Spouses moved beyond being cheerful volunteers. Regardless of gender or sexual orientation, both male and female spouses want, and in some cases, need a career of their own. Thus, we demand better opportunities for themselves and a better life for their families (Alt & Stone, 1991).

This chapter is an autoethnography, a methodology that emerged from ethnography, one of many methodologies found within social research today (Hammersley & Atkinson, 2007). Spry (2001) defines autoethnography as a "self-narrative that critiques the situations of self with others in social contexts" (p. 710). Hammersley and Atkinson (2007) argue that while it has its roots in nineteenth-century Western anthropology, there is little difference between ethnography and the "study of individual life histories" (p. 1). Unlike conventional academic writing, users of this method write in the first person. Autoethnography is a robust and relevant method. In addition to increasing use, it pays particular attention to and acknowledgment of the role of context (Golding & Foley, 2017). In order to keep this chapter in theoretical context, I will establish the context in which the military spouse finds herself or himself. I will start by introducing relevant, key concepts that impact the military spouse such as *tied migration*, role conflict, and greedy institutions. I will begin with tied migration since this factor effects everything else. Where an individual migrates to or lives influences everything else related to quality of life. Examples include overall economic stability, employment opportunities, education options, as well as social support resources like relatives and friends.

TIED MIGRATION

An example of a quality of life issue addressed by the Army in 2003 is the employment challenges spouses face because of geographic mobility. These frequent moves result in *tied migration*, where one spouse moves for employment and career reasons and the other spouse follows (Mincer, 1978). According to Bird and Bird (1985), *tied migration* implies that there is career advancement and economic gain for one of the spouses; however, the other spouse may incur losses because of the geographic relocation. When the family moves the other spouse is then "tied" to the "migration" and called the "trailing spouse." Mincer (1978) suggested that the trailing or tied partner was the wife, though this may not always be the case now. Boyle, Kulu, Cooke, Gayle, and Mulder (2008) brought forth the outcome of union dissolution because of migration, which Mincer (1978) speculated as a possible consequence.

In a 2014 study, Maury and Stone posit that *tied migration* results in loss of income because of permanent-change-of-station/relocation (p. 71), the mismatch between education level and jobs available, with underemployment on equal ground with unemployment as an issue (p. 50), and the ongoing perception that prospective employers are not interested in hiring military spouses (p. 69). In short, tied migration can have negative ramifications for the marital unit as a whole.

ROLE CONFLICT

Boyle, Cooke, Halfacree, and Smith (2001) argued that in tied migration, "partnered women are more likely than men to be economically inactive or underemployed" (p. 211). This raises the question about the financial impact of *tied migration* on the trailing spouse when the family model is dual income (Bruck, Allen & Spector, 2002). Civilian spouses then have to find new jobs each time they relocate, often with periods of unemployment (Spitze, 1984) or accepting positions that are a mismatch for an individual's skills or preferred work schedule (Booth, 2000), which increases role conflict (Kalleberg, 2008).

Spector (1997) described two types of role conflict: (a) intra-role, where the conflict is between people at work or competing work demands; and, (b) extra-role conflict, which is conflict between work and non-work demands. In the case of long separations of spouses, the extra-role conflict is between family responsibilities and work (Booth, Segal, & Bell 2007). On the other hand, Kalleberg (2008) argued that the heart of role-conflict is a mismatch between the individual and their job. This work mismatch included skills mismatch, which is the under-utilization of a person's abilities or under qualified workers (Greenhaus & Beutell, 1985; Kalleberg, 2008). These role conflicts are an added stress on the marriage.

GREEDY INSTITUTIONS

A frequently cited article in dissertations, RAND publications, and other scholarly works is Segal's (1986) article "The Military and the Family as Greedy Institutions." In this theoretical article, Segal argued that the military and the family make "great demands of individuals in terms of commitments, loyalty, time, and energy" (p. 9). Segal provided examples of the demands on military families, such as long separations. These separations added to role conflict for the civilian spouse between being a single parent and expectations to fulfill volunteer duties. Segal also included a positive side to being a military spouse. She explained how being tied to a spouse's rank gives immediate identity and allows for quick integration into an institutionalized system, which includes networks. Although referencing rank when dealing with spouses is part of the old Army mentality, Segal's article provides theoretical evidence of the network advantages of being a military spouse.

The following is my personal journey as a military spouse. It is broken down into a chronology of military assignments interwoven with aspects of my schooling and research. Also included are short personal reflections under sub-headings "Lessons Learned." Golding and Foley (2017) describe these reflections as "autoethnography and wisdom beyond the academy" (p. 397). It goes beyond theories, methods, and constraints of academic writing, and is about making sense of life and sharing insights.

PERSONAL JOURNEY

My *tied migration* began in April 1987 when I married Ron Bouchard, a fellow native of the Granite State, graduate of the University of New Hampshire, and career United States Army officer. Prior to our marriage, we agreed that I would be the trailing spouse for the next ten years. At that point, we would assess our options. Fortunately, the first move from my hometown in Laconia, New Hampshire, to the Northern Virginia area was career enhancing, as I became vice president of real estate lending at a bank located in Tysons Corner, Virginia.

The 12 years I spent after high school working at the local savings and loan association served me well as I continued my banking career in Northern Virginia. I began in banking as a teller and when I left my hometown, I had mastered the complexities of real estate lending. Equally as important were the lessons I learned delivering exceptional customer service. This, coupled with nurturing and valuing personal relationships with co-workers and customers, provided me with an invaluable foundation that I would draw on countless times as a military spouse in academia.

The Quonset Hut

My two years working in Northern Virginia were fulfilling both professionally and economically. It was summer 1989. Ron just completed a year of Command and General Staff College at Fort Leavenworth, Kansas. Together we made the decision that I would continue working in Virginia—it made financial sense—and he returned home most weekends. Much to our surprise, the promised Germany unit ended up being an assignment to South Korea. The options then were a one-year hardship tour or a two-year tour with family, if he could convince the commander to give him a command-sponsored billet. The Tuesday before Thanksgiving, I arrived at Kimpo Airport with Ron waiting to take me to our apartment outside the gate of Yongsan Army Garrison in Seoul. It was a true Korean apartment. There were ondol-heated floors and a pink tile bathroom with rodents residing in the walls and ceiling. However, Ron had placed on the government-issued kitchen table an enrollment form from the education center for the University of Maryland University College (UMUC). It was time to fill the void of not having a college degree. This form was my passport for an education journey that began with English 101 in a quonset hut in South Korea.

School was my focus. While I did the usual volunteer work, including treasurer of the Officer Wives' Club, volunteering at Army Community Services, and being active with the Catholic Women of the Chapel, I treated school as if it were a job. I set hours each day for studying, attending classes, going to the library, and arranging for group study sessions for midterms and finals. This all got easier when we moved on post—it also included Ron occasionally meeting me after evening classes and carrying my books as we walked home. My 22 months in Korea flew by. It was now August 1991 and we were heading back to the DC area. I had a little over 60 credit hours and our family now included two-month-old Michael.

Between the move and having a baby, I took a semester off. My studies resumed at UMUC's stateside campus next to College Park, Maryland. Fortunately, there was the EXCEL program, which was the taking of prior/workplace learning, documenting it, and having it translate into college credits. This was an onerous chore, and my completed submission, with all supporting documentation, was two volumes. The result was 29 credit hours, across multiple disciplines including accounting, financial management, and business law—this all related to my 15 years as a banker, and to my surprise, some of my volunteer work.

At this point, my goal was to get to the finish line. I met with an academic counselor to chart out the most direct route. While my passion was history, the practical side agreed with the recommendation to pursue a degree in business. In May of 1994, I graduated with a Bachelor of Science in Business Administration and was UMUC's first student commencement speaker. Ron was waiting for me at the foot of the stairs as I exited the stage. He handed me a card with a note written inside. The note was my present, "Graduate school."

Lessons Learned

Because of *tied migration*, I found myself living in a foreign country. Being a trailing spouse allowed me to take advantage of the education opportunities on military installations and pursue a college degree. There is evidence that more educated spouses (i.e., those with graduate degree) have lower unemployment rates or are less likely to be underemployed than spouses without college degrees (Gonzalez, Matthews, Posard, Roshan, & Ross, 2015, p. 2; Maury & Stone, 2014). However, my desire to complete my education went beyond employment. The absence of a Bachelor degree was a void in my life. It was something that I desired and in all truthfulness, I was embarrassed that I did not have one. In addition, my husband was well educated and I wanted to be his equal in terms of educational achievement. According to Blakely, Hennessy, Chung and Skirton (2014) in their ethnographic study on foreign postings and military spouses, "activities such as academic studies, employment or simply through retaining some form of independence were seen as improving self-worth" (p. 74).

My advice is to keep focused, take the direct route, and fill the void. Remember that it does not matter what you major in because there is always graduate school.

GRADUATE SCHOOL

As with most military families, long-term planning for the trailing spouse remains elusive. We were headed back to South Korea for Ron's next assignment the following spring and graduate school would have to wait—or maybe not. It was late summer 1994 and the start of a new academic year. I told Ron on an August morning that I wanted to start graduate work now. While I filled the void of not having a bachelor's degree, a new one opened while doing my undergraduate work. My longing was for a Master of Arts and to study the humanities—religion, art, and literature. His response was "Okay. If you are going to go to graduate school, then go to Georgetown." With that said, I did the fiscally responsible thing: checked out the state schools and got nowhere. It was too late to begin the application process. On the other hand, Georgetown sent me a packet to complete. I called my references and they quickly submitted the required letters. The Director of the Liberal Studies Program, graciously gave me an appointment to meet and review my completed packet, save the Graduate Record Examination (GRE). My question to the director was "Is it possible to begin this fall with a conditional acceptance pending my taking of the GRE?" She responded that the GRE was not necessary as my packet told her everything she needed to know. I was fully accepted into the Master of Arts in Liberal Studies program. Three days later, accompanied by my three-year-old son Michael, I was back on campus registering for classes and purchasing books.

Two things happened that day: one prophetic, and the other was one of the best things I could have done for managing a huge reading requirement. It was Reserve Officer Training Corp (ROTC) day on campus with ROTC cadets from Georgetown and surrounding universities attending military classes and wearing battle dress uniforms (BDUs). As we walked around the campus holding hands, Michael said, "Mom, I want to go to school here so I can be a soldier like Daddy." In response, I told him that that was a wonderful thing to want to do; however, there was an even a better school on the Hudson River. Nineteen years later Michael graduated from the United States Military Academy, class of 2013. The second thing was how overwhelmed I was with required reading and the number of books, not to mention the expense. Upon leaving the bookstore, Michael and I returned to the registration tables where I signed up for an Evelyn Woods speed-reading course. The skills learned are invaluable and I continue to use them daily.

Georgetown's Healy Hall

The following week, with heartfelt gratitude and anticipation, I walked into historic Healy Hall and began my graduate work. My first two classes were a course on the Old Testament and a course on the history of American art. It needs noting that my choice of courses was limited to offerings on Tuesday evenings and Saturday mornings. Ron could reasonably commit to being home at those times. For the next two semesters on Tuesdays, I drove from our home in Alexandria, met Ron in the Pentagon parking lot, switched cars, and continued onto Georgetown. Ron returned home with Michael in his car seat. While there were some Tuesdays and Saturdays that required alternative arrangements for Michael, it worked. I scheduled reading, researching, thinking, and writing time while Michael was at nursery school and in the evenings.

My second appointment with the Director of Georgetown's Liberal Studies Program was at the end of the winter semester to ask for another exception. The master's program had a five-year limit from start to finish. We were heading to South Korea for the second time and did not know when we would be back in the DC area. The director listened, understood my circumstances, and graciously stopped the clock as long as we were overseas.

South Korea, Hawaii, and Carlisle Barracks

The three years that we were out of the country quickly passed. While I was standing in the receiving line on Camp Carroll when Ron took battalion command in June 1995, the principal of the Department of Defense Dependent School (K–12) asked me if I would please consider tutoring and substitute teaching. I did and the second year the principal knocked on my front door and asked if I could please teach 6th grade as they had a larger enrollment than planned. Again, I said yes. It was not banking, nor was I studying religion, art, or literature at Georgetown, but it was good. We departed Korea in June 1997 for a year in Hawaii. That year I continued substitute teaching at Holy Family Catholic Academy, where Michael was in first grade. I also took six credit hours of graduate courses that were transferable to Georgetown at Chaminade University in Honolulu.

We returned to the continental United States the summer of 1998 so Ron could attend War College in Carlisle, Pennsylvania. While not ideal, I was within "striking range" of Georgetown and drove the 224 mile round trip every Tuesday and Saturday for one year. I had access to the two libraries at the War College for research and embraced being back in the classroom, researching, reading, thinking, and writing. Ron requested a follow-on assignment to the Pentagon and I had it all planned—I would be back in Virginia to finish course work and write my thesis. Then Ron came home with his orders and told me that we were going to Fort Bliss in El Paso, Texas. I asked him "Who have you irritated and why are they sending us into exile?" In hindsight, I regret those words, as it was one of our best assignments.

However, there were two small issues. First, I was three credit hours short on course work; and second, the expectation and tradition was to be on campus with a thesis mentor while writing a graduate thesis. The three credit hours were fulfilled with a two-week intensive course on the Renaissance with two Georgetown professors in Florence, Italy. The second issue also resolved. Fortunately, I was a student of one of the first female professors at Georgetown, and a graduate of the University of Texas. She agreed to be my thesis mentor and to talk with the liberal studies program director about an exception to write my thesis from Texas. For the third time, the gracious director granted me an exception. Since I was a student, the University of Texas at El Paso gave me full library privileges. Through the mail, I sent thesis chapters to my mentor and in turn received her comments via mail. Ron, Michael, and I flew back to the East Coast to attend my Georgetown commencement in 2000 and I received a Master of Arts in Liberal Studies.

Lessons Learned

Much has changed in the delivery of higher education since the 1990s. The physical mailing of thesis chapters is old school and obsolete. Online education is rapidly becoming a significant method of course delivery with the majority of courses having an online component (Carver, Mukherjee & Lucio, 2017). The online platform replaces, or more accurately enhances, the delivery of teaching what was once limited to the confines of brick and mortar institutions. At UMUC, where I teach, textbooks were eliminated and moved to open-educational resources that ensure up-to-date material. These sources connect directly to learning outcomes (Ludwig, 2015). On the other hand, much is the same, especially the procedural protocol.

First, state your circumstances, make your case, and ask for an exception. As I learned working at my hometown savings and loan, take the time to develop relationships. Academic administrators and professors, including me, want you to succeed. Also, never discount an elite academic institution as being a stretch. A military spouse's experiences and insights, along with being adaptable, resilient, and determined are an asset and add to collegial discourse. You will be a welcomed member of any program. Remember to think outside the box—do not get discouraged—sometimes coming up short three credit hours results in a trip of a lifetime to Florence.

TWO QUICK MOVES

The moves came quickly. For the school year 1999–2000, I was a substitute teacher at Loretto Academy in El Paso, Texas, while writing my graduate thesis. The following school year, I taught 3rd grade. It was an ideal situation. Michael attended Loretto Academy and we would go to school together every morning, and at the end of the day, he met me in my classroom and we would leave together. I discovered that I truly enjoyed teaching; however, it was short lived. Ron departed Fort Bliss after 18 months and Michael and I followed at the end of the school year. We were at Fort Monroe, Virginia, for less than a year. My time at Fort Monroe was what I refer to as "the year of self-improvement." I became a Weight Watchers lifetime member, spent hours walking on the seawall and reading on the beach.

At that point, we were well beyond the initial 10-year commitment I made to being a trailing spouse. We assessed our options and the plan was for Ron to transition out of the Army in 2003 at the 26-year mark. Then we received what we call a "blessing from God." We were again heading to South Korea for Ron to command the First Signal Brigade.

Back to South Korea

The summer of 2002, I immersed myself in all things related to both the brigade and the Yongsan Army Garrison community. A professor of philosophy at Georgetown commented one day in class that once you receive a solid liberal arts education, you have an obligation to teach. He went on to state that teaching is not limited to the classroom and is through influence on boards and community work. I heeded his advice.

As always, Ron and Michael came first, and I made it a point to lead by example. My only guidance to the spouses in the unit was to "Take care of yourselves so you can take care of your children and soldier." I let everyone know that they were free to participate, or not, in any way that suited them in unit and community activities. Ron and I also viewed my role as one of validator—to let family members know that we appreciated and valued them. I did this by attending countless changes-of-command at the battalion and company level, and attending unit events. In addition to being the senior advisor/mentor for the battalion Family Readiness Groups, president of the parish council, and Parent Teacher Organization board member, I had my very personal hospital ministry and was a volunteer member of the hospital chaplain's staff.

In September 2003, after three decades of tremendous growth, the Chosun Gift Shop (CGS) needed to restructure or close. The CGS, an institution in its own right, was the fund-raising arm of the spouses' club and operated a 13,000-square-foot gift shop on Yongsan Army Garrison. The items sold were goods imported from throughout Asia. The Commanding General's spouse asked if I could help with the restructuring. It was a welcomed challenge and I took on the role of chairperson of the board and set the vision and guidance for the rewriting of all policies, procedures, and enabling documents. Over the next two years, new business practices were implemented as a result of my overhauling of the policies, procedures, and documentation. In addition, the accounting and inventory systems were automated. I identified staffing requirements and implemented changes involving 75 volunteers and 10 paid staff members. This work brought my years of banking, undergraduate study of business, and my values-based graduate work together. It also included my understanding of the transient nature of military families and provided for the continuity of the organization during the rotation cycle of personnel. With limited employment opportunities for spouses, the 10 paid positions and volunteer jobs were designed to be resume building experiences. One example is the head buyer having letters of credit totaling $250,000 to purchase inventory on a buying trip to Hong Kong with three CGS volunteers, all trailing spouses.

The bottom line was that the CGS increased charitable contributions made to American and Korean charities. The amount donated went from $150,000 in 2002 to $350,000 in 2005. The amount awarded in scholarships to military family members living in South Korea increased by 90% to $75,000. Spouses were encouraged to apply for scholarships. I advocated getting spouses into the classroom.

Lessons Learned

With overseas assignments, there is often a loss of support systems. The CGS volunteers and staff became my friends and part of my personal support network. Having this support is critical as researchers have stated "pivotal for a trailing spouse's re-adjustment," and support from friends is a predictor of cross-cultural adjustment (Blakely, Hennessy, Chung & Skirton, 2014; Ramos, Mustafa & Haddad, 2017). There is great value in work and being part of an organization.

PURSUIT OF A TERMINAL DEGREE

The Bouchard family moved from South Korea to Fort Gordon, Georgia, in June 2005. That year, UMUC sent a newsletter to alumni announcing the start of a Doctor of Management program. This was a hybrid program and from my perspective, this delivery of education finally caught up with being a military family member. There were three required residency weekends a semester in addition to the online component and research. I began my doctoral work on September 7, 2006, driving 1,140 miles round-trip three times that semester. While there were implied and traditional roles that I was expected to fill at Fort Gordon, I chose carefully. Priority was always Ron and Michael then my studies. While in South Korea, I embraced being a military spouse and all of the volunteer community leadership roles that I held. However, at Fort Gordon, I had no problems regretting social invitations or suggesting another person to take on an honorary role for an organization. The one volunteer role I continued and cherish was my hospital ministry and spending time at Eisenhower Medical Center with our returning heroes from Iraq and Afghanistan.

Two of the three first-year terms of doctoral work and 6,840 driven miles were behind me. It was the summer of 2007; Ron was on orders to move back to the DC area, and I was pleased for two reasons. First, my mother was terminally ill and my plan was to fly often from Baltimore Washington Airport to Manchester, New Hampshire, to help my father care for her. Second, I would be 17 miles from campus for the required residencies. I was moving full steam ahead. Contractors were lined up to do work on our house. All the major administrative duties had been accomplished: address changes done, dental appoints made, Michael was enrolled at Bishop Ireton High School with tuition paid, the *Washington Post* was scheduled for delivery, the moving van was packed and we were 11 hours from "rolling." Then, orders changed without notice and the Bouchard family headed to Hawaii. Ron traveled to Hawaii, signed in, and started work. Michael and I drove to New Hampshire and he summered at Camp Mi-Te-Na in Alton. I then spent the summer completing the third term of the first year's course work in the basement of our Alexandria, Virginia, home. The various trades then completed the agreed-upon contracted work. I was 20 minutes from UMUC's campus and enjoyed quick trips to campus for the three required residencies and visits to the McKeldin Library.

Many details surrounding that time are now humorous. On example is using the basement workbench as my desk and the ceiling electrical outlets meant for power tools for my computer and printer. Moreover, there are blessings that are beyond anything that I had the wisdom or knowledge to ask for or envision. To begin, UMUC made a program change reducing the required term residencies to one two-day requirement. Each semester, I flew home from Hawaii a week early and spent quality time with my beloved mother in New Hampshire. Michael attended Damien Memorial, a wonderful academic-focused high school in Honolulu, run by the Christian Brothers. Ron and I became speech and debate parents and I coached the team. We lived on Hickham Air Force Base and had neighbors who were beyond caring, thoughtful, and giving.

A Dissertation

With course work and comprehensive examinations complete, I began the dissertation sequence in September 2008. The expectation for UMUC's Doctor of Management program was a completed dissertation in three terms (one year). There was much advice freely given from colleagues who had completed the program, professors, and friends on the approach to take. The two best pieces of advice were: a) it is "a" dissertation and not "the" dissertation, and b) the best dissertation is a done dissertation.

My initial topic focused on management issues related to a volunteer workforce since I had two decades of volunteering in multiple locations. I had taken the attitude that I wanted my research topic to be something that I liked and enjoyed. I thought of my dissertation in terms of having a "good roommate." Unfortunately, I was not enjoying the volunteer topic and I lacked the needed motivation to get through the process. Fortunately, while standing in the kitchen of my dissertation chair's home during an evening social in October 2008, Dr. Claudine SchWeber asked, "How do you manage a group of military spouses in the workforce?" This was the start of my new dissertation topic that evolved into "Geographic Mobility and Employment: An Investigation of Tied Migration Issues Among Employed Military Spouses" (Bouchard, 2009).

The following month, November 2008, I received a call from my father saying that he needed help with Mother. Two days later, I was on a plane to New Hampshire. Ron's job had extensive travel requirements throughout Asia. Fortunately, Michael had never given us a reason not to trust him home alone; he was very busy with school activities, and had received his appointment to West Point. He had just gotten his driver's license, so he could drive himself to and from school. Ron gave medical power of attorney for Michael to our dear neighbor. When Ron was away, we asked Michael to knock on our neighbor's door to let her know he was home safe from school. My good neighbor would open the door and hand Michael a tray with a hot home-cooked meal. Michael was so touched with her kindness. This wonderful neighbor also watched my dog Sam. I am forever grateful to her. Because we moved half a world away from where I thought my family should live, I was blessed with an angel living next door. I was able to spend the last 60 days of my mother's life caring for her.

Lessons Learned

Stay true to your family priorities. Get to know your neighbors—you never know when they will be a blessing. Additionally, do not fret over last-minute orders—keep the faith—it will work out better than anything you had planned.

REVISITING MY DISSERTATION

Revisiting my dissertation for this book chapter, and in particular the theoretical perspective section of my literature review, was like sitting down with a delightful roommate and reminiscing. As discussed in the introduction, a key concept from my literature review was *tied migration*. The identified gap in the literature at the time of my research was a need for studies designed to specifically measure the outcomes or perceived job satisfaction as a result of Army employment initiatives that circumstances and not just attitudes have improved (Houppert, 2005). The 2002 GAO report stated that there was a need to evaluate an employment program for military spouses from the military spouses' perspective. The Army Spouse Employment Partnership (ASEP) was the program chosen to evaluate from the spouse's perspective.

ASEP moved beyond assistance in résumé writing and employment searches and was a partnership between the Army and corporations. It rolled out in the Fiscal Year 2002 National Defense Authorization Act (NDAA). This act included provisions to enhance quality of life for military families. One of the requirements was for the Secretary of Defense to work with the private sector to advance training and employment opportunities for military spouses. Army Chief-of-Staff General Shinseki held an employment summit with Fortune 500 companies in December 2002. The outcome was 11 Fortune 500 companies and two military agencies entered into a private/public partnership to provide meaningful and long-term employment for military spouses.

Research Question and Survey

The literature review, management problem, purpose statement, and stated argument were completed in December 2008. Guiding my research was the question: "Is an employer initiative designed to mitigate the problems associated with *tied migration* accomplishing what it intended from the perspective of the trailing spouse" (Bouchard, 2009, p. 41)? In retrospect, I would edit the question to start with "In what ways is an employer . . ."

In order to answer the research question and fill the gap in the literature, I surveyed 647 military spouses, from May 9, 2009, through July 9, 2009, using a web-based survey. Sixteen of the measures were from Spector's (1997) job satisfaction survey, and the remaining items I developed. The survey consisted of 38 items using a Likert-type scale, 20 demographic questions, and 3 open-ended questions.[1] I had 502 useable surveys. However, getting to this point was a challenge.

Roadblocks

There comes a time during the dissertation process that calls for sheer determination and perseverance. Initially my proposed study had the full support of the Commander of the Family, Morale, Welfare, and Recreation Command (FMWRC), which included the ASEP program. The Commander wrote:

> I see this as a win-win. Marcia gets to do a study she has wanted to do for a while to help the Army Family and we get the benefit of the adjustments to the program as she determines the input, output and OUTCOME of the employment program. (Personal e-mail correspondence, dated May 28, 2008)

As with all commands, the commanders change. With a change in commander, my study came to an abrupt halt in February 2009. For reasons that I never fully understood, a career government service (GS) employee and overseer of the ASEP program notified me that I could no longer survey spouses. Fortunately, my husband Ron was attending a conference along with the new FMWRC commander. I had Ron hand-deliver my letter of introduction with the purpose of my study and I asked for the new commander's support. While it appeared everything was back on track, there continued to be several subtle attempts to stop my study.

I was discussing with the manager of the ASEP program ways to distribute the survey to some of the ASEP-reported 42,100 spouses hired by corporate partners ("U.S. Army," 2009). She was adamant that the corporate partners could not send out the survey to individuals hired by ASEP because of privacy issues and was reluctant to provide me with the corporate partner's human resource points-of-contact. Next, she inadvertently mentioned that it was too bad I was living in Hawaii because the following week, May 17–21, 2009, there was a convention of ASEP corporate partners and Employment Readiness Program Managers from military installation employment offices. I responded that traveling from Hawaii to Fort Hood, Texas, was not a problem and I would love to attend. I got off the phone and made plane and hotel reservations.

The ASEP program manager politely greeted me upon arrival. She also informed me that the Deputy Assistant Secretary of the Army for Personnel Oversight was overscheduled and I would not be able to meet with her. What is interesting is that I did not know the Secretary was attending—it was another unintentional comment. I responded with complete understanding, then took a step back and found the Secretary's assistant—the gatekeeper—and befriended her at a social gathering that evening. After telling the assistant about my study, I asked for help from her boss. I met briefly with the Secretary the next morning and had her permission to send my survey to the two ASEP government partners' human resource departments. The respective human resource departments in turn sent the survey out to their military spouses.

I noted on the conference agenda that there was a social the second evening hosted by the III Corp commander and his wife on Fort Hood. I called a friend who made my introduction to the commander and described my study. Upon arrival, the commander's spouse asked what she could do to help. I sent her my web-page link and survey access password, and she in turn sent the information to the Family Readiness Group leaders at Fort Hood to send to their members. While the surveyed population expanded beyond spouses employed through the ASEP program, it was a huge help and provided data for additional analysis. My ability to network was in keeping with Segal's (1986) theory that with military rank there are networking advantages for the spouses, and I used these connections.

There was another important piece to my research. Employment Readiness Program managers are located at Army installations throughout the world. Those in attendance at the conference were eager to help. Several sent the survey link to spouses hired through the ASEP program and four posted the introduction and link on their web pages (Bouchard, 2009). Of interest is how the Employment Readiness Program managers wanted to talk one-on-one. We did so over coffee during breaks, waiting for a bus, on the bus, at the tables during breakout sessions, and in the halls going back to our rooms in the evening. There is much information that I gleaned during these exchanges, which led to a clearer understanding of the program and issues.

After I returned home from the conference, I received a phone call from the GS employee overseeing the ASEP program. The same person that told me I could not survey the ASEP spouses now told me that the data I was gathering belonged to the government, and that I needed permission to use it. I ignored the call and decided not to worry about it until I received something more formal. I never received a formal request to turn over my data.

Lessons Learned

Listen, watch, network, and ignore. Take advantage of the smallest openings, or in my case, crash the party. At that point, I had nothing to lose and a dissertation to complete.

NEW HAMPSHIRE THEN THE FIVE STAR INN

While working on my dissertation, military life continued. Michael and I returned to the mainland the following month, June 2009, ahead of Ron. There were several moving pieces, including a permanent-change-of-station to Fort McPherson in Atlanta. Ron handled the pack-out in Hawaii and met Michael and me on the East Coast. Together, along with my father, we traveled from New Hampshire to West Point for Michael's report day (R-day). Ron headed to Atlanta to begin work and wait for quarters. I returned to my childhood home to finish the statistical analysis and writing of my dissertation. I took over the dining room table and tried to remain focused. The issue was that there was too much activity. My sisters and nieces dropped in throughout the day and wanted me to join them for whatever activities they had planned. Dad was always eager to go out for dinner; however, this usually was before I was at a good stopping point. I ended up packing everything, including my dog Sam, and drove to West Point. Sam boarded at the kennel there and I took up residency at the Five Star Inn. For the next 60 days, I conducted data analysis, wrote, edited, and edited repeatedly my findings, discussion, conclusion, implications for management practice, and limitations sections of my dissertation.

On August 14, 2009, and on schedule for a one-year completion, I successfully defended my dissertation at UMUC's Maryland campus. The Bouchards were back together for Michael's formal acceptance into the Corp of Cadets on August 15. After the cadet battalion cookout for families, Michael was able to return to my small suite at the Five Star Inn for a couple of hours. He asked for permission to use the desk in the bedroom, as he wanted to get a start on his studies. At that moment, my education journey went full circle—the desk I completed my formal education at was the same desk that Michael began his college studies.

Lessons Learned

There will never be a perfect time or ideal circumstances to return to school or write a dissertation. While I did not always have control of my circumstances, I did have control on how I adapted and did what I needed to do to keep moving forward. I often reminded myself of St. Francis de Sales' 16th-century quote, "Bloom where you are planted."

ADJUNCT PROFESSOR

One of the things that I always enjoyed about commencements is that I felt like a bride again. There is ceremony, formal music, procession, caps and gowns, flowers, food and celebrations—a joyous time. Commencement for my doctorate was even more memorable. I have referred to my formal education as a personal journey, albeit it one that is not undertaken alone, and for me involvement in academia did not stop with hooding at commencement by my dissertation chair.

After my dissertation chair placed the olive drab doctorate hood over my head, I turned and we hugged. My dear mentor added the appropriate kiss on both checks, which is in keeping with her French heritage. She then said, "Call me Claudine. I want you to work with me." Moreover, that began my continued academic journey on the teaching side. After working as a teaching assistant, I was hired to teach Intercultural Communication and Leadership in the graduate school based on having my terminal degree and my time living in Korea and running an Asian import business as a community volunteer. I also went to work for another of my doctorate professors teaching Foundations of Management, and Organizational Behavior undergraduate courses in a traditional brick and mortar setting. Then I co-taught with my dissertation chair in the Doctor of Management program. She has since retired; however, my eight-year affiliation as an adjunct faculty member with UMUC's doctor of management program continues. I now teach six credit hours a semester, three semesters a year. My course load varied from teaching Foundations of Management Theory to Leadership and Change to Managing Organizational Environments to Innovation Process and Strategy. I have now settled into a nice pattern of teaching Interpreting and Translating Management Theory in Practice, and Designing Evidence-Based Management Solutions.

ONE MORE MOVE

In December 2010, Ron retired from the Army after 33 years and 7 months of service. We made the decision to settle where the best career opportunity came together with location (needed to be East Coast), near a major airport, and with any luck, easy driving distance to UMUC's campus in Maryland. With Ron being a signal officer, it only made sense to settle in the high technology corridor in Northern Virginia—a continuation of tied migration on my part. We now call Herndon, Virginia, home and I drive to UMUC for the required residencies in 40 minutes. My work as a volunteer community leader continues and I serve on the Parish Advisory Council and as a Planning Commissioner for the Town of Herndon. In addition, I am exploring running for Town Council.

RESEARCH UPDATE

The absence of detailed findings from my research in this chapter was deliberate. However, it is worth noting that:

> "One problem was in identifying military spouses because there are no definitive guidelines for ASEP corporate partners regarding reporting and tracking of spouses hired. Difficulties in identifying military spouses employed by ASEP corporate partners suggest that the systems for record keeping were not adequate for program evaluation. In addition, the majority of military spouses in the sample population did not (a) recognize the ASEP program, or (b) use it. Findings also suggest that metrics to evaluate outcomes from the spouses' perspective are missing." (Bouchard, 2009, Abstract)

It is nearly 10 years since I completed my research; however, it appears progress is slow concerning employment program evaluation from the trailing spouses' perspective. In 2011, the ASEP program expanded to include the Navy, Marine Corps, and Air Force spouses and evolved into Military Spouse Employment Partnership (MSEP). In 2015, Congress mandated evaluation of the MSEP program as part of the National Defense Authorization Act Department (Gonzalez et al., 2015, p. ix). The Office of the Deputy Assistant Secretary of Defense for Military Community and Family Policy sponsored the RAND National Defense Research Institute to examine programs related to spouse education and career opportunities. Of interest is that two RAND reports, published six and seven years after my study (Gonzalez et al., 2105; Gonzalez, Miller, & Trail, 2016), track closely with my findings and recommendations. In a 2015 RAND publication titled "Evaluation of the Military Spouse Employment Partnership: Progress Report on First Stage of Analysis" the authors list five tasks that RAND supports. Task 4 is:

> To ensure that the Military Community and Family Policy office is able to conduct future evaluations of the Military Spouse Employment Partnership, RAND will assess the office's data collection efforts and provide guidance on what data collection systems or processes could be put in place so that an evaluation of spouses' outcomes can occur in the future. (Gonzalez et al., 2015, p. 42)

Until practices are in place that allow for the measuring and assessment of an employment program for military spouses, which includes the end-user outcomes, it will not be possible to determine if it is attitudes or circumstances that are being improved (Houppert, 2005). If the goal is to improve attitudes and not circumstances, the question then becomes: Is it the attitudes of military spouses or the attitudes of military leadership?

LIMITATIONS

To begin, the research done for my dissertation discussed throughout this chapter is considered dated. While recent inquiry was done to identify new studies and trends, it is not intended to take the place of an updated literature review. Another limitation is that the use of autoethnography comes with shortfalls. One example is the time between events and writing and reflecting on them could lead to selective memory. Also not addressed were my frustrations and disappointment that Army leadership did not heed the findings of my dissertation research at that time. In addition, discerning what would be helpful to others based on my experiences and trying to maintain privacy proved to be a challenge. I even hesitated disclosing my age in the closing reflection section. Finally, there are nuggets of wisdom that I did not write about and reflections that I could have, but chose not to, expanded upon. For those omissions, I apologize.

FUTURE STUDY

Military spouses are a unique and traceable population. Many are trailing spouses over multiple decades. In order to understand better the outcomes of tied migration, which includes the overall economic impact and career progression of the civilian spouse (Mincer, 1978; Spitze, 1984), a longitudinal study is needed. This study should include spouses married to junior members of the military, which would allow for examination of tied migration from the beginning of a military career. In addition, research studies that are short in duration should be done on military employment programs from the end user's perspective. These studies should include both employed and unemployed members of the labor force in order to gain insights into the effectiveness of employment programs.[2]

Research on work-family role conflict needs improvement by studying the actual migration or move timeframe and the impact of the unsettled period on civilian spouses' employment. In addition, further study is needed on job-skills match. Measures for these variables would allow for the testing of Kalleberg's (2008) theory, that work-family role conflict is rooted in job-skills mismatch.

Another area recommended for future research is job satisfaction and support of a military career. The findings of my study suggest a positive relationship between job satisfaction and support of a military career (Bouchard, 2009, p. 70). However, job satisfaction is a construct with multiple factors that influence it. Military spouses are diverse and talented; however, they have needs and goals as diverse as their talents. Needed are studies that identify career expectations of military spouses and how these expectations relate to job satisfaction and in turn support of a military career.

CLOSING REFLECTIONS

While I studied the issues related to *tied migration*, and being a trailing spouse, I never felt that I was on the losing end of the moves; and I argue that the opposite happened. The horizon of my worldview broadened as I lived and traveled throughout Asia and the United States. Education opportunities were plentiful, as long as I remained flexible. I never thought for a minute that I was too old to go back to school. I received my undergraduate degree at age 37, a Master of Arts in Liberal Studies at age 42, and my Doctor of Management at the age of 53. Moreover, in keeping things in context, I wrote this book chapter at the age of 62.

I continue to thrive being in an academic environment and teaching. I also enjoy family, traveling, community, and my home. It is about balance. I have the ability of working at my passion, which is teaching, and the flexibility that teaching as an adjunct professor provides.

More importantly are the relationships made along the way. One example of these relationships is from my community volunteer work while living in South Korea. Over the past 15 years, the friendships that I made have been a constant part of my life. Ron and I visited numerous friends from this time, and hosted friends in turn, traveled with some, shared in the joys of their children's graduations, weddings, becoming grandparents, and the sad gathering at Arlington National Cemetery where we laid to rest one of our dear friends and mentor.

My personal journey is nothing extraordinary;[3] however, it is my story about perseverance and determination. I hope it will inspire military spouses in some small way and if nothing else brings a smile to their face. I also hope it will inspire a fellow military spouse and researcher to continue and build upon the existing research on military spouses. Military spouses are a talented, adaptable, resilient, and complex group of individuals. Their role is constantly evolving. Their story needs to be told.

NOTES

1. See Bouchard (2009) Appendix A for Operationalization of Variables and Survey Items, and Appendix B for the Survey Instrument.

2. This Future Study section is directly from my dissertation. It is one example of how the later reports published by the RAND Corporation track closely with my work (Gonzalez et al., 2015; Gonzalez et al., 2016).

3. This is an opinion with which the editors of this volume vehemently disagree. Dr. Bouchard is extraordinary, but the editors believe that all spouses, ourselves included, can aspire to live up to the incredible journey she has traveled.

REFERENCES

Alt, B. S., & Stone, B. D. (1991). *Campfollowing: A history of the military wife.* New York: Praeger.

Bird, G. A., & Bird, G. W. (1985). Determinants of mobility in two-earner families: Does the wife's income count? *Journal of Marriage and the Family, 47*(3), 753–758. doi:10.2307/352279.

Blakely, G., Hennessy, C., Chung, M. C. & Skirton, H. (2014). The impact of foreign postings on accompanying military spouses: An ethnographic study. *Health Psychology Research, 2*(2:1468), 73–77. doi:10.4081/hpr.2014.1468.

Booth, B. (2000). *The impact of military presence in local labor markets on unemployment rates, individual earnings, and returns to education.* Doctoral dissertation, University of Maryland at College Park. Retrieved from ProQuest Dissertations & Theses Global (Order No. 3001353).

Booth, B., Segal, M. W., & Bell, D. B. (2007). What we know about Army families: 2007 update. Prepared for the Family and Morale, Welfare and Recreation Command by Caliber, an ICF International Company. https://www.mwrbrandcentral.com/images/uploads/whatweknow2007.pdf.

Bouchard, M. M. (2009). *Geographic mobility and employment: An investigation of tied migration issues among employed military spouses.* Doctoral dissertation, University of Maryland University College. Retrieved from ProQuest Dissertations and Theses Global (Order No. 3387631).

Boyle, P., Cooke, T. J., Halfacree, K., & Smith, D. (2001). A cross-national comparison of the impact of family migration on women's employment status. *Demography, 38*(2), 201–213. https://doi.org/10.1353/dem.2001.0012.

Boyle, P. J., Kulu, H., Cooke, T., Gayle, V., & Mulder, C. H. (2008). Moving and union dissolution. *Demography, 45*(1), 209–222. https://doi.org/10.1353/dem.2008.0000.

Bruck, C. S., Allen, T. D., & Spector, P. E. (2002). The relation between work-family conflict and job satisfaction: A finer-grained analysis. *Journal of Vocational Behavior, 60*(3), 336–353. https://doi.org/10.1006/jvbe.2001.1836.

Carver, L. B., Mukherjee, K., & Lucio, R. (2017). Relationship between grades earned and time in online courses. *Online Learning, 21*(4), 303–314. https://onlinelearningconsortium.org/read/olc-online-learning-journal/.

Golding, B. & Foley, A. (2017). Constructing narratives in later life: Autoethnography beyond the academy. *Australian Journal of Adult Learning, 57*(3), 384–400. https://www.ajal.net.au/.

Gonzalez, G. C., Matthews, L. J., Posard, M., Roshan, P., & Ross, S. (2015). Evaluation of the Military Spouse Employment Partnership: Progress Report on First Stage of Analysis. Santa Monica, CA: RAND Corporation. https://www.rand.org/pubs/research_reports/RR1349.html.

Gonzalez, G. C., Miller, L. L., & Trail, T. E. (2016). The military spouse education and career opportunities program: Recommendation for an internal monitoring system. Santa Monica, CA: RAND Corporation. https://www.rand.org/pubs/research_reports/RR1013.html.

Greenhaus, J. H., & Beutell, N. J. (1985). Sources of conflict between work and family roles. *Academy of Management Review, 10*(1), 76–88. doi:10.5465/AMR.1985.4277352.

Hammersley, M. & Atkinson, P. (2007). *Ethnography: Principles in practice* (3rd ed.). London: Routledge.

Houppert, K. (2005). *Home fires burning: Married to the military for better or worse.* New York: Ballantine Books.

Kalleberg, A. L. (2008). The mismatched worker: When people don't fit their jobs. *The Academy of Management Perspectives, 22*(1), 24–40. doi:10.5465/AMP.2008.31217510.

Ludwig, B. (2015). UMUC receives top honor from Open Education Consortium. Accessed on August 20, 2017 at https://globalmedia.umuc.edu/2015/04/24/umuc-receives-top-honor-from-open-education-consortium/.

Maury, R., & Stone, B. (2014). *Military Spouse Employment Report,* Syracuse, N.Y. Institute for Veterans and Military Families, February 2014. https://ivmf.syracuse.edu/article/military-spouse-employment-survey/.

Mincer, J. (1978). Family migration decisions. *The Journal of Political Economy, 86*(5), 749–773. https://www.jstor.org/stable/1828408.

National Defense Authorization Act (NDAA) of 2002. Public Law 107-107-December 28, 2001. https://www.congress.gov/107/plaws/publ107/PLAW-107publ107.pdf.

Ramos, H. L., Mustafa, M., & Haddad, A. R. (2017). Social support and expatriate spouses' wellbeing: The mediating role of cross-cultural adjustment. *International Journal of Employment Studies, 25*(2), 6–24. https://search.informit.com.au/browseJournalTitle;res=IELBUS;issn=1039-6993.

Segal, M. W. (1986.) The military and the family as greedy institutions. *Armed Forces and Society, 13*(1), 9–38. https://doi.org/10.1177/0095327X8601300101.

Spector, P. E. (1997). *Job satisfaction: Application, assessment, causes, and consequences* (Vol. 3). Thousand Oaks, CA: Sage publications.

Spitze, G. (1984). The effect of family migration on wives' employment: How long does it last? *Social Science Quarterly, 65*(11), 21–36.

Spry, T. (2001). Performing autoethnography: An embodied methodological praxis. *Qualitative Inquiry, 7*(6), 706–732. https://doi.org/10.1177/107780040100700605.

U.S. Army Posture Statement. (2009). Information paper, published by the Department of the Army. https://www.army.mil/aps/09/2009_army_posture_statement_web.pdf.

Chapter Two

Military Spouse Strategies for Navigating Academic and Personal Life

A Collaborative Autoethnographic Review of Post Graduate Pursuits

Alissa E. Harrison, Annette Maldonado, Beth van Kan, and Henrì Cooper

Today's military spouses represent a distinct cross-section of higher education's graduate population. According to the U.S. Chamber of Commerce Foundation (2017), military spouses tend to be more highly educated than their working-class American counterparts with more than 34% having earned a college degree and 15% continuing to a post-graduate degree. This cohort's distinction extends to time that they need to complete a degree. Harrell, Lim, Castaneda, and Golinelli's (2004) study of military spouse challenges in employment and education showed that spouses who persist generally take much longer than their civilian counterparts to complete their bachelor's degrees, as much as six to eight years for an undergraduate degree. Nevill and Chen's (2007) analysis of civilian postsecondary education found that students overall took an average of three years to complete a master's degree, about four years to achieve the first-professional degree, and up to six years to complete doctoral coursework and research and achieve a terminal degree (p. 43). The greatest impact on this timeline is caused by permanent changes in station (PCS) moves. A PCS is a routine aspect of military life. Typically, a new assignment translates to two to four years of physical stability. Such frequent moves are disruptive for many military spouses and often negatively affect completing higher college education.

    Harrell et al. (2004) found that out of a desire for personal fulfillment, military spouses tended to persevere to achieve a graduate-level degree, keep skills current, and ultimately enjoy a return on investment from higher-level education. What Harrell's study does not address are the strategies used by these military spouses to accomplish their goal. To initiate research that addresses how military spouses successfully exceed the graduation rates of their non-military counterparts despite unique challenges associated with military life, this study sought to identify military spouses' strategies by looking specifically at the necessary motivators and challenges referred to in Harrell et al.'s (2004) study. To do so, four military spouses, as participant researchers, used a collaborative autoethnographic methodology to explore their first-person narratives as military spouses who have navigated academia. The researchers' background, experience, motivation, and military perceptions offered a compelling opportunity to move research forward on this issue. The common themes generated from this collaborative process have implications for military spouses' future efforts to obtain a post-graduate degree.

From the research, a conceptual framework (Figure 2.1) was developed to explain how military spouses successfully pursue post-graduate study. By reviewing research participants' backgrounds, experiences, and values, it is possible to present how achievement motivators and challenges unique to military spouses might provide a platform for identifying essential strategies for achieving a graduate degree. The conceptual framework relates individual backgrounds, experiences, and values to the motivators (e.g., need for achievement) and challenges (e.g., family demands, financial demands, deployments, frequent PCS moves, etc.) faced by many military spouses. These motivators and challenges are then further linked to specific strategies identified from data generated by the participant researchers.

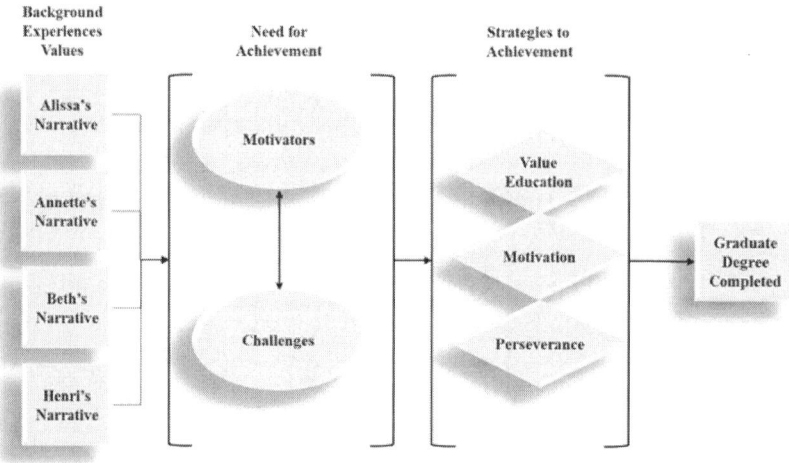

Figure 2.1. Conceptual Framework

LITERATURE REVIEW

Research has shown that military spouses face unique challenges in completing their graduate studies and earning an advanced degree. However, limited scholarly data exists on the motivational strategies that military spouses bring to bear to exceed the graduation rates of their civilian peers. The Research and Development (RAND) Corporation is a global policy think tank that studies U.S. Armed Forces' topics. The RAND project provides virtually the only in-depth research and analysis on military spouses' challenges when working toward an advanced degree and that research serves as the foundation for this study (Harrell et al., 2004).

Motivation is a decision-making process defined as "the forces within an individual that can push or propel him to satisfy basic needs" (Yorks, 1976, p. 21). Specifically, motivation prompts individuals to develop an inclination for specific behaviors (Kast & Rosenzweig, 1985, p. 296; Khurana & Joshi, 2017, p. 111). To understand those motivational factors and resulting behavior of military spouses, two theories of human motivation were applied. Herzberg's motivation-hygiene theory linked motivation and satisfaction and was used to examine military life challenges in ascertaining whether motivators (e.g., achievement) affect military spouse graduation (DeShields, Kara, & Kaynak, 2005). McClelland's (1987) theory of human motivation allowed for a more specific exploration of what drives so many military spouses to navigate military life and pursue a graduate level degree. McClelland (1987) focuses on three key factors—affiliation, power, and achievement. While affiliation and power offer compelling factors that could drive individuals to pursue a graduate level degree, the researchers used the lens of achievement to focus the analysis of motivational factors for this study. Indeed, the motivation required to attain a graduate level degree culminates in personal achievement. Yet, no matter how motivated a military spouse is to achieve a graduate degree, strategies are needed to support the need for flexibility and mitigate some of the barriers and inherent motivational factors that underpin academic success in achieving a graduate degree (Clever & Segal, 2013).

MILITARY SPOUSE ACADEMIC DEGREE CHALLENGES

Navigating academia while subject to the unique challenges posed by military life is a reality for military spouses at all levels of educational attainment. Frequent and disruptive moves, deployments, temporary absences of the service member, financial setbacks (e.g., in-state versus out-of-state tuition and childcare), and employment challenges represent a few noteworthy factors affecting military spouses who decide to navigate post-graduate educational opportunities. For many, the struggle is first taken up when earning an undergraduate degree and continues when pursuing a graduate degree.

Initial Challenges to Graduate Degree Success

Attaining an Undergraduate Degree

According to Harrell et al. (2004), many military spouses view the challenges they face as a significant hindrance to their undergraduate pursuits. For example, an Army E-7 spouse with a college degree lamented, "I've gone to four different colleges to get my degree because I followed him wherever he moved. So instead of four years to get my degree, it took six" (Harrell et al., 2004, p. 135). Echoing similar sentiments, other spouses claimed, "But who would watch the kids?" and "We'll PCS next year and I won't be able to finish the degree . . . then what?" (The Military Spouse Team, 2017, para. 3).

Challenges at the Graduate Degree Level

While many spouses are interested in pursuing a graduate or terminal degree, the heightened demands of family, work, and personal challenges are ubiquitous to the ever-changing military climate (Harrell et al., 2004). Often, the military lifestyle impacts military spouses' educational and career goals. Unlike many of their civilian counterparts, military spouses face frequent PCS moves, service member deployments, and financial barriers when seeking to attain higher education degrees (Ott, Morgan, & Akroyd, 2018). As a result, many military spouses' desire advanced graduate level degrees in portable fields like healthcare, business, mental health, and education (Ott et al., 2018, p. 30).

Upon attaining a bachelor's degree, research shows that many spouses demonstrate an intensification of motivation factors—personal achievement, graduate affiliations, or the power and control over their careers—a desire for that can be partially attributed to their ultimate success in attaining a graduate degree (McBride & Cleymans, 2014). Yet, according to the U.S. Chamber of Commerce Foundation (2017), many military spouses with degrees often face higher levels of unemployment when trying to find meaningful work. Given that many spouses have attained some measure of financial stability by the time they decide to pursue a graduate level degree, even the most motivated individual may hesitate risking that stability, given how PCS moves can extend the time and cost of pursuing a degree. Offering financial benefits is a tangible way that the military community supports the educational needs of spouses. For example, programs like the Post-911/GI Bill transfer offer a pathway for spouses to continue education pursuits (Taylor et al., 2011).

At the core of the challenges to earning a degree are the institutional culture and policies of higher education that present barriers for most military spouses (Gleiman & Swearengen, 2012, p. 83). Military spouses may often be relatively non-traditional students for most institutions of higher education and many spouses look for options that make education more accessible on military installations. Options that support education on the military base can minimize some of the barriers and thereby motivate spouses to continue their journey to higher education. Institutions that offer online and hybrid programs also create opportunities for military spouses to navigate post-graduate academics with greater success. Often, educational institutions that seek to support the military member do succeed in increasing the availability of post-graduate study opportunities to military spouses. Actively recruiting and supporting service members and their spouses through offering online programs, conducting classes during evening and weekends, and providing coaching, mentoring, and academic resources are needed examples of some of the services that might prove relevant when pursuing an advanced degree.

However, it is noteworthy that many spouses with graduate or terminal degrees claim military life supported their pursuits in achieving their degree (Harrell et al., 2004). After military spouses achieved their undergraduate degree, the impact of being a part of the military community did not impede the decision to continue and achieve a post-graduate degree (Harrell et al., 2004). According to the RAND study, normalizing the financial barrier by offering in-state tuition offered many spouses the opportunity to continue their education and post-undergraduate study. As one Air Force spouse surmised, "Education-wise, it's been a benefit because he's in the military, so active duty and spouses don't have to pay out-of-state tuition in Florida. Since I'm not a native Floridian, I would have had to pay greater tuition here" (Harrell et al., 2004, p. 131). While the RAND study focused on the financial barriers that challenged individuals seeking higher education, this study extends the discussion to understanding how motivation factors affect military spouse success in achieving their graduate degree.

Challenges to achieving a graduate degree begin at the undergraduate level for many military spouses. Succeeding in their first efforts to navigate the intersection of academia and military life provides strong motivational factors in pursuit of a graduate degree. Success in earning a graduate degree depends upon the support of the military community and the academic institution of choice—both academically and financially. The reality of military life is that you will PCS and that those moves can increase the time and cost of achieving your degree.

In the present study, we critically examined the challenges we faced and strategies we used to achieve our respective graduate degrees while our spouses served in the military. We reviewed, assessed, and discuss how our lives as military spouses influenced our educational journeys.

METHODOLOGY

As participant researchers, we chose a collaborative autoethnographic inquiry to explore our individual post-undergraduate experiences that span 30 years, collectively. Chang, Ngunjiri, and Hernandez (2013) define autoethnography as an approach to research and writing that seeks to describe personal experiences (auto) and systematically analyze (graphy) them to identify a common cultural experience (ethno). This study is an intimate version of collaborative autoethnography where a group of participant researchers constructed a culture and reality that engenders "a sense of community amongst the researchers" (Chang et al., 2013, p. 49). Additionally, "the process becomes as much of team-building activity as it is an approach to the production of knowledge" (Toyosaki, Pensoneau-Conway, Wendt, & Leathers, 2009, p. 58). This approach allows a narrative inquiry that further legitimizes the personal stories and experiences shared by a community of military spouse and post-graduate learners as we navigated academia. It is a methodology that is exactly suited to the sense of community with a team-building approach to military life that defines military spouses' interactions.

An abundance of non-peer reviewed literature and scholarly research explores the challenges many military spouses encounter as they pursue an undergraduate degree. Yet, limited data exists that explicitly addresses military spouses' achievement of a graduate or terminal degree. Recent research found that nearly three-quarters of spouses with graduate degrees identified several potential pitfalls associated with pursing post-graduate study (Harrell et al., 2004). What we're missing from the research are the specific motivators and challenges that were critical to success or failure. To that point, we found that our experiences aligned with several recurring themes identified through our individual data collection, data analysis, and interpretation.

DATA COLLECTION

Collaborative autoethnography requires group interaction (Figure 2.2). The researchers' aim was to (a) examine the similarities and differences in our post-graduate pursuits, (b) highlight the themes that underpinned our experiences, and (c) document the findings. To generate the data, we created a consistent format for data collection and entry. Each of the four researchers reviewed personal archives and located data from memory and recollection, self-observation, self-reflection, self-analysis, and populated the narratives in our data collection forms. Using first-person narratives, researchers presented their experiences as follows:

1. Early years (0–18): discussion of family life before college, decision to pursue higher education, and thoughts of marrying someone in the military.
2. Undergraduate through graduate school years and marriage: discussions of the undergraduate experience, the when and where of meeting your spouse, and getting married.
3. Graduate through terminal degree years and marriage: discussions of the decision to pursue a terminal degree and the graduate experience.
4. Reflections: what or how you would change the educational journey, how marriage impacted the educational journey, and the decision to pursue (or not) a terminal degree.

At an initial meeting, the researchers defined the type and format for the data needed for the study. Over the course of three months, each researcher collected the data and populated the data collection forms. Regular email and follow-up WebEx meetings provided a forum to discuss progress, ask questions, and exchange ideas. While brief, these discussions supported collaboration and self-examination through conversation and the exchange of stories. Moreover, a review of the initial product allowed for interpretation and responses to each researcher's reflections on the graduate experience in pursuit of their degree.

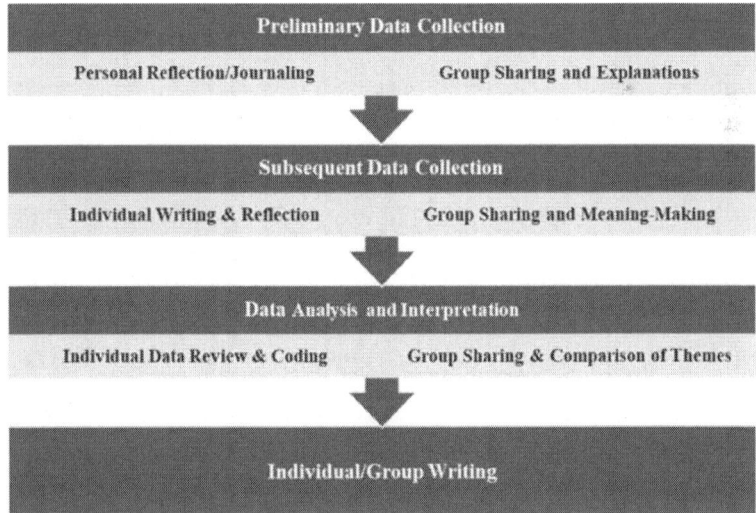

Figure 2.2. Collaborative Autoethnography Process
Adapted with permission from H. Chang, F. W. Ngunjiri, and K. C. Hernandez, 2013, Collaborative autoethnography, Walnut Creek, CA: Left Coast Press, Inc.

Upon completion of the preliminary data collection and the initial draft, each researcher reviewed the narratives and analyses of the collaborative accounts. Next, we reviewed the data for common themes contained in the narratives and commented on the cohort of experiences. The preliminary data collection, subsequent data collection, data analysis and interpretation process, and subsequent individual and group writing are illustrated in Figure 2.2.

RESULTS

To fully comprehend the nuances of completing graduate study for military spouses, a more in-depth understanding of the unique military life challenges is needed. Recognizing the distinctions starts with understanding the nature, challenges, culture, and motivations of those who chose to navigate the challenging demands of military family life combined with graduate studies. More importantly, our personal narratives recount specific strategies that kept each of us motivated as we achieved our goal.

Alissa's Narrative

No one in my immediate family had ever attended college. Still, I knew that I was destined from an early age to attend a university or college. In fifth grade, my teacher took an interest and encouraged me to explore science and math. My junior high school teacher thought my technical aptitude warranted placement in higher-level math. While accepted to Yale and other universities in my home state of Connecticut, my mom was excited when I decided to attend Howard University. With consistent positive feedback from my family and friends, I achieved an undergraduate degree in chemistry within four years. I wasn't certain where my education would lead me, but I was curious and enjoyed research and teaching. Having an undergraduate degree was a necessary first step to any future career pursuits.

My first encounter with the military in any formative way was as a freshman at Howard University. While my father served in the Korean War years before my birth, no one in my immediate family had any recent experiences with the military. So, my thoughts on whom I might marry as an adult did not include the military life as an option. Even as a college student, Michael embodied many of the traits that I was looking for in a future partner. Intelligence, competitiveness, sense of humor, and a deep love for family and friends were all attributes that changed my mind about the military and our future. I attended and participated in his commissioning ceremony, and we married on my birthday approximately one year after graduation. That decision changed my career direction and subsequently my academic goal timeline.

Many military spouses encounter unique challenges when they attempt to continue to a graduate-level degree. Notwithstanding frequent moves, the three-legged stool that presented barriers during the early years of our marriage were balancing family, military spouse commitments, and professional work commitments. Our first duty station was Fort Campbell, Kentucky. The logistics to attend a state university—limited finances and one car—resulted in me attending Austin Peay State University to pursue a post-bachelor certification in education instead of a master's degree in science. However, by the time we saved enough money for me to start my master's, we received orders to PCS to Washington, DC. Consequently, progress on what to study stalled as I tried to decide what field would be of interest to pursue a graduate degree as well as figuring out what I might want to do in the workplace. As a result, my interest in science, math, and technology coupled with a second bachelor's degree in computer science became the impetus for pursuing my graduate degree.

Early in our marriage, we had decided to wait to start a family. This decision, along with the postponement of my Master's degree study in Kentucky, increased savings for education. Coupled with my employer tuition benefits and flexible work scheduling, I selected and attended George Washington University to pursue a Master's degree in Administrative Sciences. However, our next PCS move almost derailed completing graduate studies. My military spouse received his orders to our next duty station earlier than expected, a full six months before my graduate studies were complete. Fortunately, a sympathetic advisor supported an exception to university policy and allowed me to take more than the allowed course load. The waiver enabled me to complete the requirements during that summer, and I joined him later that fall at Fort Benning, Georgia. Had it not been for a few accommodating professors at George Washington University, my postgraduate studies and subsequent master's degree pursuit might have ended that summer.

While I wanted to complete my doctoral studies by the time I was 30, that achievement did not come until I was well into my 50s. By then, we had three boys, several deployments, family care issues, and a few more military moves. The challenges of military life had extended my self-imposed timeline. Waiting until my children had completed high school to re-engage and seek out a Ph.D. program was the correct decision.

Unlike many spouses, my employers have been supportive at every stage of my educational journey. My education benefits covered nearly all the required tuition and fees at the graduate level, though I paid for my books and various fees. Additionally, my direct supervisor encouraged me to pursue a doctorate. In seeing the value that a terminal degree offered the company, my personal goal became a corporate objective in my annual review. As we were nearing military retirement, I decided during our last overseas tour in Japan to start my doctoral program. So while our family was stationed overseas, I selected a stateside school in Maryland for my doctoral program.

I am not sure what I was thinking at the time, but I was able to balance the role of senior military spouse and mom of two children in school overseas, and one stateside college student as I started work on achieving a terminal degree. My employer's decision to have me continue working part-time in a remote senior position provided the financial stability needed to pursue my degree. Since the doctoral program has a semester face-to-face residency requirement, I was able to coordinate that visit with my employer's requirement for me to return once a quarter for stateside team meetings and training. With all perceived barriers removed, I made completing my doctoral pursuit in three years a personal objective. I met that objective in December 2015.

Annette's Narrative

Before college, I lived in Puerto Rico. I was born and raised there in a small town on the west side of the island about three hours from the capital. My family comes from a lower socioeconomic group. While my mom finished her high school degree and my dad did not complete his elementary school education, I became the first-generation college graduate in our family. Our family experienced several setbacks, and when I was in middle school, my mom lost her job as a factory worker. Consequently, there were a lot of economic struggles in the family during my formative years. But, as my parents always told me, if you do not want to remain stuck in a cycle of poverty, you need to go to college and get a degree. That advice, along with noting the success of friends and their parents with degrees and successful professions guided me on my path to go to college.

Even though the location of a military reserve base was three hours away from my home, the component and function of the active-duty military structure are different from the National Guard and Reserve Units. I was not thinking about the military when I graduated from high school and went directly to college to pursue my undergraduate degree. I met my husband at college, and we dated throughout the four years of college and decided to get married after graduation. Entering the military via the ROTC route, he was commissioned as an officer in the Air Force and was assigned to our first duty station in Clovis, New Mexico. Clovis is a small town in eastern New Mexico located about two hours from Lubbock, Texas.

Clovis derailed my dream to continue to graduate school right after achieving my bachelor's degree. I wanted to study science and to pursue a graduate degree in biology, my undergraduate minor area. Unfortunately, the military impacted my educational journey because my preference was to attend a brick-and-mortar school, but an online institution was the only option available at our new duty station. Because I was unable to identify a program that matched my desires, I decided to wait. The inability to find a suitable program coupled with my husband's multiple deployments to Afghanistan and Iraq solidified my decision to wait. Upon his return, we received orders to Dayton, Ohio's, Air Force School of Technology where he finished his master's degree in 18 months. While there, I took advantage of the proximity of Wright State University to our duty station and earned my MBA degree. I made a personal goal to leave Dayton with my degree to align with our next PCS move. Fortunately, I achieved that goal and on time.

We recognized early in our marriage that children and PCS moves might introduce challenges in completing higher education. We decided to postpone having children until we completed our graduate degrees. We had our first child after 10 years of marriage and by that time I had achieved my MBA. As a supportive spouse, my husband was always very sensitive to my professional career aspirations and educational goals. He committed to supporting my educational goals while balancing his professional career objectives. Routine military moves for our family presented challenges to continue my educational journey and professional endeavors at the next level graduate school. Overall, these relocations presented such a significant barrier that we often discussed leaving the military so I could pursue continuing my education and have a professional career.

As I completed my MBA and my husband finished school at the Air Force Institute of Technology, the economy declined. Securing suitable employment was difficult. However, I accepted an internship and worked full-time for the government in financial management. While working on my MBA, I planned to enter the government system and become a GS-9, and eventually a GS-12. The program's process was a known as a pathway to GS-12. This program assists spouses with navigating federal employment opportunities. As it worked out, my husband received orders to PCS and I was unable complete the process for this government job. All attempts to modify the agreement and an agreement that aligned with the next PCS and a federal job at the new duty station did not work either. The employer informed me that there were no similar positions. Sadly, I was not able to find employment after graduate school.

Financial challenges are omnipresent barriers to my achieving a Ph.D. With the internship program, I was able to complete about half of the coursework for my master's degree and the reimbursement was approximately 75%

for the second half of my degree; I had to pay 100% of costs for the first half. In the end, the costs exceeded thirty thousand dollars and I have struggled to find employment after graduation due to the PCS moves. Because it required nearly ten years to pay back the educational loans, the associated costs were economically draining even without children at that time. As a young couple trying to save funds and "do the right thing" for our future, the cost of a full-time doctoral program when my job prospects are limited is highly prohibitive. Given the student loans that were incurred during my MBA degree journey, paying for a terminal degree is the most significant barrier to continuing my education. After our next move to the DC area, I was able to obtain a rewarding position in the federal sector that uses my MBA and positions me to continue with my goal of achieving a Ph.D.

Beth's Narrative

I believe that it was my success in middle school and high school that led me to believe I could succeed in college . . . and I do not mean academic success. I was a participant in many social activities and very successful in those activities. I was only an okay student during my secondary years. I had a newspaper route from grades 5 through 11 and babysat for a few of the families on my route. During my junior year of high school, I began working as a grocery store clerk, bagging groceries, returning carts, and was successively promoted to checker and then to the administrative office. During this time, I also played school sports, held class offices, participated in several clubs (and was President of more than one of those), including Ski Club, Computer Club, and Political Affairs Club. I was a very successful social student, which may have led my teachers and peers to see me as a successful academic student. However, I was only average because I did not prioritize academics.

There was never a time when my parents mentioned college in my future. Neither of them had gone to college, and we had a good, if modest, family life. I am not sure if my mother ever wanted us to leave our family home. It was my sister, four years older, who led the path to college and was an example of what to do. She studied hard and did well in school. She was accepted into an accounting program at Ohio State University and then switched her studies to nursing at a private nursing college. It was her journey that made me realize I would have to struggle with my parents for the opportunity to go to school.

I am not sure I would have chosen differently, but Ohio State University (OSU) worked well for my circumstances. I was not considering marriage at this point in my life nor was the military lifestyle in my realm of knowledge. Our family did not have any military members in it, and I did not know anyone in the service. I did have people I worked with to engage with socially, and a few friends from college classes. OSU is a big university, and it was the classes I took in Russian Language and Literature that brought me into a smaller group of people with a common interest and with whom I was able to spend some of my spare time socially. One of those people was my future husband.

John and I met my freshman year. He had already served in the U.S. Army for four years before he began his college career. It may have been we would have dated sooner, but John was intermittently absent for entire quarters at OSU. While at OSU, he served with a Reserve Unit and would miss whole quarters of classes intermittently to attend military training. I remember having a discussion with him about his military service and being surprised by it. One of his last duty stations had been with the 3rd U.S. Infantry Regiment, The Old Guard, as a Tomb Guard Sentinel. I must admit, even with my limited military knowledge and almost nonexistent travels, I had been to the Tomb of the Unknown Soldier, and I was impressed with his commitment to our nation and the obvious reverence he had for the position. I knew then that after he finished his studies at OSU, he would return to the Army.

We married six months after I graduated. John graduated from OSU in 1992. At my insistence, he had applied for an ROTC Scholarship and received it. I worked as a full-time Financial Aid Counselor for OSU while John completed his degree. I accepted my position anticipating John would be commissioned into the Army, and he was. When I left my first professional job, I was 23, four months pregnant, and would be moving more than 30 minutes away from my parents for the first time in my life. Our first duty station was Ft. Huachuca, Arizona. With a PCS move to Germany next in our forecast, we made the decision that I would become a stay-at-home mom. I planned to return to the workforce once the kids were out of the home. Given the military lifestyle and moves, I did not regret delaying pursuing my education and employment.

It was 2006 when I was accepted into a Master of Science program to study school library media at McDaniel College in Maryland. I reasoned that if I completed the program by 2010, I would graduate the same year our oldest would graduate from high school. When I began my studies, John was serving an unaccompanied 12-month tour at the U.S. Embassy in Pakistan. I had been working for a high school as a part-time registrar for two years. This is when the county I worked for advertised a cohort group for an M.S. in school library media. I applied and was accepted into the program. While John was away, I began not only the program but also began to work full time in the middle school library where my youngest child attended school. Keeping busy was always key to enduring his absences and working full-time in the school library kept me on the kids' schedules. Evening, weekend, and online courses were now added to the schedule along with the responsibility of getting the kids to karate, swimming, three different music lessons, volleyball, marching band, and other various activities. These things fulfilled my keeping busy requirement.

With a mixture of courses in education from the community college and master's degree courses from McDaniel College, I completed my degree in 2010 and went on to be certified to teach and administer school libraries in Maryland in grades K–12. Even though John retired from the Army on his return from Pakistan in 2008, I received my degree just in time for him to come home and say, "Do you want to move to the Philippines?" I said, "Yes!" And so my educational journey culminated in a Master's Degree and a guaranteed full-time school librarian job offer in Howard County, Maryland. It also included a move to the Philippines so that my husband, the now civilian, could serve in the U.S. Embassy in Manila. Once again, we uprooted our lives and carried on.

Henrì's Narrative

I grew up in a military town, with Army, Air Force, and Navy facilities nearby. My father, now long retired, had enlisted in the Air Force. Because of my father's PCS moves, my older sister and I received two years of our elementary education in Okinawa, Japan, while my mother taught adult education at the nearby Kadena Air Force Base. Though I grew up and was exposed to a military community, the thought of marriage, much less to a service member, was not something I consciously entertained.

Many of the people with whom I interacted while growing up were educators. Education was of great importance to my family and associates. My maternal grandparents, great-aunts, great-uncles, mother, aunts, and uncles were all college educated, many with degrees beyond the baccalaureate. Many of my family members were educators themselves. One source of family pride was that my grandfather was a doctoral candidate and was all but dissertation (ABD). His pursuit of this advanced degree was delayed because of a growing family. College attendance was not something I gave great thought. In my family, it was a natural progression after high school. The decision was which college to attend.

Throughout my high school and college years, I maintained a relationship with my boyfriend, who became my husband. The discussion of marriage came up at the end of my senior year of high school, but we both decided that we were much too young and should wait a while longer. I intended to acquire a college degree. My dream after graduation was to become a lawyer. Upon graduation from high school, I received a scholarship to a prestigious college that had a law school in its affiliation. During my first semester, I realized that this was not the place for me. I enjoyed the diversity of my classmates, and the climate within the college was amicable; however, I found the surrounding environment and attitudes to be less than welcoming. Following the advice of my mother to "give it at least a year," I "survived" my freshman year. Nearing the completion of my freshman year, after having convinced my mother of my need to relocate, I eagerly anticipated my transfer to another institution of higher learning.

While in college, I maintained a respectable academic GPA, was involved in several organizations and activities, and even pledged a national sorority. I took it upon myself to find a job, unbeknownst to my parents, to help supplement my finances. Once they became aware of my working, they were not pleased and stipulated that I was to "quit" should my grades begin to suffer. In my home, it was made abundantly clear that neither the pursuit of finances nor romance was to interfere with the acquisition of a college degree.

Sometime during my sophomore year, my boyfriend decided to join the Army ROTC program at our college. I observed a "no one tells me what to do" type individual transform into a military leader. This changed the trajectory of our relationship over the next few years as he became a "gung-ho" military cadet, with a greater vision of his future and potential to establish and care for a wife and family. Because of the ROTC, our talks of marriage increased, and I was faced with the real possibility of becoming a military spouse. Directly after graduation, I entered graduate school and simultaneously began my career as a teacher. During that time, I had applied for a teaching position in Northern Virginia. The year he acquired his degree and commissioned, we officially confirmed plans to marry. I received an offer from the Northern Virginia school system, and my soon-to-be husband received orders for his first duty assignment.

I thought I was prepared for this journey, having grown up as a military "brat." It was during this time that I first became aware of the implications of being a military spouse. As a result of my future husband's orders, we decided that I would not accept the teaching position, but instead look for employment where he was stationed. Wedding planning was no easy feat, as we had to arrange our wedding date around his three-day leave during an officer basic course at Fort Benning, Georgia. Because of military obligations and our desire to reside as one household, I withdrew from graduate school and turned down my offer of a job.

My husband and I married during a holiday weekend. We married on a Saturday and were on the road from Virginia to Fort Benning, Georgia, on Sunday, so my husband could return by 0600 on Monday. My arrival at Fort Campbell, Kentucky, after his Fort Benning training was greeted with my husband's deployment for an unspecified amount of time to an unspecified location in the Middle East. I was quickly introduced to military spouses of other officers in the battalion.

Aside from the other battalion spouses, there developed a closeness among family members because of common PCS assignments, interests, family dynamics, being neighbors, or necessity. Military deployments were frequent and long, resulting in family members of the service members relying on one another as a source of support, information, and comfort. There were significant increases in family sizes upon the service members' return from deployment. Many military spouses gave birth when their husbands were deployed, causing them to depend on the support of other spouses or family members. We decided to delay children and graduate school until we could have greater assurance that my husband would be around for delivery. The arrival of the first child came after 4½ years in the military and the second child arrived at year 8½.

At each PCS, the idea of graduate school was addressed. Always present in my mind was the possibility of not completing a program in the required time, thus having to transfer (and again lose credits hours) due to a possible PCS, monetary obligations, and children. Though courses were taken to recertify in my field, I never actively pursued graduate school until my husband's separation from the military. At that time, I was in my 40s, my children had completed high school, my husband was self-employed, and we were financially stable and well established. With family, career, and leaving the military aligned, I was able to complete my graduate degree in Education.

CONNECTING REFLECTIONS TO THE NARRATIVE

The data for this study combined scholarly research on challenges and motivations for achieving higher-level education with personal narratives, memories, and reflections for data analysis and interpretation. Thomas and Harden (2008) suggest three stages for thematic synthesis, all which support connecting narrative reflections to literature: coding text "line-by-line," developing descriptive themes, and generating analytical themes (p. 45). For this study, there was no intrinsic narrative coding. As an alternative, we identified three consistent themes throughout the narratives: the value of education, motivation, and perseverance.

Value of Education

The commonalities in our backgrounds included the value of education. Our diverse backgrounds mirror that of the military community. In fact, two participants in this study are African American, one is White, and another is Puerto Rican. Raised in the north, south, east, and an island territory of the United States, what we had in common were parents who valued and expected college to be a factor in our success. For example, Annette recognized the importance in pursuing education as a child: "I knew that not having a degree would be the difference between getting stuck there and not being able to be successful and to be able to provide more." Similarly, Beth and Henrí experienced family pressure to obtain undergraduate degrees; however, the impetus was more that graduating from college was a given. Annette and Alissa were the first to receive a degree in their families. Both came from a lower socio-economic stratum, and the motivation to achieve was a predominant driver in degree completion. Comparatively, all four met or dated a military service member in college.

According to Alexander and Reilly's (1981) research of the effects on marriage timing and educational attainment, marrying early often proves detrimental to achieving a higher level degree. Given a recent study exploring underemployment and educational attainment, our combined experiences strengthen the case for military spouses who obtain degrees prior to marrying (Maury & Stone, 2014). In contrast to much of the research, we all completed our undergraduate education before getting married. We recognized education as valuable and that understanding offered broad implications for our future success in finishing our undergraduate degree. Application of early lessons learned to graduate level pursuit might have supported or facilitated moving us to the next level, either graduate school or entering a doctoral program.

Motivation

Motivation evolved as the second common theme as the military spouse moved from undergraduate to graduate level study. Clearly, military spouses are motivated; however, mitigating the inherent motivational factors espoused by Clever & Segal (2013) typically underscore academic success. Specifically, how to intrinsically link education with the extrinsic benefits of career and employment was a prevalent factor for all four narratives. In navigating frequent PCS moves, deployments, and family and friends, military spouses have mastered the art of adaptability, creativity, patience, and flexibility in the face of personal challenges to complete graduate study. As Yager (2006) said, over-achievers have a high sense of task significance, urgency, and tend to work hard and are more efficient performers.

Perhaps coincidently, we each delayed the start of our graduate studies due to PCS moves. Alissa and Annette, both science undergraduate majors, wanted to start their graduate studies immediately upon receiving their undergraduate degrees. Unfortunately, their first PCS to base installations were in remote locations and more than an hour's commute to a suitable university to continue their studies. Alissa stated, "The closest school with a graduate program of interest was in Nashville, Tennessee." Similarly, Annette commented, "But, because we moved to this location, I was unable to do that due to the lack of higher education institutions nearby."

Despite the motivation to complete the graduate program, disruptive moves presented a more significant barrier than financial constraints. Balancing the military lifestyle challenges while remaining motivated typically determines whether the spouse achieves graduate level success. While all narratives exhibited strong achievement motivations that resulted in success, the narratives suggest that lack of availability of the right programs drives most military spouses to delay education pursuits. Due to the frequency of PCS moves, Henrì waited until her spouse left military service. Even Beth delayed completion and tied getting her graduate degree with her spouse's retirement. Quite simply, base installations are not typically located near suitable universities. Our shared experience showed that achieving at the graduate level required flexibility and adaptability to align the right university as we moved with our service member.

Perseverance

The third theme showed how perseverance factored into navigating military and personal life. Due to the contextual effects of military base locations and surrounding labor markets, military spouses encounter employment challenges (Clever & Segal, 2013, p. 27). A higher-level degree helped to secure and further career goals. As Beth stated: "Though it took me four more years than I had expected, I have reached the goal I was seeking in 2010, and one of the goals I had set for myself in 1992. My four-year hiatus after completing my master's degree did not impede my hiring potential." Alissa noted that she received her terminal degree in three years; however, military moves slowed plans to start that journey by nearly three decades. Annette, the only researcher with a spouse currently on active duty, remains strongly motivated and plans to continue. She states: "I have not been able to pursue a Ph.D., which is my goal. But, right now I am lucky that we moved to the DC area, and I was able to find an awesome opportunity."

SUMMARY

Through collaborative autoethnography, we identified several strategies from the collection process and analysis of the data. With a deeper understanding of our individual selves and our collective selves as military spouses, we arrived at a common understanding of the military spouse's needs as interest in graduate study evolves (Chang et al., 2013). As military leaders respond to the challenges of supporting the military member and their families, this institution needs to develop innovative solutions to support military spouse education and career requirements. Areas of consideration include deployments, frequency, and location of base installations for PCS during relocation, issues that extend the undergraduate and graduate level experience, and financial challenges associated with tuition and fees.

A recurring theme, frequent PCS moves, highlighted the financial barrier of tuition, fees, and general costs because of restarting education. Clearly, the mobile military lifestyle can hinder obtaining higher-level degrees because of the inability to transfer credits, completing the course, or completing of the degree (McBride & Cleymans, 2014, p. 97). Exploring each researcher's personal experiences in navigating life as a military spouse while achieving a graduate degree provided the impetus for this project. Reflecting upon narrative discussions through an autoethnographic review of our post-graduate pursuits offers spouses ways to mitigate some of the present-day barriers through an analysis of the lessons learned.

CONCLUSIONS AND FINAL REFLECTIONS

A review of the literature found that there is little to no academic literature that presents findings in terms of the military spouse's motivation strategies for graduate study. Scholarly research primarily analyzed education and employment at the undergraduate level or from the service member perspective. In selecting a collaborative autoethnographic methodology to identify motivators of military spouses' successful graduate degree achievement, we sought to add to this limited body of literature by looking through the lens of the military community. Four participant researchers contributed to the data collection process by providing narratives that reflected our diverse backgrounds, experiences and positions, analysis, explanation, writing, and review process.

In our inquiry, we found that the uniqueness of our individual experiences, identified through group sharing, were attributable to the transient nature of military life, as was found by Chang et al. (2013). Multiple deployments, the inconvenient and remote locations of most military bases, frequent moves with little or minimal notice, limited transportation options, and costs of education represent some of the common challenges experienced by military spouses.

Our collaborative autoethnographic study involved three distinct layers of self-discovery and reflection. Our personal narratives as military spouses on the topic of obtaining a graduate degree included consistent factors that underpinned our individual journeys, which spanned several decades. Analysis of the research revealed three common themes in the experience of military spouses meeting the challenges inherent in the pursuit of a graduate degree. First, we all had an undergraduate degree before marriage and a determination to obtain a master's degree. Next, we were self-motivated and highly focused achievers academically and in our professional careers. Lastly, a persistent, creative, and resilient drive in our pursuits of graduate education motivated us through completion of graduate studies.

This collaborative autoethnographic experience was successful for two reasons. First, it was paramount that military spouses develop a sense of solidarity through discovery of self and others in meeting the challenges of achieving a graduate degree as a military spouse (Chang et al., 2013). In sharing our narratives, we offer strategies that can be used by other military spouses. Second, the authors were able to highlight the use of collaborative autoethnography as a tool to support developing a sense of community (p. 144).

Although our experiences are not unique for military spouses, we recognize that the challenges can have an impact on the collective military community. Navigating collaborative autoethnography is an enabling tool that offered a view beyond our individual perspectives to create a shared sense of how our individual journeys have parallels within the military community at large. As we continue to share our experiences, we will use our collective voices to identify strategies that might help motivate other military spouses to persevere and obtain their graduate degree.

REFERENCES

Alexander, K. L., & Reilly, T. W. (1981). Estimating the effects of marriage timing on educational attainment: Some procedural issues and substantive clarifications. *American Journal of Sociology*, *87*(1), 143–156. http://dx.doi.org/10.1086/227422.

Chang, H., Ngunjiri, F., & Hernandez, K. (2013). *Collaborative autoethnography*. Walnut Creek, CA: Left Coast Press, Inc.

Clever, M., & Segal, D. (2013). The demographics of military children and families. *The Future of Children*, *23*(2), 13–39. https://doi.org/10.1353/foc.2013.0018.

DeShields, O. J., Kara, A., & Kaynak, E. (2005). Determinants of business student satisfaction and retention in higher education: Applying Herzberg's two-factor theory. *International Journal of Educational Management, 19*(2), 128–139. https://doi.org/10.1108/09513540510582426.

Gleiman, A., & Swearengen, S. (2012). Understanding the military spouse learner using theory and personal narratives. *New Directions for Adult and Continuing Education, 136,* 77–88. https://doi.org/10.1002/ace.20037.

Harrell, M. C., Lim, N., Castaneda, L. W., & Golinelli, D. (2004). *Working around the military: Challenges to military spouse employment and education.* Santa Monica, CA: RAND Corporation.

Herzberg, F. (1968). One more time: How do you motivate employees? *Harvard Business Review, 46*(1), 53. https://doi.org/10.1007/978-1-349-02701-9_2.

Kast, F. & Rosenzweig, J. (1985). *Organization and management : A systems and contingency approach.* New York, NY: McGraw-Hill.

Khurana, H., & Joshi, V. (2017). Motivation and its impact on individual performance: A comparative study based on McClelland's three need model. *CLEAR International Journal of Research in Commerce & Management, 8*(7), 110–116. Retrieved from http://www.clear-research.in/.

Maury, R., & Stone, B. (2014). *Military spouse employment report.* Institute for Veterans and Military Families. Retrieved from http://www.moaa.org/Content/Publications-and-Media/MOAA-Blog/Military-Spouse-Employment-Report.aspx.

McBride, P., & Cleymans, L. (2014). A paradigm shift: Strategies for assisting military spouses in obtaining a successful career path. *Career Planning and Adult Development Journal, 30*(3), 92–102. Retrieved from https://www.questia.com/read/1P3-345604903 1/a.

McClelland, D. (1987). *Human motivation.* New York, NY: Cambidge University Press.

Nevill, S. C., & Chen, X. (2007). The path through graduate school: A longitudinal examination 10 years after bachelor's degree. Postsecondary Education Descriptive Analysis Report. NCES 2007-162. *National Center for Education Statistics.* Retrieved from https://files.eric.ed.gov/fulltext/ED495661.pdf.

Ott, L. E., & Morgan, K. & Akroyd, H. D. (2018). Impact of military lifestyle on military spouses' educational and career goals. *Journal of Research in Education, 28*(1), 30–61. Retrieved from https://files.eric.ed.gov/fulltext/EJ1168179.pdf.

Pardee, R. L. (1990, February). *Motivation theories of Maslow, Herzberg, McGregor & McClelland. A literature review of selected theories dealing with job satisfaction and motivation.* Retrieved from ERIC database (ED316767).

Taylor, P., Morin, R., Parker, K., Cohn, D., Funk, C., & Mokrzycki, M. (2011). *The military-civilian gap: War and sacrifice in the post-9/11 era.* Retrieved from http://www.pewsocialtrends.org/.

The Military Spouse Team. (2017). The pursuit of education as a military spouse [Web log post]. Retrieved from https://militaryspouse.com/career/education/the-pursuit-of-education-as-a-military-spouse/.

Thomas, J., & Harden, A. (2008). Methods for the thematic synthesis of qualitative research in systematic review. *BMC Medical Research Methodology, 8*(45). https://doi.org/10.1186/1471-2288-8-45.

Toyosaki, S., Pensoneau-Conway, S. L., Wendt, N. A., & Leathers, K. (2009). Community autoethnography: Compiling the personal and resituating whiteness. *Cultural Studies-Critical Methodologies*, *9*(1), 56–83. https://doi.org/10.1177/1532708608321498.

U.S. Chamber of Commerce Foundation. (2017, June). *Military spouse in the workplace: Understanding the impact of military spouse employment on military recruitment, retention, and readiness* [Hire Our Heroes series]. Retrieved from U.S. Chamber of Commerce Foundation website: www.uschamberfoundation.org/sites.

Yager, E. (2006, April 14–20). Controlling achievement overdrive. *The Enterprise/Salt Lake*, p. 9.

Yorks, L. (1976). *A radical approach to job enrichment*. New York, NY: Amacom.

Chapter Three

Cultural Collision
A Review of Literature
Amy May and Victoria McDermott

The military and the academy are two distinct cultures with clearly defined norms, values, and beliefs. Historically, the military has been defined by conformity and uniformity, while the academy has pushed for freedom of thought and social change. For married couples attempting to bridge the cultural divide, competing and conflicting ideologies have the potential to negatively impact interpersonal communication and the overall level of relationship satisfaction. To understand the impact of the military and academic cultures on marital communication and relational outcomes, it is important to consider the norms and values of these cultures, the greedy nature of both institutions, and the communication challenges that occur when cultures collide. As such, in this chapter, we address historical tenets associated with military culture and academic culture, and we consider how these cultures collide for military/academic spouses in relational and organizational contexts. We begin by reviewing concepts of both military and academic systems independently and then juxtapose them to attempt to understand the experiences of military spouses with advanced degrees. Throughout this review of literature, we focus on how these concepts may affect communication between members of the military family.

MILITARY CULTURE

Since 1775, United States military has been tasked with "[deterring] war and [protecting] the security of our country" (DoD, 2017, para. 9). This elite force is comprised of "the few, the proud, the brave" who volunteer to serve their country across five distinct branches: Army, Navy, Air Force, Marine Corps, and Coast Guard. Today, 1.3 million active-duty troops, roughly 0.04% of the population, and 865,000 reservists serve as members of the armed forces (Lai, Griggs, Fisher, & Carlsen, 2017; Parker, Cilluffo, & Stepler, 2017). As a functioning unit, the military has a rich history and complex culture. While the policies and practices of the military have changed to reflect an evolving and more diverse society, many of the foundational cultural values remain steadfast, creating opportunity for both inclusion and conflict.

Military culture, defined by a strict hierarchy, order-based decision making, and the emphasis on acting in favor of the greater good (Halvorson, Whitter, & Taitt, 2010) creates inclusion and loyalty within its ranks. Moreover, these operational values help maintain status quo and reinforce homogeneity. In part, military culture is defined by conservative and moral ideologies (Taber, 2009), isolationism, defined gender norms, and the threat of violence.

Conservative and Moral Ideologies

Ideologies guide how an individual interprets and responds to aspects of political and social environments (Malka & Lelkes, 2010). Conservative ideology is characterized as supporting a large military with heavy military intervention in world affairs, maintaining the status quo, and limited government welfare (Malka & Lelkes, 2010). Liberal ideologies, on the other hand, coincide with the belief of a smaller military with limited military intervention in world affairs, change, and the support of social welfare (Malka & Lelkes, 2010).

As an institution, the military honors traditional institutions and practices, reflecting a more conservative ideology. Since 1789, soldiers have pledged to "bear true faith and allegiance . . . so help [them] God" (Title 10 of 1956; 2018) to their country and core. Loyalty, duty, respect, selfless service, honor, integrity, and personal courage provide the framework for the military code of conduct and the standard by which soldiers are judged personally, professionally, and legally, within the military justice system (Uniform Code of Military Justice of 1951; 2018).

These rules are in place to train service members to be effective at following orders and defending one's country, while heavily reinforcing the culture the military wants to perpetuate (Turchik & Wilson, 2010). Ethical standards and rules of conduct guide personal and professional behavior, reinforcing morality and patriotism as core values (Dunivin, 1994). Soldiers who demonstrate unethical behavior or act in an immoral way may be punished and/or discharged from service (Uniform Code of Military Justice of 1951; 2018). For example, in the civilian world, a cheating spouse is not likely to affect a person's career trajectory. Under the Uniform Code of Military Justice, however, a service member caught cheating on a spouse can be punished for breaching Article 134 with loss of rank, tarnished reputation, extra guard hours, forfeiture of pay, or even dishonorable discharge (Uniform Code of Military Justice of 1951; 2018).

Isolationism in the Military Community

Due to the current self-selected nature of the military and the specific eligibility requirements, the military tends to draw from a select sample of the population (Turchik & Wilson, 2010). The United States military is comprised of younger individuals, more people with high school degrees than those with higher education, and fewer women than is reflected in the overall population; furthermore, the military is mostly white (70%; DoD, ODASD, & MC&FP, 2016). Additionally, the recruitment strategies used by the military suggest a clear and targeted attempt to reach a masculine audience, focusing on physical strength, a "warrior strong" mentality, and masculine pride (Reit, 2017).

Along with the defining demographic profile, military bases or posts are designed to be self-sufficient, complete with their own police, courts, schools, and medical systems (Turchik & Wilson, 2010). Correspondingly, bases have specific amenities that are consistent from site to site to provide a semblance of familiarity. Military posts and bases contain everything from grocery stores to fast food chains that can be found throughout the United States and across the globe (Zucchino & Cloud, 2015; Carter & Barno, 2013). "Military bases are our most exclusive gated communities" (Zucchino & Cloud, 2015, para. 29) with many bases and posts largely off-limits to civilians. Entrances with locked gates, concrete barricades and armed soldiers further provide evidence of their exclusivity.

Military families are separated geographically, socially, and economically from the outside society they serve (Carter & Barno, 2013, para. 2). While not all active-duty military families may live on base, many families are bound to military installation for health care and other services. Moreover, communities surrounding bases tend to be heavily military oriented with neighborhoods containing large numbers of active-duty military families and veterans (Zucchino & Cloud, 2015; Carter & Barno, 2013). Through this, military branches are able to create fully immersive socialization processes where service members and their families are heavily co-dependent on the military to provide everything, while simultaneously creating a further divide between military and civilian life (Zucchino & Cloud, 2015; Carter & Barno, 2013; Drummet, Coleman, & Cable, 2003).

Defined Gender Norms

Despite the increased presence of women and the LGBTQ community, the military remains a masculinist institution (Weitz, 2015; Silva, 2008; Cohn, 2000). Historically, the profession of war, defense and combat have been defined in terms of the masculine (Binkin & Bach, 1977; Enloe, 1983) with an idealized, hypermasculine warrior-image (Archer, 2013; Dunivin, 1994). Hyper-masculinity is an extreme form of masculinity based on polarized traditional gender roles, power, competition, control, toleration of pain, and mandatory heterosexuality (Hunter, 2007). The hyper-masculine military male should exemplify the ideal qualities of heroism, strength, and endurance, leaving no room for weakness or vulnerability (Keats, 2010). Moreover, through the identity of the masculine warrior, the military is able to achieve exclusion and homogeneity, creating a tighter bond among active service members (Weitz, 2015).

Soldiers who fall outside the hypermasculine, warrior identity are often scrutinized or ostracized regardless of gender identity (Johnson, Rosenstein, Buhrke, & Haldeman, 2015; Weitz, 2015; Fassinger, 2008; Decew, 1995; Dunivin, 1994). As such, any behavior that might be "interpreted as the slightest bit feminine . . . is considered weak and unfit for military service" (Johnson et al., 2015, p. 47), and soldiers falling outside of the masculine norm are expected to adapt. As noted by one female veteran, women are:

> "Expected to behave and perform in traditionally masculine ways—demonstrating strength, displaying confidence in their abilities, expecting to be judged on their merits and performance. . . . The military doesn't just urge women, it requires them—especially if they want to succeed—to view themselves on the same playing field as their male counterparts." (Maples, 2017, para. 2)

In addition to a narrow definition of the masculine, women are still overlooked for specific military occupational specialties (MOSs), and women may face obstacles when attempting to gain organizational power (Turchik & Wilson, 2010). While women are transitioning into more combat-related roles, they are still excluded from particular jobs with the argument of preserving combat effectiveness (WIIS, 2017; Decew, 1995). As of 2017, no women had been selected for armor training, or for any special operation teams (e.g., Army Special Forces, Navy SEALS, Marine Raiders, or Battlefield Airmen) (WIIS, 2017). Moreover, while official DoD policy may remove formal barriers and token examples of successful female recruits appease the masses, informal barriers, including sexual harassment and social ostracism, still exist, making it difficult for women to compete (O'Malley, 2015).

Threat of Violence

Violence exists in the military and may be viewed as a legitimized way to achieve a means to an end endorsed by the government. Over the years, the approach to training soldiers for violence in battle has evolved. During World War II, for example, most service members were not shooting to hit or kill the enemy (Grossman, 1996). Training methods over time, however, have been revised and now use desensitization and conditioning to increase firing and killing rates. Service members are now trained to accept a culture of violence and to understand that killing is part of their job in active combat (Turchik & Wilson, 2010). Off the field, a combination of desensitization, specialized training, culture-specific rewards, and validations reinforces hyper-masculine violence and a subculture with little room for tolerance or difference (O'Malley, 2015), which may be problematic as the military becomes more gender inclusive. Specifically, evidence suggests "the hypermasculine culture of the military is the core issue perpetuating sexual assault" (O'Malley, 2015, p. 20) and may contribute to the acceptance of rape myths (Aosved & Long, 2006).

The military has responded in recent years to the threat of violence and a desire to improve the safety of all service members by implementing mandated training programs, such as Sexual Harassment and Assault Response and Prevention (SHARP) in the Army and Sexual Assault Response and Prevention (SARP) Program in the Navy (Turchik & Wilson, 2010). These programs encourage soldiers to intervene, act, and motivate each other to "denounce sexual misconduct" and ". . . take action" (U.S. Army, n.d., Motivate, para. 1). Despite increasing awareness, the overall effectiveness of these programs is unclear. As evidenced by a 2008 joint investigation by the DoD and the Government Accountability Office, 13% to 43% of military personnel were not sure how to report an assault, even after training (Government Accountability Office, 2008; U.S. Department of Defense, 2018). One-third of women in the military did not know how to formally report a rape and only 26% of victims reported their sexual assault to the chain of command (Sadler et al., 2003). Fear of retaliation and/or negative impact to future career aspirations may also be of concern for reporters (O'Malley, 2015).

In recent years, programs have been implemented to increase reporting with noted success. Throughout fiscal year 2017, an upsurge of sexual assault reports was seen across all branches (U.S. Department of Defense, 2018; Cohen & Browne, 2018; Saintsing, 2018; Ferdinando, 2018), ranging from an 8% increase in the Army[1] to an alarming 14.7% increase in the Marine Corps, flagging the attention of the Sexual Assault Prevention and Response Office (SAPRO; Cohen & Browne, 2018; U.S. Department of Defense, 2018;

Saintsing, 2018; Ferdinando, 2018). These rates do not account for service members who may not feel comfortable reporting harassment or barriers that prevent people from reporting (U.S. Department of Defense, 2018). While this increase in sexual assault reports for Fiscal Year 2017 may not indicate an increase in sexual assaults or harassment, the Department of Defense recognizes sexual assault and harassment as prevalent issues (Cohen & Browne, 2018; Ferdinando, 2018).

Cultural norms regarding violence are changing as evidenced by recent policy changes. Victims of sexual assault have "increased control over the release and management of their personal information, . . . [empowering] them to make more informed decisions" about reporting and participating in the investigative process (DoD, n.d., para. 3). Military personnel can now file a restricted report, which allows them to receive care and treatment services for their sexual assault but does not spur an investigation or identify the victim to his or her chain of command (MCCS Forward, 2016; DoD, n.d.). A person may choose restricted reporting over unrestricted reporting because of the fear of negative career outcomes and retaliation (Rosellini et al., 2017; Darehshori et al., 2015; Burns et al., 2014; Mengeling et al., 2014).

Summation

Overall, military organizations "represent a specific occupational culture which is relatively isolated from society" (Soeters, Winslow, & Weibull, 2006, p. 237). Cultural norms, values, and beliefs reinforce service to country and strong bonds between brothers/sisters in arms. The job of a Soldier, Airman, Sailor, or Marine becomes less of a job and more of a lifestyle requiring obedience, conformity, and respect for the chain of command. Traditional gender norms and the threat of violence have long defined military service; however, evolving policies and practices are evidence of an evolving culture.

ACADEMIC CULTURE

Academia, much like the military, is steeped in tradition and requires much of its service members. In opposition to the military, the academy facilitates academic freedom and liberal ways of thinking for constant questioning of the status quo. Within the academy there is also an underlying desire to bring about social change, and an expectation of freedom to practice without unreasonable interference from a chain of command.

As an institution, academia has a rich history and dynamic culture. Originally tasked with ensuring clergy were educated in their mission to serve

God and the people (Kaufman, 2018; Eckel & King, 2004), the focus of higher education quickly broadened (Kaufman, 2018; Eckel & King, 2004) as revolutionaries pushed to separate church and state and educate the general populous (Chan, 2016). Today, over 20.4 million students enroll in higher education each year (U.S. Department of Education, 2017a). As with the military, the academy has attempted to evolve to reflect the increasingly diverse populations they serve; however, many of the foundational cultural values remain unchanged, creating both the opportunity for growth and strife.

One of the primary pillars of the culture of higher education is the development and refinement of critical thinking (Kurfiss, 1988), allowing students to challenge traditional institutions and advocate for change. While these cultural norms may seek to challenge society outside of the ivory tower, the academy remains a hierarchy rich, status-driven institution. Collectively, the academy espouses liberal ideologies, advocates for inclusion/diversity, and strives to change narratives regarding violence.

Liberal Ways of Thinking

The specific mission and ideologies within the academic setting may change based on the institution and/or individual faculty member; however, the overall assumption is that higher education functions as a catalyst for initiating social change, stimulating economic growth and increasing people's quality of life (Stier, 2011). As an institution, the academy reflects a more liberal ideological way of thinking. While the academy is not a liberal hegemony (Zipp & Fenwick, 2006) but a trend toward moderation from both ends of the spectrum, many professors and instructors prescribe to the traditional ideals of higher education, including "an appreciation of literature and the arts, creative thinking, and the free exchange" (Zipp & Fenwick, 2006, p. 320).

Generally speaking, the role of higher education is to support the welfare of future generations through the fostering of knowledge and increasing people's quality of life through education. Through the more liberal ideologies within the academy, people are given the space to think more freely to initiate change, critically analyze the status quo, and challenge the privilege of those in/with power. The academy is fueled by the appreciation of critical thinking and the construction of new knowledge (Stier, 2011; Zipp & Fenwick, 2006).

Academic Community

Communally, academia strives for diversity, inclusion, and access, pushing members to think, challenge, and support social change (Harvard, 2018). When there is limited access to higher education, social inequality is sustained

(Stier, 2011). To improve access and completion, four-year-degree-granting post-secondary institutions offer grants, merit-based scholarships, and strategic campus resources. For the 2014–2015 academic year, 86% of first-time, full-time degree/certificate-seeking undergraduates received some sort of financial aid, making college more affordable and accessible (U.S. Department of Education, 2017c). Likewise, most colleges and universities offer student support services to meet the needs of diverse populations of learners. Veterans, LGBTQ, and countless other groups are represented on campus by departments and student organizations designed to improve student retention and completion rates. While pushing for increased access and providing aid is noble, there are contradictions that challenge espoused values and liberal ideologies for students, faculty, and staff. Students and faculty of color often have challenging and adverse experiences within the academy as they attempt to navigate structural inequities, institutionalized racism, and lack of cultural understanding within the academy (Dade et al., 2015; Pilkington, 2011).

Racism

The average cost of college tuition across institutions averages over $22,000 per year and continues to result in mounting debt for students across the United States (U.S. Department of Education, 2018a), fueling a divide along racial and socioeconomic lines. The majority of students in post-secondary institutions are white (U.S. Department of Education, 2018b) with incomes above the federal poverty level (U.S. Department of Education, 2018c). Correspondingly, the majority of faculty are also white (U.S. Department of Education, 2017b), potentially limiting diversity of thought and access to critical cultural approaches that challenge privilege. These racial and socioeconomic disparities create significant tension on campuses and perpetuate institutionalized racism (Eisenkraft, 2010; Pilkington, 2011; Dade, Tartakov, Hargrave, & Leigh, 2015).

Fraternity members in Blackface (Branson-Potts, 2018), racial slurs on doors (Staff Reports, 2018), and police being called on black students for appearing "out of place" (Whitford, 2018, para. 3) highlight deeply rooted issues in the academy and reinforce the privileged ivory tower. Not only must students of color navigate the tricky lines of racism from peers, but the lack of minority faculty also leaves a gap for students looking for role models within their future career paths (Eisenkraft, 2010). Students of color across the country must deal with the institutionalized racism that is still occurring, such as the 2017 White Nationalist and Ku Klux Klan march at the University of Virginia (Spencer & Stolberg, 2017). While this march was met with much backlash and anti–White Nationalist protesters, the fact that there were enough people to create this hateful atmosphere on a college campus signals the on-going battle many students of color face on a daily basis. The ivory tower continues to be a place of privilege and elitism.

Stereotyping and discrimination against faculty of color significantly impact new faculty recruitment, faculty retention, and promotion (Dade et al., 2015). The lack of inclusion that can occur within the academy may lead to imposter syndrome. This imposter syndrome creates a false narrative for faculty of color, causing them to doubt their accomplishments and successes, as well as perpetuates institutional racism (Dancy & Jean-Marie, 2014; Dade et al., 2015). Moreover, faculty of color may have to work within a "chilly climate" (Eisenkraft, 2010, p. 3) from both colleagues and students. Faculty must deal with the disrespect and automatic judgements from students claiming they got to their faculty position as a diversity hire or having their work and opinions disregarded by colleagues (Eisenkraft, 2010). The lack of diversity among faculty maintains the status quo of archaic racist undertones and elitism within academia.

Academic Politics

Academic freedom has long been touted as a fundamental right, charging scholars to research or critically analyze anything they feel needs to be explored or challenged. The American Association of University Professors (AAUP) (2018) advocates at the level of the federal government for freedom of research, advancing the rights of academics and ensuring higher education's contribution to the common good. However, the academy is facing a new reality, defined by declining student enrollment, cuts to funding at the state and federal levels, and increased competition from for-profit institutions.

Over the years, there has been a noted shift to bolster commercial motivations, shying away from certain topics or methods of research for the financial benefits of universities and publishers (Fyfe, Coate, Curry, Lawson, Moxham, Mork Rostvik, 2017). Until recently, publishing was a means for academics to share their research with fellow scholars (Fyfe et al., 2017). With the rise in profitable research publications coupled with an increasingly consumeristic mind-set of students (Delucchi & Korgen, 2002; Naidoo, Shankar, & Veer, 2011), scholars are feeling the pressure to produce research that will bring in large grants, entice students, and positively impact the university's reputation. Professors and scholars are being forced to adapt and play the political game at work to further their own careers and maintain their funding (Vigoda-Gadot & Drory, 2016). Learning for the sake of learning is being replaced with learning for the sake of funding and playing the tenure game (Brechelmacher, Park, Ates, & Campbell, 2015).

Gender Norms

The culture of academia challenges traditional gender roles. In 2014, women outnumbered men in graduate school 136 to 100 and in 7 of the 11 graduate fields of study for a doctoral degree (Perry, 2015). The dominance of females in the academy is in stark contrast with the female representation in the military; however, this is discipline specific. While certain disciplines, primarily the humanities, are dominated by women, across all ranks, white males have majority share (U.S. Department of Education, 2017b).

Unlike the military and its changing/not clearly defined policy regarding gender inclusion (e.g., stemming from President Trump's twitter proclamations, 2017), transgender students and professors face less uncertainty in the academy as many institutions push for trans-inclusive/gender fluid admissions policies (Campus Pride, 2018), gender neutral pronouns, gender neutral bathrooms/housing, and adopt inclusive hiring policies. With departments and campus organizations devoted to the study of gender and sexuality, there is at least some recognition and acceptance of the gender spectrum and validation of the unique needs of the LGBTQ community. These open-minded and more liberal ideologies provide an outlet for those outside of mainstream (i.e., white, heterosexual, masculine) to be accepted, advocated for, and supported. Despite a desire to be open and inclusive, there are structural inequalities that continue to challenge the academy (Eckel & King, 2004).

Changing Narratives of Violence

Although social change takes time, the academy advocates for equality and changing the narratives surrounding violence and sexual assault, stressing social change through knowledge rather than violence. In 1972, Title IX was introduced prohibiting discrimination based on biological sex in education programs or activities that receive federal financial assistance (Education Amendment of 1972; 2018). The impact of academic research has shed light on a multitude of social issues across the decades from the psychological effects of sexual violence to uncovering and understanding the gender and sexuality spectrums for a more inclusive learning environment (Johnson, 2013). Social movements like #MeToo have been critically analyzed and embraced on campuses across the United States, shaming perpetrators of sexual violence and giving a voice to victims (Rodino-Colocino, 2018).

Like the military, the academy has a hierarchy to rank students, instructors, and professors in specific positions of power based on degree attainment, perceived prestige, and notoriety within their field (Burris, 2004; Fyfe et al., 2017). When power differentials exist, there will be people who seek to take advantage. In the academy, the professor-student relationship may be abused.

"A professor is kind of like a priest" (Hsu & Stone, 2017, para.15) in the eyes of an undergraduate or graduate student; the trust fostered in an academic relationship is paramount for a successful career in academia (Hsu & Stone, 2017; Brown, 2015). Graduate students look to professors for strong letters of recommendation, mentorship, and emotional as well as academic support for research and career guidance (Hsu & Stone, 2017) The stark power deferential of professors and graduate students, and strong dependency on mentorship required for graduate students to succeed in a harsh job market add to the potential for abuse.

Sexual Assault and Harassment

While the academy strives to create an inclusive learning environment, some archaic practices are still in place and sexual assault still happens (Burris, 2004). As with the military, sexual assault has been and continues to be a prevalent issue within the academy. From sexual harassment between students to the sexual assault and harassment between students and faculty, the problem of under-reporting and the lack of support for victims by the university continue to be an issue (Taylor & Gassner, 2010; Perkins & Warner, 2017).

A recent high-profile sexual assault case found a female professor guilty of sexual harassment of a gay former graduate student (Greenberg, 2018). This Title IX case is still being hotly debated as other professors continue to defend the perpetrator and shame the victim for standing up and reporting his case (Greenberg, 2018). For decades, universities and colleges across the globe have been called out for mishandling Title IX complaints and under reporting rates of sexual assault on campuses to protect the universities' reputations (Kitchener, 2014). More transparency from universities means more recorded victims damaging the reputation of the university. Through this mentality, victims of sexual assault and harassment in the academy are left unsupported without justice and the perpetrators are left without consequences to continue harassing.

Summation

Collectively, the academy strives to further society's understanding of social issues to bring about change. As with the military, clearly defined values reflect both history and a changing landscape in which the academy must evolve, adapt, and address significant issues that plague espoused values. With a focus on academic freedom, inclusion, and changing the narrative on violence, the academy has a different structural core that is, at times, diametrically opposed to the military. Moreover, members of both cultures often are deeply entrenched, committing to a career that requires loyalty and full immersion to survive and thrive. As such, intimate partners may experience conflict as they navigate the complexities of a cultural collision on the home front.

COLLISION OF TWO CULTURES

Cross-cultural communication theory dictates that when communicating from the position of two distinct cultures, barriers to communication and marital dissatisfaction may occur (Spencer-Rodgers & McGovern, 2002). Intercultural communication barriers arise from group differences in cognition, emotions, and patterns of behavior (Spencer-Rodgers & McGovern, 2002). The norms, values, and beliefs of the military and the academy represent two distinct, complex cultural groups, requiring skillful negotiation as divergent core ideologies may create conflict for spouses attempting to bridge the cultural divide. Adding a layer of complexity is the all-encompassing nature of both institutions, requiring heavy investment of time, creative energy, and personal capital for institutional gain. For romantic partners heavily invested in either culture, little energy and time may be left at the end of the workday for cross-cultural understanding, increasing the potential for conflict, misunderstanding, and eventually, resentment. When the military and academy collide, partners may be forced to choose between family or career goals and renegotiate ideological norms that define gender roles. In the end, these institutions, despite conflicting norms, values, and beliefs, demand much of their members, underscoring the need for intercultural competency.

Family vs. Career

Both the military and academia are "greedy" (Coser, 1974, p. 3), leaving little time or energy to devote to family or other institutions (Segal, 1986; Coser, 1974). Before 1973, the military could afford to be greedy, primarily drafting single male soldiers. Today's military is comprised mostly of soldiers with spouses and/or dependents (DoD, ODASD, & MC&FP, 2016). Deployments and frequent duty station relocations (i.e., permanent changes of station [PCS]) make it challenging for couples and families to maintain relationships and facilitate communication (see Smith, Heaven, & Ciarrochi, 2007; Gottman & Levenson, 2000; Weinstein & White, 1997; Heavey, Christensen, & Malamuth, 1995).

To support military cultural norms and promotion of the service member, military spouses, a majority of whom are female, may be forced to choose between their family and career. For military service members, deployments and relocations are not optional, thus the whole family is impacted by the military's order, either through frequent moves or separating family members. Spouses have limited options when orders come down for PCS. They must choose to either follow the military service member or decide to live apart for months to years at a time. For families with limited financial resources, living apart is not feasible, and may serve as an unacceptable disruption to the relationship with their intimate partner and/or dependents. Furthermore, during deployments and service-related separations, military spouses must take on more than just one household role, perpetuating the idea that the military requires everyone to serve in every way (Weinstein & White, 1997). For spouses in the academy, military service often results in either staying behind or embracing life as the trailing spouse, as Bouchard's chapter in this volume illustrates. A trailing spouse follows along as the career of the military spouse drives relocation. Often, the trailing spouse sacrifices academic and career goals to meet the needs of their partner's career (Bernhagen, 2017).

Academic Goals

Access to higher education is an important consideration, and some military spouses may feel their educational opportunities are negatively impacted by the military lifestyle (Orthner, 2005). With frequent moves, spouses may struggle to transfer credits and complete degrees (DoD, ODASD, & MC&FP, 2016). Earning a bachelor's degree is challenging enough, and for many military spouses, the idea of attaining a graduate level degree may seem dubious or even impossible. As a graduate student, researchers are expected to dedicate two years for a master's degree and four to six years for a Ph.D.; many programs will not accept transfer credits. As such, this further limits the ability to compete in the academy's culture of terminal degree attainment as a basic requirement for a tenure-track position.

Career Goals

The goal for many academics is a tenure-track position. Tenure is a five-to-seven-year journey that requires demonstrated proficiency in three areas: research, service, and teaching. However, tenure is challenging for academic military spouses to achieve when the average duty station shifts every two to three years. The result can be a life as an adjunct, picking up teaching assignments, typically introductory classes, at local colleges in the duty station area. However, since a significant number of duty stations are rural (DoD, ODASD, & MC&FP, 2016), these teaching assignments may be limited, especially for certain disciplines. Moreover, adjunct pay is low. Funding for travel is non-existent, and adjuncts are often excluded from departmental decision making and development. The other option is life as a term faculty member, contracting year to year. Similar to the adjunct experience, term faculty members are often "work horses," teaching a heavy load of introductory courses. Often, pay is less than tenure-track peers and little time is left for research. The final option the trailing spouse has is to selectively disclose military affiliation. Without disclosing the military affiliation, it may be easier for a military spouse to maintain competitiveness and ensure job security (The Council of Economic Advisors, 2018).

For academics or Ph.D.s working outside of higher education, finding a job can be difficult and limiting as a result of frequent relocations, lack of career progression, and conditions of the local job market (DoD, ODASD, & MC&FP, 2016); collectively, the unemployment rate for military spouses is four times higher than the national average (MOAA, 2017; The Council of Economic Advisors, 2018). For spouses with professional licenses, such as nurses, lawyers, or educators, moving to a new duty station in a different state requires additional testing and out of pocket expense to obtain a license (The Council of Economic Advisors, 2018). Finally, employers may be reluctant to hire military spouses because they assume lack of permanency and high turnover (The Council of Economic Advisors, 2018). Spouses who do find employment often earn less than non-military peers, which has been estimated to be roughly $200,000 less over the course of a spouse's 20-year military career regardless of degree level and would likely be higher for those with advanced degrees (The Council of Economic Advisors, 2018).

Work-life Balance

As with the military, the academy requires an unspoken, yet extremely high level of commitment. Graduate students, faculty, and professors are expected to work seven days a week while the academic year is in session, including late nights, weekends, and personal time volunteering for the department or university. While working in the university setting is not seen as a nine-to-five job, academic freedom is, "the freedom to work all the time" (Tierney, 1997, p. 11). Even in the summer months, members are expected to research, teach, or work to make money to survive during the school year. Women especially may feel obligated to work even longer hours to prove themselves in a historically patriarchal institution (Tierney, 1997; Schultz, 2008). Toth (1995) argues that prior to attaining tenure status, women are encouraged to pick their battles and make sacrifices to increase job promotion potential. The AAUP (2001) asserts "the lack of a clear boundary in academic lives between work and family has meant that work has been all-pervasive often to the detriment of family" (p. 2).

With greedy institutions to satisfy, the time spent with significant others and family becomes more valuable and the implications of ineffective intercultural communication have greater meaning. Trailing spouses or spouses forced to choose between career and family may feel resentful over time as opportunity for advancement is repeatedly sacrificed for the service member. Academic spouses may engage in social comparison, for example, analyzing their career progression against stationary peers. If academic spouses are not able to effectively communicate their feelings or perceive a lack of validation/recognition for their career sacrifice from their military partner, resentment and a negative impact on martial satisfaction may result.

Ideological Gender Role Differences

Communicated gender role differences are a potential source of conflict for romantic partners navigating the military and the academy. The disparity of traditional gender roles (i.e., male breadwinner and female caretaker) versus non-traditional gender roles (e.g., men staying home, the male military spouse, or women working outside of the home in a position of power) may lead to martial conflict among spouses because of the gap in expected versus performed spousal roles. Additionally, couples made up of two individuals subscribing to different ideologies related to gender performance may face barriers to effective communication.

As previously argued, traditional gender roles are perpetuated within the military (Cynar, 2005; Keats, 2010; Mosher & Tomkins, 1988); however, they are evolving as women gain more prominence in the military. For heterosexual female service members, this means the increased presence of the male spouse. Men comprise roughly 15% of the military spouse community, a noted shift from previous generations (DoD, ODASD, & MC&FP, 2016). Regardless of gender, spouses are especially important as they have been known to influence the strength and effectiveness of service members (Clever & Segal, 2013). Moreover, the military culture includes specific formal and informal expectations that military spouses are required to meet. These formal and informal expectations may be based on the service member's rank, which some use to determine a military spouse's position in the "unwritten" spousal hierarchy (Redmond et al., 2015).[2] Along with this categorization of military spouses, a service member's rank may come with specific social responsibilities for military spouses, such as planning specific gatherings, hosting events, or mentoring new military spouses (Redmond et al., 2015). Military spouses also play a critical role in leading the unit's Family Readiness Group (FRG) or planning monthly parties for other military spouses (Cynar, 2005). Groups like FRGs and Family Centers are staffed by spouses offering training and social support to family members of active-duty military personnel. The structure of the FRGs tends to follow a hierarchy based on traditional gender roles and is comprised mostly of female spouses (DoD, ODASD, & MC&FP, 2016). Spouses who identify in the masculine may be challenged to find their place in a group dominated by women providing support to mostly female spouses. Male spouses have been described as "invisible" and some may struggle with gender role reversals such as those experienced in FRGs, in part because ". . . the military environment . . . emphasizes traditional ideas of masculinity (Weinstock, 2016, para. 3).

While FRGs may be a helpful outlet for some military spouses, it requires time from its members to hold social events, meetings, and to volunteer when needed (Pincus, House, Christenson, & Alder, 2001). For military spouses who already have a graduate degree or are seeking to complete one, there is little time left between completing the tasks necessary to excel in academic life and making time for their marriage and family to participate in any other outside activities. Moreover, an academic spouse in a position of power at work may be reduced to Mrs./Mr. So-and-so, the military spouse's partner, once they reenter the military's domain. Being stripped of power may be perceived by the academic spouse as problematic, resulting in conflict.

In addition to the spousal expectations, historically, and ever-present within the military culture, men have dominated the work role and women have dominated the family role (Fletcher & Bailyn, 2005; Redmond et al., 2015). Males who prescribe to the restrictive traditional gender role ideologies have been found to be less likely to accept help and more likely to believe that there are certain characteristics and emotions that are specific to each gender (Good, Dell, & Mintz 1989; Livingston & Judge, 2008). Correspondingly, men and women who follow traditional gender roles may have problems with communication in their relationships over time (Lamke, 1989; Ickes, 1993). Violations of gender norms can lead to unmet expectations regarding household chores, dual vs. single household earners, and financial and familial responsibilities (Ickes, 1993; Leaper & Friedman, 2007). Over time, small communication conflicts and unmet expectations can lead to larger problems within a marriage (Fincham, 2003; Amato, 2010).

In contrast to the military, academia attempts to shift away from traditional gender roles and promote more integrative gender roles. While this may not completely unshackle spouses from gendered stereotypes or norms, it may open more opportunities for integrative gender roles within the couple. Since traditional gender roles are more frequently challenged within the culture of academia (e.g., degree programs focused on women & gender studies, research & publication, social justice campaigns such as #MeToo, student-led demonstrations), couples with one spouse who does not fit the traditional gendered personality traits may be at a higher risk of relationship dissatisfaction. Military spouses with graduate degrees must both navigate the strict traditional gender roles invoked by the military culture while thriving in the more integrative gender role structure required to succeed in the academic world (Malka & Lelkes, 2010). For a military spouse with a graduate degree the gaps between the expected and performed roles in each culture may lead to miscommunications or the feelings of half-involvement within both cultures (Ott, Kelley Morgan, & Akroyd, 2018).

CONCLUSION

In the end, the military and the academy may be at odds not because of their conflicting cultural ideologies but because of their greediness. These institutions are all-encompassing, challenging members to give more, do more, and be more to survive and thrive. Both the military and the academy operate based on a hierarchy that has been in place since their inception. Both cultures value length of service as an important criterion for promotion and celebrity (Burris, 2004; Redmond et al., 2015). These rankings in both the military and academy create a power deferential to reinforce cultural norms. For members of both cultures, starting at the bottom and rising through the ranks is revered as the most legitimate way to reach the peak of their professional career. To start out at the lowest rank and achieve success, the service member must be fully committed to serve country; likewise, the academic must serve the discipline and host institution.

For military spouses straddling the divide between the military and the academy, collisions can create conflict and negatively impact communication and the overall level of relationship satisfaction. Military spouses with graduate degrees are simultaneously members of the military and academy, while uniquely positioned on the fringes of both all-encompassing cultures. The military focuses on deindividualization, the benefit of the group, and violence as a means to an end (Turchik & Wilson, 2010). The academy focuses on an individual's ability to critically analyze and contribute to their discipline by increasing the overall body of academic research, individual achievements, and research as a means to initiate social change (Tierney, 1997). With all this in mind, the operational definition of "toughness" is quite different for both cultures, leading to a potential lack of understanding between spouses. Misunderstandings that arise from cultural variation may lead to alienation or an inability to develop trust and rapport (Sue & Sue, 1977). These misunderstandings can lead to communication barriers, impacting communication within a romantic couple.

Military spouses with graduate degrees may feel like they are leading two lives, one within the academy and the life of military spouse at home. When home and work life overlap, there is potential for conflict if the military spouse brings either of the valued traits from the academy into the military culture or vice versa and these values are not accepted by their spouse or colleagues. Teetering on the line between the military and the academy could lead to eventual burnout of the military spouse as it has the potential to lead to alienation of the couple within their own cultures and miscommunications within their marriage, resulting in marital discord. With limited time every day, it is impossible to satisfy both greedy institutions daily; therefore, military spouses with graduate degrees must precariously navigate the line between cultures to thrive amidst uncertainty.

FUTURE RESEARCH

In the literature, there is a plethora of research on the communication dynamics that occur on long deployments and at the height of war. Research has also focused on the high levels of stress military families experience during and after deployments as they renegotiate spousal roles, responsibilities, and boundaries (Drummet, Coleman, & Cable, 2003; Riggs, 1990). There is, however, a dearth of research on everyday communication exchanges and challenges military couples must navigate as the communication dynamics change. Even more insufficient is the research regarding the communication among couples with one spouse in the military and one spouse in academia regarding day to day interactions and the delicate equilibrium required between spouses to maintain a healthy marriage and worklife balance. The all-encompassing nature of both cultures places a great deal of stress and need for intercultural competence to promote effective communication and cross-cultural understanding. More research is needed on the impacts of the military on military spouses with graduate degrees. Another area for future research is the impact of military ideologies on spouses' academic careers and area of research interests. The strategic communication required between both spouses during long periods of separation also needs to be researched further. Researching the specific characteristics that make the military and higher education different could also lead to important information to help better integrate military spouses and veterans into the culture of higher education after service. Better understanding the communication boundaries of spouses within the military and higher education could lead to new research on ways to overcome the communication boundaries and more effective communication techniques.

NOTES

1. This breakdown does not include the number of restricted reports that may include one or more victims. Restricted reporting is a confidential form of reporting that does not trigger an investigation or command involvement, but allows the victim to receive medical care. Unrestricted reporting starts an official law enforcement investigation and enlists the support of the chain of command and provides the victim with a full range of support services (MCCS Forward, 2016).

2. While the authors of this chapter do not want to perpetuate the stereotype of the spousal hierarchy, one of the contributing authors, as an enlisted spouse, has firsthand experience with the power dynamics and feels that it is an important aspect of military spouse life that needs to be acknowledged.

REFERENCES

American Academy of University Professors. (2001). Statement of principles on family responsibilities and academic work. Retrieved from http://www.aaup.org/statements/REPORTS/re01fam.htm.

American Academy of University Professors. (2018). About the AAUP. Retrieved from https://www.aaup.org/about-aaup.

Amato, P. R. (2010). Research on divorce: continuing trends and new developments. *Journal of Marriage and Family*, *72*(3), 650–666.

Aosved, A. C., & Long, J. (2006). Co-occurrence of rape myth acceptance, sexism, racism, homophobia, ageism, classism, and religious intolerance. *Sex Roles*, *55*, 481–492.

Archer, E. M. (2013). The power of gendered stereotypes in the U.S. Marine Corps. *Armed Forces & Society*, *39*(4), 647–668.

Bernhagen, L. (2017, November 30). What the "trailing spouse" teaches us about the stickiness of gender inequality. *Slate*. Retrieved from http://www.slate.com/blogs/better_life_lab/2017/11/30/trailing_spouses_what_female_ph_d_s_teach_us_about_lasting_workplace_gender.html.

Binkin, M., & Bach, S. S. (1977). *Women and the Military*. Washington, D.C.: The Brookings Institution.

Branson-Potts, H. (2018, April 25). After blackface incident, minority students at Cal Poly San Luis Obispo say they don't feel welcome. Retrieved from http://www.latimes.com/local/lanow/la-me-ln-cal-poly-racism-20180425-story.html.

Brechelmacher, A., Park, E., Ates, G., & Campbell, D.F.J. (2015). The rocky road to tenure—Early paths in academia. In Fumsaoli, T., Goastellec, G., & Kehm, B. M. (Eds.), *Academic Work and Careers in Europe: Trends, Challenges, Perspectives* (13–40). Switzerland: Springer International Publishing.

Brown, S. (2015, October 22). Why colleges have a hard time handling professors who harass. *The Chronicle of Higher Education: Sexual Boundaries for Professors*. 15–17. Retrieved from https://www.chronicle.com/items/biz/resource/Chron-Focus_SexualBoundaries_v2_i.pdf.

Burns, B., Grindlay, K., Holt, K., Manski, R., & Grossman, D. (2014). Military sexual trauma among US servicewomen during deployment: A qualitative study. *American Journal Public Health, 104*(2), 345–349.

Burris, V. (2004). The academic caste system: Prestige hierarchies in PhD exchange networks. *American Sociological Review, 69*, 239–264.

Carter, P., & Barno, D. (2013, November 8). Military bases are our most exclusive gated communities—and that hurts veterans. *The Washington Post*. Retrieved from https://www.washingtonpost.com/opinions/military-bases-are-our-most-exclusive-gated-communities—and-that-hurts-veterans/2013/11/08/27841b1e-47cb-11e3-a196-3544a03c2351_story.html?noredirect=on&utm_term=.b52888a5a752.

Carter, S. P., & Renshaw, K. D. (2016). Spousal communication during military deployments: A review. *Journal of Family Issues, 37*(16), 2309–2332. doi:10.1177/0192513X14567956.

Campus Pride. (2018). 13 women's colleges have formal policies to admit at least some trans students. Retrieved from https://www.campuspride.org/tpc/womens-colleges/.

Chan, R. Y. (2016). Understanding the purpose of higher education: An analysis of the economic and social benefits for completing a college degree. *JEPPA, 6*(5), 1-41. Retrieved from https://scholar.harvard.edu/files/roychan/files/chan_r._y._2016._understanding_the_purpose_aim_function_of_higher_education._jeppa_65_1-40.pdf.

Clever, M., & Segal, D. R. (2013). The demographics of military children and families. *The Future of Children, 23*(2), 13–39.

Cohen, Z., & Browne, R. (2018, April 30). US military sees spike in sexual assault reports. *CNN*. Retrieved from https://www.cnn.com/2018/04/30/politics/dod-sexual-assault-report2017/index.html.

Cohn, C. (2000). "How can she claim equal rights when she doesn't have to do as many push ups as I do?": The framing of men's opposition to women's equality in the military. *Men and Masculinities, 3*(2), 131–115.

Coser, L. A. (1974). *Greedy institutions: Patterns of undivided commitment*. New York, NY: Free Press.

Cynar, D. J. (2005). *Keeping the home fires burning: The effects of military induced separations on marital intimacy from a female perspective*. (Unpublished master's thesis). The University of Alaska Fairbanks, Fairbanks, Alaska.

Dade, K., Tartakov, C., Hargrave, C., & Leigh, P. (2015). Assessing the impact of racism on black faculty in white academe: A collective case study of African American female faculty. *Western Journal of Black Studies, 39*(2), 134–146.

Dancy II, T. E., & Jean-Marie, G. (2014). Faculty of color in higher education: Exploring the intersections of identity, impostorship, and internalized racism. *Mentoring & Tutoring: Partnership in Learning, 22*(4), 354–372.

Darehshori, S., Rhoad, M., Root, B., Parker, A., Gerntholtz, L., Ross, J., Haas, D., Saunders, J., Rau Barriga, S., Reiser, S., Kotowski, A., Mills, K., & Hepkins, F. (2015, 18 May). Embattles: Retaliation against sexual assault survivors in the US military. *Human Rights Watch*. Retrieved from https://www.hrw.org/report/2015/05/18/embattled/retaliation-against-sexual-assault-survivors-us-military.

Decew, J. W. (1995). The combat exclusion and the role of women in the military. *Hypatia, 10*(1), 56–73.

Delucchi, M., & Korgen, K. (2002). "We're the customer—we pay the tuition": Student consumerism among undergraduate sociology majors. *Teaching Sociology, 30*(1), 100–107.

DoD, ODASD, & MC&FP (2016). 2016 Demographics profile of the military community. Retrieved from http://download.militaryonesource.mil/12038/MOS/Reports/2016-Demographics-Report.pdf.

DoD. (2017, January 27). About the Department of Defense (DoD). Retrieved from https://www.defense.gov/About/.

DoD. (n.d.). Restricted reporting. Retrieved from http://sapr.mil/index.php/restricted-reporting.

Drummet, A. R., Coleman, M., & Cable, S. (2003). Military families under stress: Implications for family life education. *Family Relations, 52*(3), 279–287.

Dunivin, K. O. (1994). Military culture: Change and continuity. *Armed Forces & Society, 20*(4), 531–547.

Eckel, P. D., & King, J. E. (2004). An overview of higher education in the United States: Diversity, access, and the role of the marketplace. *American Council on Education*. Retreived from http://www.acenet.edu/news-room/Documents/Overview-of-Higher-Education-in-the-United-States-Diversity-Access-and-the-Role-of-the-Marketplace-2004.pdf.

Education Amendment of 1972, 20 U.S.C. §§ 1681–1688 (2018).

Eisenkraft, H. (2010, 12 October). Racism in the academy. *AU University Affairs*. Retrieved from https://s3.amazonaws.com/academia.edu.documents/32071801/UAffairs_Racism-in-the-Academy_VP-Equity_12Oct2010.pdf?AWSAccessKeyId=AKIAIWOWYYGZ2Y53UL3A&Expires=1536698571&Signature=tT7R5ubuqwe5Mx968%2FBZ5Qbxdw0%3D&response-content-disposition=inline%3B%20filename%3DVP_Equity_FHSS_-_University_Affairs_inte.pdf.

Enloe, C. (1983). *Does khaki become you?* London, UK: South End Press, 7–15.

Fassinger, R. E. (2008). Workplace diversity and public policy: Challenges and opportunities for psychology. *American Psychologist, 63*, 252–268.

Ferdinando, L. (2018, May 1). DoD release annual report on sexual assault in the military. *Department of Defense*. Retrieved from https://www.defense.gov/News/Article/Article/1508127/dod-releases-annual-report-on-sexual-assault-in-military/.

Fincham, F. D. (2003). Marital conflict: Correlates, structure, and context. *Current Directions in Psychological Science, 12*(1), 23–27.

Fletcher, J. K., & Bailyn, L. (2005). The equity imperative: Redesigning work for work–family integration. In E. E. Kossek & S. J. Lambert (Eds.), *Work and life integration: Organizational, cultural, and individual perspectives,* 171–190. Mahwah, NJ: Erlbaum.

Fyfe, A., Coate, K., Curry, S., Lawson, S., Moxham, N., & Mork Rostvik, C. (2017). Untangling academic publishing: A history of the relationship between commercial interests, academic prestige and the circulation of research. *History Research*. Retrieved from https://research-repository.standrews.ac.uk/bitstream/handle/10023/10884/Fyfe_etal_UntanglingAcPub_CC.pdf?sequence=1.

Good, G. E., Dell, D. M., & Mintz, L. B. (1989). Male role and gender role conflict: Relations to help seeking in men. *Journal of Counseling Psychology, 36*(3), 295–300.

Gottman, J. M., & Levenson, R. W. (2000). The timing of divorce: Predicting when a couple will divorce over a 14-year period. *Journal of Marriage and the Family, 62*, 737–745.

Government Accountability Office. (2008, August 29). DOD's and the Coast Guard's sexual assault prevention and response programs face implementation and oversight challenges. Retrieved from http://www.gao.gov/new.items/d08924.pdf.

Greenberg, Z. (2018, August 13). What happens to #MeToo when a feminist is the accused? *The New York Times*. Retrieved from https://www.nytimes.com/2018/08/13/nyregion/sexual-harassment-nyu-female-professor.html.

Grossman, D. (1996). *On killing: The psychological cost of learning to kill in war and society*. New York, NY: Little Brown and Co.

Halvorson, A., Whitter, M., & Taitt, S. B. (2010). *Understanding the military: The institution, the culture and the people*. Retrieved from https://www.samhsa.gov/sites/default/files/military_white_paper_final.pdf.

Harvard. (2018). Mission, vision, and history. Retrieved from https://college.harvard.edu/about/mission-and-vision.

Heavey, C. L., Christensen, A., & Malamuth, N. M. (1995). The longitudinal impact of demand and withdrawal during marital conflict. *Journal of Consulting and Clinical Psychology, 63*, 797–801.

Hsu., I. & Stone, R. (2017, November 30). "A professor is kind of like a priest." *The New Republic*. Retrieved from https://newrepublic.com/article/146049/a-professor-kind-like-priest.

Hunter, M. (2007). *Honor betrayed: Sexual abuse in America's military*. Fort Lee, NJ: Barricade Books.

Ickes, W. (1993). Traditional gender roles: Do they make and then break? Our relationships? *Journal of Social Issues, 49*(3), 71–85.

Johnson, J. R. (2013). Cisgender privilege, intersectionality, and the criminalization of CeCe McDonald: Why intercultural communication needs transgender studies. *Journal of International and Intercultural Communication, 6*(2), 135–144.

Johnson, W. B., Rosenstein, J. E., Buhrke, R. A., & Haldeman, D. C. (2015). After "Don't ask don't tell": Competent care of lesbian, gay and bisexual military personnel during the DoD policy transition. *Professional Psychology: Research and Practice, 46*(2), 107–115.

Kaufman, C. (2018). The history of higher education in the United States. Worldwide Learn. Retrieved from https://www.worldwidelearn.com/education-advisor/indepth/history-higher-education.php.

Keats, P. A. (2010). Soldiers working internationally: Impacts of masculinity, military culture, and operational stress on cross-cultural adaptation. *International Journal for the Advancement of Counselling, 32*(4), 290–303.

Kitchener, C. (2014, December 17). When helping rape victims hurts a college's reputation. *The Atlantic*. Retrieved from https://www.theatlantic.com/education/archive/2014/12/when-helping-rape-victims-hurts-a-universitys-reputation/383820/.

Kurfiss, J. G. (1988). *Critical thinking: Theory, research, practice and possibilities.* Washington, D.C.: Eric Clearinghouse on Higher Education.

Lai, K. K. R., Griggs, T., Fisher, M., & Carlsen, A. (2017, March 22). Is America's military big enough? *New York Times.* Retrieved from https://www.nytimes.com/interactive/2017/03/22/us/is-americas-military-big-enough.html.

Lamke, L. (1989). Marital adjustment among rural couples: The role of expressiveness. *Sex Roles, 21,* 579–590.

Leaper, C., & Friedman, C. K. (2007). The socialization of gender. In Grusec, J. E., & Hastings P. D. (Eds.), *Handbook of socialization: Theory and research* (561–587). New York, NY: Guilford Press.

Livingston, B. A., & Judge, T. A. (2008). Emotional responses to work-family conflict: An examination of gender role orientation among working men and women. *Journal of Applied Psychology, 93(1),* 207–216.

Malka, A. & Lelkes, Y. (2010). More than ideology: Conservative-liberal identity and receptivity to political cues. *Social Justice Research, 23,* 156–188.

Maples, S. (2017, November 22). The inconvenience of being a woman veteran. *The Atlantic.* Retrieved from https://www.theatlantic.com/politics/archive/2017/11/the-inconvenience-of-being-a-woman-veteran/545987/.

MCCS Forward. (2016). Restricted vs. unrestricted reports—Know your options. Retrieved from http://www.usmc-mccs.org/articles/restricted-vs-unrestricted-reports-know-your-options/.

Mengeling, M. A., Booth, B. M., Torner, J. C., & Sadler, A. G. (2014). Reporting sexual assault in the military: Who reports and why most servicewomen don't. *American Journal of Preventative Medicine, 47(1),* 17–25.

Military Officers Association of American (MOAA). (2017, October 6). Military spouse unemployment rate at least four times higher than the national average. Retrieved from http://www.moaa.org/Content/Take-Action/On-Watch/Military-Spouse-Unemployment-Rate-at-Least-Four-Times-Higher-Than-National-Average.aspx.

Moore, K. M., & Amey, M. J. (1993). Making sense of the dollars: The costs and uses of faculty compensation. *ASHE-ERIC Higher Education Report No. 5.* Washington, D.C.: The George Washington University, School of Education and Human Development.

Mosher, D. L., & Tomkins, S. (1988). Scripting the macho man: Hypermasculine socialization and enculturation. *Journal of Sex Research, 25,* 60–84.

Naidoo, R., Shankar, A., & Veer, E. (2011). The consumerist turn in higher education: Policy aspirations and outcomes. *Journal of Marketing Management, 27(11/12),* 1142–1162.

O'Malley, O. (2015). All is not fair in love and war: An exploration of the military masculinity myth. *DePaul Journal of Women, Gender and the Law, 5(1),* 1–40. Retrieved from http://via.library.depaul.edu/cgi/viewcontent.cgi?article=1022&context=jwgl.

Orthner, D. K. (2005). Deployment and separation adjustment among army civilian spouses. *Survey of Army Families [SAF IV] Survey Report.* Retrieved from http://www.armymwr.com/corporate/operations/ planning/surveys.asp.

Ott, L. E., Kelley Morgan, K., & Akroyd, H. D. (2018). Impact of military lifestyle on military spouses' educational and career goals. *Journal of Research in Education*, *28*(1), 30–61.

Parker, K., Cilluffo, A., & Stepler, R. (2017, April 3). 6 Facts about the U.S. military and its changing demographics. *Pew Research*. Retrieved from http://www.pewresearch.org/fact-tank/2017/04/13/6-facts-about-the-u-s-military-and-its-changing-demographics/.

Perkins, W., & Warner, J. (2017). Sexual violence response and prevention: Studies of campus policies and practices. *Journal of School Violence*, *16*(3), 237–242.

Perry, M. (2015, September 17). Women earned majority of doctoral degrees in 2014 for 6th straight year, and outnumber men in grad school 136 to 100. *AEI Ideas*. Retrieved from http://www.aei.org/publication/women-earned-majority-of-doctoral-degrees-in-2014-for-6th-straight-year-and-outnumber-men-in-grad-school-136-to-100/.

Pilkington, A. (2011). *Institutional racism in the academy: A case study*. London, UK: Trentham Books.

Pincus, S. H., House, R., Christenson, J., & Adler, L. E. (2001). The emotional cycle of deployment: A military family perspective. *Journal of the Army Medical Department*, *2*, 15–23.

realDonaldTrump. (2017, July 26). Transgender individuals to serve in any capacity in the U.S. Military. . . . [Twitter Post]. Retrieved from https://twitter.com/realdonaldtrump/status/890196164313833472?lang=en.

Redmond, S. A., Wilcox, S. L., Campbell, S., Kim, A., Finney, K., Barr, K., & Hassan, A. M. (2015). A brief introduction to the military workplace culture. *Work*, *50*, 9–20.

Reit, R. (2017). *The relationship between the military's masculine culture and service members' help-seeking behaviors* (Master's thesis, Marquette University). Retrieved from http://epublications.marquette.edu/theses_open/410.

Riggs, B. (1990). Routine-work-related-absence: The effects on families. *Marriage and Family Review*, *15*, 147–160.

Rodino-Colocino, M. (2018). Me too, #metoo: Countering cruelty with empathy. *Communication and Critical/Cultural Studies*, *15*(1), 96–100.

Rosellini, A. J., Street, A. E., Ursano, R. J., Chiu, W. T., Heeringa, S. G., Monahan, J., Naifeh, J. A., Petukhova, M. V., Reis, B. Y., Sampson, N. A., Bliese, P. D., Stein, M. B. Zaslavsky, A. M., & Kessler, R. C. (2017). Sexual assault victimization and mental health treatment, suicide attempts, and career outcomes among women in the US Amy. *American Journal Public Health*, *107*(5), 732–739.

Sadler, A. G., Booth, B. M., Cook, B. L., & Doebbeling, B. N. (2003). Women's military environmental risk factors for rape. *American Journal of Industrial Medicine*, *43*, 262–273.

Saintsing, M. (2018, May 1). All military branches saw upsurge of sexual assault last year. *Connecting vets*. Retrieved from www.connectingvets.com/articles/all-military-branches-saw-upsurge-sexual-assault-last-year.

Schultz, N. (2008, November). *Balancing faculty careers and family work: Tenure-track women's perceptions of and experiences with work/family issues and their relationships to job satisfaction*. Paper presented at the National Communication Association. San Diego, California.

Segal, M. W. (1986). The military and the family as greedy institutions. *Armed Forces and Society, 13*, 9–38.

Segal, D. R., & Segal, M. W. (2004). America's military population. *Population bulletin*, 4.

Silva, J. M. (2008). A new generation of women? How female ROTC cadets negotiate the tension between masculine military culture and traditional femininity. *Social Forces, 87*(2), 937–960.

Smith, L., Heaven, P. C. L., & Ciarrochi, J. (2007). Trait emotional intelligence, conflict communication patterns, and relationship satisfaction. *Personality and Individual Difference, 44*, 1314–1325.

Soeters, J. L., Winslow, D. J., & Weibull, A. (2006). Military culture. *Handbooks of Sociology and Social Research*, pp. 237–254. Boston, MA: Springer Science and Business Media, LLC.

Spencer, H., & Stolberg, S. G. (2017, August 11). White nationalists march on University of Virginia. *New York Times*. Retrieved from https://www.nytimes.com/2017/08/11/us/white-nationalists-rally-charlottesville-virginia.html.

Spencer-Rodgers, J., & McGovern, T. (2002). Attitudes toward the culturally different: the role of intercultural communication barriers, affective responses, consensual stereotypes, and perceived threat. *International Journal of Intercultural Relations, 26*(6), 609–631.

Staff Reports. (2018, April 27). Racial slur written on 300 Swift resident's door overnight. Retrieved from https://www.dukechronicle.com/article/2018/04/racial slur-written-on-300-swift-residents-door-overnight.

Stier, J. (2011). Taking a critical stance toward internationalization ideologies in higher education: idealism, instrumentalism and educationalism. *Globalisation, Societies and Education, 2*(1), 1–28.

Sue, D. W., & Sue, D. (1977). Barriers to effective cross-cultural counseling. *Journal of Counseling Psychology, 24*(5), 420–429.

Taber, N. (2009). Gender in children's books written for military families: The gendered portrayal of women and men, mothers and fathers in the Canadian military. *Journal of Integrated Social Sciences, 1*(1), 120–140.

Taylor, S. C., & Gassner, L. (2010). Stemming the flow: Challenges for policing adult sexual assault with regard to attrition rates and under-reporting of sexual offences. *Police Practice and Research, 11*(3), 240–255.

The Council of Economic Advisors. (2018, May). Military spouses in the labor market. Retrieved from www.whitehouse.gov/cea.

Tierney, W. G. (1997). Organizational socialization in higher education. *The Journal of Higher Education, 68*(1), 1–16.

Title 10, 1956, 502 U.S.C. Title 10 § 255 (2018).

Toth, E. (1995). Women in academia. In A. L. Deneef & C. D. Goodwin (Eds.), *The Academic's Handbook* (pp. 38–47). Durham, NC: Duke University Press.

Turchik, J. A., & Wilson, S. M. (2010). Sexual assault in the U.S. military: A review of the literature and recommendations for the future. *Aggression and Violent Behavior, 15*, 267–277.

Uniform Code of Military Justice, 1951, 109 U.S.C. UMCJ §§ 801-946 (2018).

U.S. Army. (n.d.). SHARP Annual Unit Refresher Training (URT). Retrieved from http://www.sexualassault.army.mil/annual_unit_refresher.aspx.

U.S. Department of Defense. (2017, May 1). DoD Releases FY 2016 Annual Report on Sexual Assault in the Military. Retrieved from https://www.defense.gov/News/News-Releases/News-Release-View/Article/1168041/dod-releases-fy-2016-annual-report-on-sexual-assault-in-the-military/.

U.S. Department of Defense (2018, May 4). Department of Defense Annual Report on Sexual Assault in the Military: Fiscal year 2017. Retrieved from http://sapr.mil/public/docs/reports/FY17_Annual/DoD_FY17_Annual_Report_on_Sexual_Assault_in_the_Military.pdf.

U.S. Department of Education, National Center for Education Statistics. (2017a). Back to school statistics. *Digest of Education Statistics.* Retrieved from https://nces.ed.gov/fastfacts/display.asp?id=372.

U.S. Department of Education, National Center for Education Statistics. (2017b). Characteristics of postsecondary faculty. *The Condition of Education 2017* (NCES 2017-144). Retrieved from https://nces.ed.gov/fastfacts/display.asp?id=61.

U.S. Department of Education, National Center for Education Statistics. (2017c). Fast facts: Financial aid. Retrieved from https://nces.ed.gov/fastfacts/display.asp?id=31.

U.S. Department of Education, National Center for Education Statistics. (2018a). Tuition costs of colleges and universities. *Digest of Education Statistics.* Retrieved from https://nces.ed.gov/fastfacts/display.asp?id=76.

U.S. Department of Education, National Center for Education Statistics. (2018b). Total fall enrollment in degree-granting postsecondary institutions, by level and control of institution and race/ethnicity of student: Selected years, 1976 through 2016. *Digest of Education Statistics.* Retrieved from https://nces.ed.gov/programs/digest/d17/tables/dt17_306.20.asp?current=yes.

U.S. Department of Education, National Center for Education Statistics. (2018c, January). Immediate college enrollment rate. Retrieved from https://nces.ed.gov/programs/coe/indicator_cpa.asp.

Vigoda-Gadot, E. & Drory, A. (2016). *Handbook of Organizational Politics: Looking Back and to the Future.* Northampton, MA: Edward Elgar Publishing, Inc.

Weinstein, L. L., & White, C. C. (1997). *Wives and Warriors: Women and the Military in the United States and Canada.* Westport, CT: Bergin & Garvey.

Weinstock, M. (2016, March 30). Staff perspective: Male military spouses—"invisible" family members? Retrieved from https://deploymentpsych.org/blog/staff-perspective-male-military-spouses-"invisible"-family-members.

Weitz, R. (2015). Vulnerable warriors: Military women, military culture and the fear of rape. *Gender Issues, 32*, 164–183.

Whitford, E. (2018, August 3). Police called on black student eating lunch. Retrieved from https://www.insidehighered.com/quicktakes/2018/08/03/police-called-black-student-eating-lunch.

WIIS. (2017, February 1). Women in ground combat: Facts and figures. Retrieved from https://www.servicewomen.org/wp-content/uploads/2017/02/Women-in-Ground-Combat-Arms-Fact-Sheet-2-1-17.pdf.

Zipp, J. F., & Fenwick, R. (2006). Is the academy a liberal hegemony? The political orientations and educational values of professors. *American Association for Public Opinion Research, 70*(3), 304–326.

Zucchino, D., & Cloud, D. S. (2015, May 24). U.S. military and civilians are increasingly divided. *Los Angeles Times.* http://www.latimes.com/nation/la-na-warrior-main-20150524-story.html.

Chapter Four

Exploring Identity, Professionalism, and Patriotism within a Multicultural Military Relationship

Intimacy Overseas

Precious Yamaguchi

TWO DIFFERENT ETHNICITIES, GENERATIONAL IDENTITIES, AND PROFESSIONS

My relationship as a professor with a spouse in the military is characterized by diverse experiences, ways of living, and a newfound respect for people serving, supporting, and participating in military life. My autoethnographic position as a Japanese American woman with a partner who is Mexican American serving in the Marines for 11 years is worth exploring because we are two ethnic-American individuals with very different culturally related histories and perspectives when it comes to our families' view on serving in the military. Moreover, our relational experiences can help shed light on intercultural relationships and communication in military contexts.

The history and the treatment of Japanese Americans during World War II plays a significant role in my family's perceptions of patriotism. My great-great grandparents immigrated by ship during the 1880's to the United States. I am a fifth-generation Japanese woman and all four of my grandparents were teenagers when they were imprisoned in the World War II internment camps in Poston, Arizona; Jerome, Arkansas; and Rohwer, Arkansas. When they were released from the internment camps, none of them were able to attend college because they had to immediately find work as domestic servants, in factories, and in a bowling alley. My grandparents always encouraged all of their grandchildren to receive a college education since it was an unobtainable dream for them.

My grandparents did not often discuss their experiences in the internment camps, and my parents grew up knowing very little about the hardships my grandparents faced. It was not until they reached their 80s and 90s that they started telling their grandchildren about the challenges they experienced during and after World War II. Seeing their peers and other people their age pass away, they began to feel a sense of urgency to share with my brother, cousins, and me details about their lives. I was always surprised how when my grandparents did speak about their internment camp and post–World War II experiences, they did so with elements of sadness as well as with a sense of strength, pride, and American patriotism. The "interlocking axes of power" are not divided between their Japanese identities and their American identities but are situated in contextual, historicized, and socialized ongoing negotiations between embracing their Japanese traditions and American patriotism (Shome, 1999, p. 109).

My background as a daughter and granddaughter of these Japanese Americans shaped how I first experienced my relationship with my husband and how, as I spent more time with my partner through his deployment and on the Miramar base in California, my views began to change. Thus, this autoethnographical chapter explores the intersectional themes surrounding my narrative as a Japanese American Communication Studies professor with my husband, a Mexican American Staff Sergeant in the U.S. Marines. In this chapter, I depict how my identity and academic interests became critically challenged when I entered into a relationship with a Marine shortly after I had completed my doctoral degree and experienced his deployment to Afghanistan during the first years of my tenure-track position as an Assistant Professor. My narrative specifically focuses on our communication when he was deployed in Afghanistan and how we navigated through our relationship, investigating our cultural identities, our careers, and the challenges of being in a long-distance, overseas relationship using insights from the Interpersonal Process Model of Intimacy (Reis & Shaver, 1988).

Through the challenges of deployment and the frequent efforts my spouse and I made to support each other through our professional lives of military service and academia, I discovered a new patriotic side of myself and an increased sense of intimacy through the disclosure shared among my spouse, his family, and a mentor of mine who was also a military spouse. The intersectional issues of being a person of color in a professional academic position, with a deployed spouse in Afghanistan, posits a trajectory of challenges that offered me new insight of navigating through issues of communication, identity, and intimacy. Through this chapter I hope to provide a narrative of how ethnicity, race, profession, nationality, and patriotism can intersect within a post-graduate and military relationship.

A FIFTH-GENERATION JAPANESE AMERICAN UPBRINGING

Leela Gandhi's (2006) philosophies on anti-colonial thought focus on how the creations of dualist perspectives striving toward utopian societies often disregard the in-between-ness of other possibilities. The multi-generations of my family and their perceptions of patriotism lie within that in-betweenness. The increments of power, stability, economy, and citizenship gained have the ability to move individuals farther and farther away from their ancestors of their own former identities of otherness (Ong, 1999). When I interviewed my grandparents for a book I wrote (Yamaguchi, 2014), I found how they have suffered in silence giving up so much of their Japanese heritage and even forgoing the use of their language. The shame that developed through their imprisonment as teenagers in the World War II internment camps has never been forgotten, only hidden and buried in their memories. Though they were imprisoned, they still saw themselves as patriotic.

On the contrary, my parents are the children of my grandparents, all four of whom were imprisoned, and expressed anti–Vietnam War sentiments. My parents knew a little bit about their parents' World War II experiences, and the lack of communication between the two generations caused them to struggle with understanding each other. My parents' identities as Japanese Americans who knew vaguely about the imprisonment and pain of their parents and the patriotism my grandparents expressed was confusing for both generations to express and understand.

As an adult I realize my mother and father have grown up and spent most of their lives not knowing much about their parents' experiences in the World War II internment camps; it was a sensitive subject. My father communicated there was tension growing up with his father, not knowing much about his parents' internment camp experience, and he often expressed that his father would lash out for unexplained reasons, inflicting verbal and physical abuse on my father. My father would recall how his father would hit him at the dinner table for an unexplained reason. It may have been some form of coping with PTSD from the internment camps or some kind of similar experience. My father would tell my brother and me how he never understood why his father would verbally insult him or hit him. Like many Japanese Americans who were imprisoned in the internment camps, there was a sense of shame deep within them that has been kept silent.

Of course it was not my grandparents' choice to be placed in internment camps but like many Japanese Americans, our families made the choice to support the American side of World War II efforts through showing their devotion, fighting for their country, and enduring their hardships. By the 1960s, my parents were very removed from the histories of their parents and grandparents and identified with the civil rights movement, anti-Vietnam protests, and embraced the hippie culture. My brother and I grew up in a household where my parents verbally expressed their distaste of war, military efforts, and violence. I often felt there was a lack of patriotism growing up. Both my mom and father would refer back to the Vietnam War, and how the government could not be trusted because they drafted innocent young men to fight a war in Vietnam.

Even when I talked to my mother about writing this chapter focused on the communication and relationship between my husband and me when he was in the Marines, my mother looked at me, teary-eyed, and said, "You should see your Auntie Marci's friends' letters who were in the Vietnam War, and the letters they wrote home. It was horrible. It would make you cry." Just the mention of the word "military" connects my mother's mind to the Vietnam War instead of the experience and lessons learned I was trying to share with her about Andres and me when he was deployed in Afghanistan. I can empathize with her because I believe that there were some heartbreaking experiences among her peers during and after the Vietnam War. Whenever there were discussions about my friends joining the military or different topics relating to the military, my parents would automatically mention their views on the Vietnam War.

A FIRST-GENERATION MEXICAN AMERICAN BACKGROUND

My husband's parents immigrated from Mexico City, Mexico, in the 1960's shortly after my husband's paternal grandfather came to work in California through the Bracero program. Andres's grandfather completed his agricultural work in California and returned back to Mexico City where the rest of his family lived, including his son, Andres's father Armando Sr. My husband pointed out, "When my grandfather came to work through the Bracero program, he was not necessarily very young; he already had children who were adults, like my father." Armando Sr. was a policeman in Mexico City and envisioned starting a life for himself, his wife, and future family in the United States. He flew to Pasadena, California, and started a new life there. His wife eventually joined him and together they had five children; my husband, Andres, is the middle child.

Andres's eldest brother, Armando Jr., enlisted in the Marine Corps after he graduated from high school. By reading old letters saved in a scrapbook, I was able to see the admiration Andres had for his older brother. Armando Jr. told him about his life in the Marines and reminded Andres to take care of the family while he was away. Although it may not have originally been in Andres's plans to join the Marines, I was able to see how his admiration of and mentorship from his elder brother led him in the direction of joining the military. When 9/11 occurred, Andres recalls he was inspired to join the Marines because, "I wanted to contribute . . . I felt like I could do something with the skills I had and provide something." During that time, Armando Jr.

was working as a recruiter for the Marines. Andres wanted to sign up for the Marines through his brother, but Armando Jr. tried to discourage him from it since military life was dangerous and difficult. Andres told his brother that he was determined to enlist in the Marines and if he couldn't do it through him, he would do it through a new recruiter on his own. Armando Jr. gave in, and enlisted Andres into the Marines. Andres was already familiar with some aspects of military life due to his older brother's involvement in the Marines.

Mexican Americans, like Andres and his brother, Armando, are just a couple of the thousands of Latinos who have joined the military throughout U.S. history. Leal's (2003) work on military service and the acculturation of Latinos and Anglos shows how the "United States armed forces acts as an instrument of acculturation for Latinos" for the nearly half a million Latino World War II veterans (p. 205). Blacks, Latinos, and white individuals have obtained intercultural experiences and acquired interracial friendships through their military experiences (Lawrence & Kane, 1996; Leal, 2003). Leal (2003) found that the military is a place where acculturation takes place and that Latino veterans were more likely to have friendships with Anglos than Latinos who were not veterans. As I became part of Andres's military life, I found this to be true. Andres's best friend, Matt, who went to Afghanistan with him during his first deployment there, was very close to him and they were even roommates when they returned back to San Diego from Afghanistan.

With two sons in the Marines, my spouse's parents expressed visible pride and patriotism for the United States and also valued their Mexican cultural heritage with regional traditions from Mexico City, Puebla, and Oaxaca. Walking through their living room, there are photos of both of their sons Andres and Armando Jr. in their Marine Corps uniforms as well as decorative artifacts and gifts from Okinawa, a photo of Andres when he traveled to Kenya and climbed Mount Kilimanjaro while he was stationed at the Guinea Embassy, and folk art from Mexico. Out of the five children, Andres and Armando Jr. are the most well traveled due to the several years they spent in the Marine Corps.

Observing my husband's family and seeing how they embraced their Mexican culture as well as exhibited patriotism and support for their sons in the Marines was the first time I began to really reflect upon the intersection of patriotism and cultural pride. For so long, I had been raised in a family with the mind-set that the majority of people of color could not trust our government and military. It was not until I became a part of my husband's family that I started to see that some people of color make up our military and we entrust much of our freedom and protection to them.

EXPERIENCING DIVERSITY IN THE MILITARY AND IN A DEPLOYMENT

Andres and I met during the summer of 1998 at a high school journalism summer camp. He was the design editor of his high school newspaper. I was the editor of my high school yearbook. We became best friends that year and graduated from our own high schools in 1999. We continued our friendship and I went to college in Northern California, while he worked and attended community college in Pasadena. After we graduated, we rarely saw each other but still kept in touch through the occasional email or phone call, especially on our birthdays, Christmas, and New Year's Eve.

The attack on September 11, 2001, made a significant impact on Andres. At the time, I was nearly finished with my bachelor's degree at Humboldt State University and Andres decided to enlist in the Marine Corps. Less than two years later, Andres was a Marine and I was starting my Communication master's degree program at Pepperdine University. The year of 2003 was a major starting point for us in embarking upon our own individual careers in the military and academia.

We were heavily engaged in our careers and gaining international experience. Andres worked his way up the ranks in the Marines and also traveled the world through his job, working and living in Japan, Burma, Egypt, and having two tours in Afghanistan. I was also consumed with my work in graduate school, teaching, and traveling the world through programs in Greece, Ghana, Vietnam, and China. I graduated from my doctoral program in August in 2010 and after 12 long years of separation, Andres and I finally saw each other again. We spent the Fourth of July in 2011 together and became boyfriend and girlfriend that week. This is where our military–academic relationship started.

Coming from a family where military life was very foreign and sometimes looked down upon due to my parents' anti–Vietnam War stance, I had very little knowledge about being in a relationship with a Marine. All the people I knew who were against the Vietnan War were also as anti-military as my parents were when I was growing up. Even though my grandparents were imprisoned in the Japanese–American World War II internment camps, my grandparents exhibited patriotism symbolically such as purchasing small American flags on the Fourth of July and singing patriotic songs. They showed their allegiance verbally when they spoke about the United States, and even when it was related to topics such as presidents, politics, and World War II; they always felt that they were true Americans. My parents, who are both Japanese-American, were very much the opposite and talked about how the government can't always be trusted: "The Vietnam War should have never happened," and "The government uses innocent young men to fight these wars." We discussed colonization, corrupt politicians, and presidents in our household whenever the military was mentioned.

The complexity of the relationship between Asian-Americans and the U.S. military goes beyond the World War II Japanese-American internment camps and the Vietnam War. Under the Immigration Act of 1790 and the Revised Statutes of 1870, "limited naturalization to those who were white or of African descent," excluded Asian Americans (Salyer, 2004, p. 847).

Asian-Americans who have served in the U.S. military were denied citizenship, contrary to the Alien Naturalization Act, also known as the Act of May 9, 1918, "which offered naturalization to any alien who had served in the [U.S.] Armed Forces during war" (Salyer, 2004, p. 847).

The concept of patriotism, especially for people of color, is multifarious due to people's ethnic, cultural, religious, regional, political, and generational histories. Coleman, Harris, Bryant, and Reif-Stice (2018) attempt to explore "patriotism from an African American cultural perspective" and how patriotism takes "seemingly antithetical concepts" of culture and how it fits together (Coleman et al., 2018, p. 177). They also investigated how "communication is used to create and maintain constructs that define patriotism, its audience, and how African Americans fit within that audience"(Coleman et al., 2018, p. 174). This chapter incorporates the complexity of patriotism within a Japanese American–Mexican American, academic and military couple, from two different generations. As found in the research of Coleman and colleagues (2018), there are "dialectical tensions between race and patriotic identity" for people of color (p. 185). Previously in this chapter I've explored some of those same tensions between my Japanese American history and my personal experiences of viewing how my grandparents and parents expressed their thoughts on patriotism.

As an academic, my research reflected the interest in post-colonial and anti-colonial studies partially due to my upbringing and my family history of my grandparents' imprisonment in the World War II internment camps, so it was surprising to even myself when I was suddenly in a relationship with a Staff Sergeant. So much of my previous research had been about how the United States imprisoned Japanese American citizens, like my grandparents. This event affected our family for generations. We lost our language because our grandparents were too ashamed to speak it. They lost all of their properties, homes, businesses, and family heirlooms when they were imprisoned. My grandparents also lost a part of themselves while they were imprisoned. They carried a certain type of silence and sadness while raising my parents. Through all of my research on the Japanese American internment as well as the overall history of the hardships people of color faced, I was upset at my country's history.

I definitely challenged Andres with questions such as the loss of Native American land, immigration, internment, and military invasions. He did not deny those tragedies of our country's past, which helped me to respect his opinions. He also shared with me how he felt pride to be an American citizen, that his family worked hard to build their life in the United States, and that he truly feels American. I could not refute his perspective because I truly feel I am an American too. I had been to Japan with my brother and we both felt very foreign not knowing the language, the customs, and we didn't even have any family back in Japan.

In 2011, I attended my very first Marine Corps Ball in San Diego, California, which was truly an eye-opening experience; it was almost shocking for me to see how diverse the Marine Corps was in terms of race and ethnicity. In writing this autoethnography, I looked at photos of our first Marine Corps Ball and I am still surprised to see two things: (1) how happy my husband looks in the group photo with his battalion and (2) how diverse his battalion was in terms of race. My perceptions of race, patriotism, and service continued to change over time. As I began to join Andres on the Marine Corps Air Station Miramar base, go shopping with him at the Marine Corps Exchange, and attend certain Family Day events with his peers, I learned more about his position as a Staff Sergeant. It was all very new to me, just as life in academia was new to him.

After our first year in our relationship passed and Andres was getting to know more about my academic life while I was getting more familiar with his work in the Marine Corps, we were hit by the jolting news that he was going to be deployed again to Afghanistan in a couple of months. This time there would be one-eighth of the staff there, so he had to work multiple jobs. I was devastated because this was unlike any other long-distance relationship I had ever experienced. It didn't matter if I had winter break, spring break, or summer break, I would not be able to visit him for 10 months while he was in Afghanistan and not even able to call him. We were only in the beginning of the second year of our relationship and now we were going to have to face one of the biggest challenges. Andres surprised me with a trip and an engagement ring a couple months before he deployed to Afghanistan and we had two months of enjoying each other's company as a newly engaged couple before he headed to Afghanistan.

Reflecting back on those months, I believe it was partially because I am an academic and aware of the communication challenges military couples face that made me not want to have a last-minute wedding before he left for Afghanistan. We knew many couples in the military who would get married right before their spouses deployed to be eligible for some of the financial and emotional benefits, and I was familiar with the challenges military service members face when returning home. As shown in the research from Wilson, Gettings, Hall, and Pastor (2015), it is not uncommon for service members who are deployed, especially in Iraq and Afghanistan, to experience PTSD and depression. Baptist, Amanor-Boadu, Garrett, Goff, Collum, Gamble, Gurss, Sanders-Hahs, Strader, and Wick (2011), wrote, "It is clear that members of military marriages have to cope with intense pressure and stress, and adapt to the myriad changes related to deployment and reintegration" (p. 200). We had only been together for a year—would we be able to endure the possibilities of physical, mental, and emotional stress associated with Andres's deployment? I wanted to make sure we could sustain our long-distance relationship throughout his deployment and after his deployment without the pressure of staying together because we were married. I had no idea what to expect when he returned home. As is shown in the research of Baptist et al. (2011), "Military marriages with ineffective adaptive processes, deployment-related stress could lead to a decline in marital quality and/or stability" (p. 201). I was worried that we may be one of those military marriages with an ineffective adaptive process.

Looking back on my decision to not get married right away, it may have been a selfish and cautious choice. I had invested so many years into my education, career, and academic goals, and having a relationship with someone in the military was so unfamiliar to me because they navigated through a completely different type of schedule than what I was used to. As an academic who just received my Ph.D. and a tenure-track position, I was not willing to do some things other spouses were willing to do (e.g., relocate to different parts of the country or the world) and I wasn't interested in receiving a stipend or benefits just for being a military spouse to a deployed Marine. Andres accepted and respected my feelings and career, and this only made me fall in love with him more. I loved Andres and wanted to be supportive, but I also knew how lucky I was to receive a tenure-track position. We had known each other for a really long time as friends though we had only been together for a year. I worried about the possibility that he may return back from Afghanistan and we may be one of those couples that couldn't make it throughout his deployment. Although I wanted our relationship to work, I knew we would be together after Afghanistan if it we were meant to be.

The second moment I began to really feel my prior beliefs and inexperience of the intersections of race, ethnicity, patriotism, and the military challenge was a few weeks before my husband deployed to Afghanistan. I attended a family information session for the spouses and families of Marines who were going to be deployed. I sat in an auditorium listening to Andres's peers and supervisors speak, who were all people of color: Vietnamese, Black, Latino, and Filipino. As I listened to the different challenges we were about to endure as our loved ones were about to be deployed to Afghanistan and looked around the auditorium, I could not help but feel a new awakening of what inclusivity, freedom, and service means in relation to patriotism. I realized my point of view of prior to becoming a spouse of a Marine was so narrow and looking at the diverse families of the Marines moved me to see how many people from families that are newly immigrated or who have immigrated from several generations ago serve our country.

Throughout Andres's deployment, I found support through our consistent communication with each other over the phone and email, with a few of my students who also had partners in the military, and through the mentorship of Andres's eldest brother, Armando Jr.'s wife Sandra. Sandra and Armando Jr. had been together since high school and he had been in the Marines for over 15 years during the time Andres was deployed. She had also experienced Armando Jr. being away overseas several of times, was a mother of four children (including a special needs child), and is Mexican American. Although she is not an academic like myself, having her support and her willingness to share her experiences of having a spouse deployed was incredibly meaningful. She shared with me a myriad of information ranging from being able to observe subtle signs of PTSD when your spouse returns home to being in a long-distance relationship as well as just a person to talk to when I was concerned or missing Andres. I learned about her identity as a very active wife, mother, and a patriotic Mexican American woman through watching and listening to her talk about her experiences.

When Andres was deployed in Afghanistan, I was only 31 years old and worked at a college where the majority of the faculty members were quite older than me; some of them even had grandchildren. None of my colleagues had spouses or partners who ever served in the military. Some days were difficult going to work, especially during the seventh, eighth, and ninth months that he was away. I would hear my colleagues talk about their children and their weekends with their spouses and I would have to tell myself that in just a short amount of time I would be having fun weekends with Andres too.

Andres used phone cards to call me almost every single day from Afghanistan. His internet connection did not work well enough for us to Skype or chat online so he purchased over $1000's worth of phone cards and would call me. One day, I received an email from him with just a URL link about his base in Afghanistan being attacked by missiles and he would not be able to call me for a while. For two days, I continued to teach class, fulfill my office hours, and attend meetings, with constant worry and concern about his safety. There were no news updates online or on the television about the missile attack on his base; it was all kept very quiet. There was an email from our Family Readiness Advisor, which gave very vague news about the attack.

For a couple days, I waited, stressed out and exhausted, hoping to hear from him. Eventually after about two days I heard from him over the phone and he let me know he was okay. These types of incidents were moments I felt I was alone at work with no one else who could relate to what I was experiencing.

Throughout Andres's deployment in Afghanistan I did find a few students and a staff member at my college who were able to discuss the challenges of military life with me. A few of my students had partners in the military and we would talk about care packages and our partners' rigorous schedules. I was thankful for a staff member and friend at my college whose brother and spouse were Marine veterans. Although her spouse and brother were not currently serving in the Marines she was able to share her experiences as well as relate to all the things I was experiencing.

RETURN FROM AFGHANISTAN

During the time when Andres returned home from Afghanistan, I was very busy with my position as a full-time professor and had a gradual introduction to military life. After 10 months of being apart, he returned home toward the end of my Spring semester. I flew to San Diego to greet him at the airport during one of the busiest weeks of the semester. At the airport we ran and hugged and kissed each other like all of the other couples around us. We had a short 48 hours together and then I had to fly back to Pennsylvania because I was scheduled to be the keynote speaker at an event at my college the next day. I was emotionally and physically exhausted from the traveling and all the feelings I experienced after seeing Andres arrive home from Afghanistan. During my keynote speech the next day, which was about support for our LGBTQ community at our college, I broke down in tears, and could almost not make it through the speech. My emotions were overwhelmed by not only how passionately I felt about the topic of LGBTQ support at our college, but by the happiness of Andres returning home and the sadness that we were still apart with him in San Diego and me in Pennsylvania. I wanted to celebrate his return but instead we both had to jump right back into our jobs and it was emotionally stressful. As shown in the research by Baptist et al. (2011), "Families must undergo this process each time the service member leaves and returns" (p. 200).

Andres moved into his older brother's house near San Diego when he returned from Afghanistan. Observing Andres and his peers transition from their lives in Afghanistan to their lives and work back in the United States, I was able to gain a new type of understanding and sympathy about the difficulties of transitioning back into a post-Afghanistan life. Like most people who live abroad and return home, figuring out the logistics of where to live, moving one's belongings out of storage, and getting back into the routines of normal life can be challenging. I saw some of Andres's colleagues who went to Afghanistan with him come home to broken relationships with partners or spouses who had broken up with them or cheated on them while they were in Afghanistan.

Though there is research on communication and military couples (Baptist et al., 2011; Doss et al., 2015; Wilson et al., 2015) and the challenges they face when their spouse returns home from deployment, there is not much research specifically on couples where one individual is in the military and the other individual is a professor in academia, as well as multicultural couples, specifically Mexican American and Japanese American. The challenges of communicating with your spouse who is deployed while working an academic position can be challenging because both careers entail multiple duties and are demanding in terms of time. Mehta and Jorgenson (2015) advise couples who are in a military relationship to inform their spouses about their work. "Simply having a conversation about what military life is like and how they feel about it is a significant way of removing a barrier" (Mehta & Jorgenson, 2015, p. 135). This basic but time-consuming task of communication really helped Andres and I navigate through our relationship during deployment. Through this autoethnography, I shared the complex familial and cultural backgrounds my husband and I experienced growing up, that shaped some of our career and personal decisions, patriotism, and our relationship. I hope some of this information can create more dialogue on the complexities of our ethnic, racial, and professional identities in our relationships, as well as offer some advice of couples who are preparing to experience separation during deployment.

THE INTERPERSONAL PROCESS MODEL OF INTIMACY FOR A MILITARY—ACADEMIC RELATIONSHIP

Parcell (2015) posits that one of the ways to categorize communication and military research is through "a) interpersonal interactions, b) mediated messages, and c) public discourses" (p. 8). This autoethnography takes an in-depth look at the relationship my husband and I maintained when he was deployed in Afghanistan for 10 months through the framework of the Interpersonal Process Model (Reis & Shaver, 1988). This model examines how the process of self-disclosure and responsiveness develop intimacy in long-distance relationships. Self-disclosure is the "the communication of personal facts, thoughts, and emotions to one another," and responsiveness is "the perception that the relationship partner recognizes, values, and behaviorally supports the core aspects of the self" (Jiang & Hancock, 2013, p. 557). The IPMI model was tested in a research study by Jiang and Hancock (2013) to investigate college students in long-distance and geographically close relationships. Results showed the students in long-distance relationships were able to have just as much satisfaction, if not more, than the students who were in geographically close relationships. This study was incredibly encouraging because it proposed that two "intimacy-enhancing mechanisms," behavioral adaption and idealization, enhanced intimacy among long-distance couples (Jiang & Hancock, 2013, p. 559). Behavioral adaption is when "LD [long-distance] daters strategically adapt their self-disclosure behaviors" and idealization is when "LD daters form intensified relational perceptions" (p. 559), sometimes intensifying perceptions that are "above and beyond" the actual "changes in a partner's self-disclosure" (p. 560).

The IPMI model emphasizes the intimacy process and development based upon the attributes and engagement of self-disclosure, perceived partner disclosure, and perceived partner responsiveness. Without my spouse even knowing about the IPMI framework when I interviewed him for this chapter, I asked him, what was the most significant way I showed him support during his deployment in Afghanistan and he replied:

"Being able to answer or respond, by picking up the phone or responding in a timely manner because a lot of times you only get so much time during the day to take care of personal stuff and if you're playing phone tag or something, it just doesn't really work. If you're not in Afghanistan or overseas or something like that, it doesn't really matter but when you're there, that time matters a lot more. Being reliable with responding is very helpful, knowing that somebody's going to be there."

In order to make sure my responses were timely, it was important for me to disclose the liberties as well as limitations of my job. For example, I gave him my class schedule, my office hours information, and let him know about meetings and conferences I may be participating in, that way we could successfully coordinate our phone calls. It can feel disappointing and anxiety-provoking if you miss the call from a deployed partner.

While my fiancé was deployed in Afghanistan, he could call me, but I could not call him, and just because I had free time, it didn't always mean he would be free to call me. On days when I would present at an academic conference, I would tell him what time my presentation was and how long a presentation panel usually lasts. This type of detail helped us to gain knowledge of how we were spending our time, information about our careers, and trust and interest in each other.

Applying a framework such as IPMI sounds simple but for two people who have jobs that are very time-consuming and filled with specific details that sometimes can and cannot be shared, it can be discouraging to disclose information about one's work. There was a lot of information Andres could not disclose about his job, such as locations, dates, and specific duties. However, due to the fact that our success in connecting with each other on the phone relied on sharing our schedules, we explained some of the intricate details of our job so we could understand our limitations. The process of disclosing, communicating, and managing our schedules with each other is an example of what Jiang and Hancock (2013) highlighted as behavioral adaption, and the positive effects it has on intimacy among couples in a long-distance relationship. Not only did Andres know my schedule, he was knowledgeable about certain events in my life, such as a colleague evaluation or a conference presentation, to show support. Hearing my daily schedule helped Andres understand how rigorous academic life can be and get to know all of the duties involved in an academic position, and it also made me feel that he really cared about my career. Likewise, sometimes he would share with me the numerous tasks he completed or the preposterous amounts of hours he had been awake to complete a task, and I would show him my support and encouragement.

One of the challenges my significant other faced that wasn't as much of a challenge for me was shifting his mind-set from work to our relationship. For example, when I was walking across campus and received a phone call from Andres, I felt engaged, relaxed, and happy to speak to him. It was the opposite for him. He felt that he had to consciously make an effort to shift from his work to connect with me on the phone. While in Afghanistan, sometimes he had incredibly stressful duties or numerous tasks he had to fulfill and taking 10 minutes out of this routine to make a phone call to me was sometimes challenging because he felt he had to take himself away from his work or military mind-set, and ask my how my day was without being in work-mode. He explained:

> "[The biggest challenge for me was] there's not enough time. If you're there, it's to work, you have to take yourself out of the mindset that you're in so you can really make a phone call that isn't just like nodding your head. [Being deployed in] Afghanistan it's more about working with one another to be supportive. You can easily do that here. But being separated by such a long distance, time, and hardship is more of a trial by fire than a regular relationship. Something that really helped was us listening to different things from each other and taking a common sense approach to everything and understanding the practicalities of calling or emailing back and forth from such a long distance and the limitations that it has, that really helps."

Interestingly, we both were working in the field of Communication, though our jobs, goals, and daily life were very different. Andres was in the Communication department in the Marines, however, his focus was on radio signal interception, encryption, networks, and creating and fixing different types of technology. Even though there was not much internet connection where he was located, on special days or holidays he would apply all of his technical skills so we could connect for a few minutes through video chat. Just seeing the backdrop of where he was, the dust, the lack of buildings, and how tired he looked, I could not help but learn about the difficult conditions he was working in Afghanistan.

In such a situation as this, I found it hard to not become a more patriotic person. I had not grown up with American flag symbols or the messages of supporting our troops, but through the disclosure from my spouse of the unbelievable amount of work he did every day, I gradually became more and more patriotic, appreciating his service and understanding why it is so important to thank people in the military for their tireless service. I began to send him care packages every other week, email him every day, and he reciprocated the same amount of effort with daily phone calls, flower deliveries, and emails. The daily amount of communication made even the most difficult days such as Christmas, birthdays, and holidays being apart still feel like they were special.

I had spent so many years in academia focusing on the mistreatment of people of color and diverse populations in our country; I realized I had failed to see how many diverse populations also feel pride for their country and are willing to serve the United States. Growing up I had imagined faceless military people, fighting in wars, and invading countries, but now I saw my fiancé dusty and tired in Afghanistan or at the Marine Corps Ball taking a photo with his battalion of Vietnamese, Latino, Black, and White peers. These images gave me new meaning to military service. Colonization, wars, and the mistreatment of people still exist, though now I understand the relationships among these occurrences differently.

Although a few years have now passed since our year when he was deployed in Afghanistan, I asked Andres what he thought was unique about being in a relationship with a professor while he was in the Marines and in Afghanistan, to which he replied:

"A person in academia usually has very long-term and short-term goals; they may be working on research projects in addition to prepping for a class they're teaching and they have all these different career-shaping goals and that makes them very productive and busy. In the military although it may seem like a person does just one job all of the time, a lot of the time you're doing your own work as well as independent research if you want to learn how to be promoted.

So the fact that both people can be pretty busy and have a very challenging career, I can see how it would help [for a person in the military to be with a person in academia] because your academic career sometimes really matches up with someone in the military who has a really crazy schedule that is not a 9 to 5 type of job."

CONCLUSION

The Interpersonal Process Model of Intimacy posits the ways self-disclosure, perceived partner self-disclosure, and the perceived partner responsiveness contributes to the development of intimacy. Although we were two people who had very demanding jobs and were immersed in our careers, we communicated and disclosed a lot of information about our schedules, work, and goals. It would have been easy for us to nonchalantly have the attitude of, "oh, you don't want to hear about my department meeting" or "you would never understand what it's like to be in Afghanistan," but instead we discussed and disclosed the information we could about our jobs, never implying that it was too mundane to discuss. I remember one time my husband even sent me an MRE (Meal Ready-to-Eat, a type of portable, preserved meal in a pouch), so we could have a "dinner date" and eat the same meal over the phone. I thought it was funny, but looking back on it in relation to the IPMI, I am thankful that we really shared so much about our careers with each other. Both of our careers were such a significant part of ourselves, lives, and who we were during that time. We were both heavily invested in our tasks, our pathways to promotion and success, and sharing the details of our work helped us see our shared values of leadership.

As shown in figure 4.1, the basic disclosure of practical information between an academic's life and a military partner's life, such as details about our schedules, worklife, daily life, future goals, and plans helps to set a foundation of how to support each other. With a bit of information about your significant other's professional life you are able to follow each other's accomplishments and meaningful milestones in each other's careers, and emotionally respond accordingly. Intimacy is much more than knowing each other's schedules and worklife, it is really listening to each other, communicating with one another, and showing empathy through the challenging times.

Through sharing our daily schedules and what was happening in our lives, we were able to achieve time together over the phone and through various types of technology such as email and video chat without the frustration of unresponsiveness or playing email/phone tag. Our timely responsiveness helped us to grow as a couple and through the experience of being an academic, I applied various communication skills and techniques I taught in

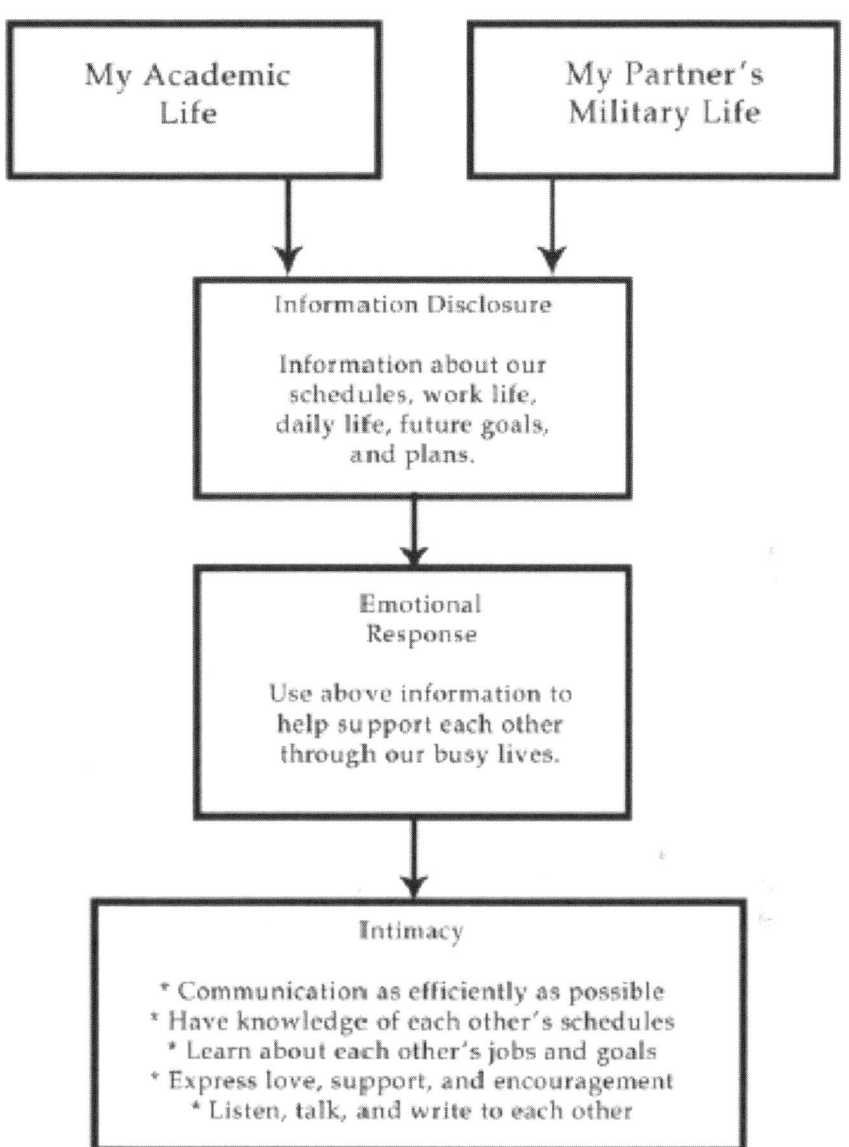

Figure 4.1. Model of Information Disclosure and Intimacy

class to one of the most challenging communication experiences of my life. I was also able to develop a sense of patriotism that was originally conflicted by my family history of my grandparents experiencing the World War II internment camps and my parents who were very much against the Vietnam War, realizing the intersectionality of beliefs can coexist as historical and cultural moments. Similar to the study by Coleman et al. (2018) of the complexity of African Americans' perception of patriotism, my Japanese American perspective of the United States is embedded in its cultural history; however, now it is also joined by the respect and appreciation for the diverse populations of people who serve in its military. This chapter displays a pathway to examining our complex cultural identities and how they adapt and change through deeper understanding and learning about our partner's profession and service, whether it is in the military or in academia.

Observing and communicating with Andres, I learned about the complexities of serving your country while embracing your heritage. Engaging in my husband's military life as a first-generation Mexican American, I gained a new sense of appreciation of being from immigrant parents and serving your country no matter how many generations your family has or has not been in the United States. I used to believe patriotism conflicted with my areas of research on post-colonialism and anti-colonialism, but now have become interested in how the pride of our country does not have to negate the hardships of ancestors. Rather, the narratives from all sides, generations, and positions helps us to create a more inclusive society and field, respecting our diverse roles and contributions to our country.

REFERENCES

Baptist, J., Amanor-Boadu, Y., Garrett, K., Nelson Goff, B., Collum, J., Gamble, P., Gurss, H., Sanders-Hans, E. M. Strader, L. & Wick, S. (2011). Military marriages: The aftermath of Operation Iraqi Freedom (OIF) and Operation Enduring Freedom (OEF) deployments. *Contemporary Family Therapy: An International Journal*, *33*(3), 199–214. doi:10.1007/s10591-011-9162-6.

Coleman, M. J., Harris, T. M., Bryant, K. L., & Reif-Stice, C. (2018). A cultural approach to patriotism. *Journal of International and Intercultural Communication*, *11*, 173–191. doi:10.1080/17513057.2018.1454974.

Doss, B. D., Mitchell, A., Georgia, E. J., Biesen, J. N., & Rowe, L. S. (2015). Improvements in closeness, communication, and psychological distress mediate effects of couple therapy for veterans. *Journal of Consulting and Clinical Psychology*, *83*, 405–415. http://dx.doi.org/10.1037/a0038541.

Gandhi, L. (2006). *Affective Communities: Anticolonial Thought, Fin-De-Siecle Radicalism, and the Politics of Friendship*. Durham: Duke University Press.

Ginosar, A. (2015). Understanding patriotic journalism: Culture, ideology, and professional behavior. *Journal of Media Ethics, 30*, 289–301. doi: 10.1080/23736992.2015.1082915.
Hafen, S. (2009). Patriots in the classroom: Performing positionalities post 9/11. *Communication and Critical/Cultural Studies, 6*, 61–83. doi: 10.1080/14791420802632111.
Jiang, C. L., & Hancock, J. T. (2013). Absence makes the communication grow fonder: Geographic separation, interpersonal media, and intimacy in dating relationships. *Journal of Communication, 63*, 556–577. doi:10.1111/jcom.12029.
Lawrence, G. H., & Kane, T. D. (1995). Military service and racial attitudes of white veterans. *Armed Forces & Society, 22*(2), 235–255.
Leal, D. L. (2003). The multicultural military: Military service and the acculturation of the Latinos and Anglos. *Armed Forces and Society, 29*, 205–226. https://doi.org/10.1177/0095327X0302900204.
Learenceau, J., Barrett, L. F., & Pietromonaco, P. R. (1998). Intimacy as an interpersonal process: The importance of self-disclosue, partner disclosure, and perceived partner responsiveness in interpersonal exchanges. *Journal of Personality and Social Psychology, 74*, 1238–1251. doi: 0022-3514/98$300.
Manne, S., Zaider, T., Kim, I. Y., Penedo, F., Kashy, D. A., Lee, D., Heckman, C., & Kissane, D. (2018). Interpersonal processes and intimacy among men with localized prostate cancer and their partners. *Journal of Family Psychology, 12*, 664–675. http://dx.doi.org/10.1037/fam0000404.
Mehta, M. S., & Jorgenson, J. (2015). Work-family predicaments of Air Force wives: A sensemaking perspective. In E. S. Parcell and L. M. Webb (Eds.), *Communication Perspective on the Military: Interactions, Messages, and Discourses* (pp. 121–138). New York: Peter Lang Publishing, Inc.
Ong, A. (1999). *Flexible citizenship: The cultural logics of transnationality*. Durham: Duke University Press.
Padilla, P. A., & Laner, M. R. (2002). Trends in military influences on army recruitment themes: 1954–1990. *Journal of Political and Military Sociology, 30*, 113–133. https://doi.org/10.1111/j.1475-682X.2001.tb01124.x.
Parcell, E. S. (2015). Research at the intersections of the military and communication: A preview and review. In E. S. Parcell and L. M. Webb (Eds.), *Communication Perspective on the Military: Interactions, Messages, and Discourses* (pp. 1–18). New York: Peter Lang Publishing, Inc.
Reis, H. T., Shaver, P. (1988). Intimacy as an interpersonal process. In S. Duck (Ed.), *Handbook of Personal Relationships* (pp. 367–389). Chichester, UK: Wiley.
Rovine, M. J. (2005). The interpersonal process model of intimacy in marriage: A daily-diary and multilevel modeling approach. *Journal of Family Psychology, 19*, 314–323. doi: 10.1037/0893-3200.19.2.314.
Salyer, L. E. (2004). Baptism by fire: Race, military service, and U.S. citizenship policy, 1918–1935. *The Journal of American History, 91*, 847–876. https://doi.org/10.2307/3662858.
Shelton, J. N., Trail, T. E., West, T. V., & Bergsierker, H. B. (2010). From strangers to friends: The interpersonal process model of intimacy in developing inter-

racial friendship. *Journal of Social and Personal Relationships, 27*, 71–90. doi: 10.1177/0265407509346422.

Shome, R. (1999). Whiteness and the politics of location: Postcolonial reflections. In T. K. Nakayama and J. N. Martin (Eds.), *Whiteness: The Communication of Social Identity*. Thousand Oaks, CA: Sage Publications.

Slatter, K., & Garner, A. C. (2007). Mothers of soldiers in wartime: A national news narrative. *Critical Studies in Media Communication, 24*, 429–445. doi: 10.1080/07393180701694655.

Smith-Osborne, A., & Jani, J. (2014). Long-distance military and civilian relationships: Women's perceptions of the impact of communication technology and military culture. *Military Behaviorial Health, 2*, 293–303. https://doi.org/10.1080/21635781.2014.963759.

United States Marine Corps. (2016, February 11). *Racial and Gender Distribution*. https://marinecorpsconceptsandprograms.com/almanacs/active-duty-officer/racial-and-gender-distribution.

Wilson, S. R., Gettings, P. E., Hall, E. D., & Pastor, R. G. (2015). Dilemmas families face in talking with returning U.S. military service members about seeking professional help for mental health issues. *Health Communication, 30*, 772–783. doi: 10.1080/10410236.2014.899659.

Yamaguchi, P. (2014). *Experiences of Japanese American Women During and After World War II: Living in Internment Camps and Rebuilding Life Afterwards*. Lanham: Lexington Books.

Part II

ACADEMIC, PROFESSIONAL, AND MILITARY CHALLENGES

Chapter Five

Becoming Whole

Balancing Dual Identities as a Graduate Student Marine Wife

Elise Dixon

Full disclosure: I never wanted to be a military wife. When my husband Dave and I first began our relationship, I worried his military career would mean I would play second fiddle in our life together. And yet, surprisingly, we have traveled across the country to two different states *not* for the military, but for my graduate education. And, to be honest, I never expected to become an academic either; still, these two identities have become an important part of my adult life. Most importantly, though, I never thought that these two identities—graduate student and military wife—would end up at odds with one another in the ways they are now. My experience juggling graduate school in rhetoric and writing while being married to a Marine has led to many negotiations, both in practice and in theory, especially as my graduate focus in queer, feminist, and cultural rhetorics has challenged my thinking around the American military's history with gender, sexuality, and imperialism.

As I developed as a scholar, I found myself becoming more critical toward the military, especially because I was often surrounded by colleagues who were critical of the military industrial complex as a whole. Everything I was learning seemed to suggest to me that the military was complicit in so many problematic systems of violence, sexism, heteronormativity, and racism. I worked to distance myself from my connection to the military, even as my Marine husband joined me at parties and events connected to my program. During that time, my husband became a recruiter for the Marine Corps. In essence, as a married couple, our careers put us perpetually at odds with each other as we become more entangled in military life. As I continually benefit from my husband's consistent paycheck and quality medical insurance, my scholarship sometimes directly challenges the military system that bankrolls my graduate career. Additionally, like many military wives, I have experienced explicitly sexist behavior from other military members and implicitly through policies, classes, and events that sometimes enculturate spouses as support staff for military members. Negotiating these tensions creates complications in my personal life as I interact with my husband and his fellow Marines outside of the walls of academe; these complexities also impact my intellectual life as I negotiate my own connection to a military system of which many of my colleagues disapprove.

In this chapter, I outline the ways in which my existence as a military wife has been changed and challenged by my life as a graduate student. Drawing from personal experiences as a military spouse and from scholarship I have learned while pursuing my master's and Ph.D. in rhetoric and writing, I illuminate the ways in which graduate school has challenged my thoughts around some of the military's heteronormative practices, its historical treatment of spouses and especially wives, and its connection to colonial and imperial power. These challenges often led me to withdraw from military family events, often leading to my nickname of "Ghost Wife" among recruiters and their own spouses. I describe how I have often felt I needed to choose between my identity as a military spouse or an academic. I conclude this chapter by discussing how I have struggled to come to terms with these sometimes seemingly incompatible identities in order to thrive as both. I offer an alternative to "picking a side" by illuminating the way in which academia and military life have much in common and much to offer one another, both theoretically and in practice.

AT ODDS

"So what do you do?" A fellow graduate student asked my husband, Dave. We were at a bar at the beginning of the summer between my first and second years of my master's degree. The graduate student we were with was a Ph.D. student I deeply admired. Her work was focused on queer theory, and I respected her radical politics and intelligence.

"I'm a recruiter for the Marine Corps," my husband replied, preparing to explain what his work entailed. Before he could begin, he was interrupted.

"Oh my God, you're evil," the graduate student blurted out. "I HATE you." She began discussing her feelings about the military as a whole, its connections to the homophobia that fueled early bans on LGBT people in the military, followed by "Don't Ask, Don't Tell." She mentioned the United States's investment in gratuitous wars, especially the interminable War on Terror. Dave smiled and listened while I squirmed in my seat, wide-eyed and silent until someone at our table changed the subject.

Later, when we made our way home, I told Dave how upset I was by this woman's abrupt contention that she hated him, having only just met him. "It's ok," he said calmly, hanging up his jacket. "I joined the Marines to defend her freedom to say that."

Instances like this one put me on edge as a graduate student, especially early in my graduate career when I wanted to belong. My focus on queer and feminist theories in my coursework often meant I was in the company of people who were staunchly anti-war and anti-military. From a feminist perspective, military violence is especially unfeminist; from a queer perspective, the military's connection to past and present oppressive anti-LGBT policies speaks for itself. As a bisexual woman married to a man, I felt and understood these issues both intellectually and personally. I worried my connection to the military through my husband would strip me of my credibility as a scholar in these fields.

During this time, I was first introduced to the work of Althusser, whose discussion of the military as an Ideological State Apparatus (Althusser, 1968) caused me to consider the ways in which a military is made and developed through the perpetuation of sometimes problematic ideologies. Learning this theory and others sent me into a tailspin—how could I negotiate the tensions I saw in my scholarship and in my own life as a military spouse?

As I learned in my graduate classes, the military acts as a "Repressive State Apparatus" (RSA), fueled and perpetuated by ideologies we often see connected to the military (Althusser, 1968). For instance, "the Army and the Police . . . function by ideology both to ensure their own cohesion and reproduction" (Althusser, 1968, p. 7). For example, I began to think about the ways in which the American military is informed by Ideological State Apparatuses (ISA) like tradition, family, and freedom, concepts we use to defend why the military is so necessary in society. ISAs themselves are created through what Althusser calls "an imaginary assemblage" (p. 23) of various concepts and realities that give us an idea of an abstract idea. ISAs—like the concept of freedom—are a conglomerate of many separate individual meanings made into a pastiche of singular meaning, used to inform a set of values. These values, then, can be enforced through violence (like war) to become RSAs. Where might I, as a military spouse, be inculcated in this repressive state apparatus?

As I learned more, I saw how ideologies of family and marriage—which are often connected to stories we tell about military life (in terms of military families themselves, and the military's defense of the safety of the American family)—certainly include me as a spouse, in ways I don't always feel comfortable with, especially as a bisexual woman. According to Althusser (1968) and others I was learning about in my classes (e.g., Foucault, 1980;

1995), the military RSA is informed also by the ISA of marriage, a concept enforced and reinforced through generations of heteronormative rituals and norms. Thus, though according to Hyde (2015), "It is perhaps easy to forget that the 'military wife' is a compound figure of both military and marital status, whose subjectivity is doubly defined by two heteronormative institutions" (p. 32). The conjunction of these two heteronormative ideologies create a mutually beneficial relationship, though one might argue many women benefit from neither.

Perpetuated by Ideological State Apparatuses, the military system uses violence (or at least violent training to be used in war) to produce military members who then reproduce the system in which they themselves were inculcated. Althusser (1968) indicates that structures of power like this often function well because they can reproduce the ideologies necessary to perpetuate the system. He asserts, ". . . the reproduction of labour power requires not only the reproduction of its skills, but also, at the same time, a reproduction of its submission to the rules of the established order" (p. 5).

Thus, the military is able to reproduce itself as a structure of power, not just because it is reproduced by outside forces, but also because it reproduces a submission of the ruling ideology in military members themselves (and by proxy, those intimately connected to them). For example, much rhetoric exists (through commercials, recruiting materials, and news production) around the military's necessity for the purpose of the defending American freedoms. Military members' individual buy-in of the value of freedom and the belief that war can sustain such a freedom helps to maintain the military system at large. Thus, the ideology of the military relies on particular metanarratives of freedom, family, heteronormative marriage, protection, and capitalism to maintain its supposed singularity.

As I learned about Ideological State Apparatuses, I felt I was forced to contend with my own implication into the American military's power in the world. I knew that the military did not always fight wars that I agreed with, and yet my position as a military spouse made me part of that community, for better or for worse. Furthermore, the symbolism I carried as a military spouse—a wife especially—was one of heteronormativity and family, concepts that politicians I didn't always agree with used to fund wars and programs I myself did not support. Regardless of how I felt about myself or my own personal politics, my position as a woman married into the military was a part of the ideology that built and perpetuated the military, both the parts of it I supported and the parts I did not. Such a realization made me want to avoid my status as a military wife. Further, when I was forced to contend with what it meant to be a military spouse, I wanted to dismantle all the connections to heteronormativity and sexism I could find, even if it meant withdrawing altogether from a sense of community with my husband, the military, or other military spouses.

"WIFEY" CLASS

At my first Marine Corps Ball as a recruiter's wife, I was surprised to discover that I was highly encouraged to attend a class scheduled before the Ball and led by the Family Readiness Officer on how to cope with recruiting duty as a spouse. At balls I had been to in the past, classes had never been offered and I was curious. I sat in the back, among wives I had never met before, as we listened to a two-hour-long lecture on the intricacies of recruiting duty. In the first hour, we learned how many phone calls recruiters made daily, how many visits they made to prospective recruits, how the quota system worked, etc. I noticed quickly that these details were provided to us as explanation for why our husbands left our homes at 6 am and did not return until 11 pm or later, unwilling to talk with us and emotionally exhausted.

In the second hour, we were offered suggestions for how to "cope" on recruiting duty. At this point, my master's in rhetoric and writing with a focus on feminist and queer theory led me to consider the gendered history of domestic work often seen as women's work: we were encouraged to bake them cookies, carry around and pass out our husbands' business cards at the grocery store, leave them alone when they got home to allow them to decompress, etc. These coping skills struck me not as things that would help *me* cope, but rather help my Marine husband do his job better. This made no sense to me; if my husband worked in sales in the civilian world, I don't think I would be invited to a seminar about how to help him be better at his job. Why would that be my responsibility, since he was receiving the paycheck, not me? I felt as if the assumption of the audience in the room was that we were all stay-at-home wives with a great deal of free time to do this additional work. There were no men in the room, and many of the women *were* stay-at-home wives, but they were busy with their children, their homes, their hobbies, and side-businesses. Was it fair to provide coping strategies that only added additional labor to all of our busy lives? Was there a similar workshop for the Marines on how to be more considerate to the stress recruiting might put on their spouses?

At the end of the class, I stormed up to our hotel room to angrily describe the scene to my husband. He informed me that the man who had taught the class—who had given us all tips on how to be better wives to our husbands—had been divorced four times. And no, there was no equivalent spousal class for Marines themselves.

The next year, I volunteered to teach the class myself alongside another wife as a way to focus the course more toward needs of the spouses, instead of the military members. Instead of "Coping During Recruiting Duty" we titled the course "Empowering Yourself Through Recruiting Duty," and we filled out goal sheets, discussed how recruitment could be a useful career step for their spouses, and provided information on community activities and post-secondary education opportunities for military wives. At the end of the class, however, we found ourselves fielding questions from wives about how they might make recruitment duty easier for their husbands. One wife asked me who I gave out my husband's business cards to. Despite my best efforts to focus the course on the spouses, the spouses themselves *wanted* the content from the previous class I had hated so much. After the class, as we headed to our hotel rooms, we ran into the wife of the Executive Officer and asked her how she thought the class went. "It was ok," she said, as the elevator doors closed in our faces. I realized that my desire to critically change the design of the course based on the feminist work I had done in graduate school was relatively unwanted. I felt very alone.

I am the only wife of an enlisted military member pursuing her Ph.D. that I have ever met. Additionally, my work on LGBT and feminist rhetorics further separates me from the traditionally conservative, male-centered, heteronormative values of the military. While I always expected to not be every Marine's cup of tea, I was surprised to find little in common with other wives. At this writing, I currently have no children and I am not a stay-at-home spouse or military member myself; my radical queer politics are nearly always poorly received among other military members and spouses. At military family functions, I have learned to stay quiet about my interests and political leanings in order to blend in. When spouses ask me what I do, I tread lightly, tell them I'm still in school, studying writing, never say the word "queer" to describe my studies, and mention hoping to have a baby someday. I have learned to stop by my husband's office in the summers when I have more time. Once, on his birthday, I brought him a homemade steak lunch. I have learned to live in the tension between being the person I know I am and being the wife the military wants me to be. Most often, though, I have also learned to stay away from military functions out of self-preservation, feeling far too much like I do not belong.

My graduate education further complicated my understanding of who I was or should be as a military spouse. I began to read the work of Butler (1994, 2006), Foucault (1995), Bartky (1990), and Enloe (2000, 2014), all who complicated my understanding of the representation of gender and sexuality, causing me to think especially of how those representations impacted military spouses. One-dimensional representations of military spouses as heterosexual stay-at-home mothers only perpetuate sexist and heteronormative tropes that the military has embodied in the past: strong man going to war while weak woman waits at home. My graduate work allowed me to see these representations as problematic for the first time, which only caused further dissonance between my two identities as graduate student and military wife.

When I think of military wives, I think of the media representations of women who are both moveable and immobile: easily whisked away after a shotgun wedding to her husband's duty station, stalwartly and faithfully waiting alone in her on-base housing as she anticipates her husband's return from deployment. These representations are depicted in countless television shows and movies like *Army Wives*, where the wives' on-base waiting is a key plot point, or in *American Sniper* as Taya Kyle, portrayed by Sienna Miller, bravely and pregnantly awaits her husband Chris's calls from the desert. In these representations, military spouses are treated in one-dimensional ways: they are nearly always portrayed as white, heterosexual women, who patiently twiddle their thumbs in waiting while their husbands are away.

The military itself, through programs aimed at providing information and support to spouses and family members, such as Family Readiness Groups and Military OneSource, sometimes also provide an understanding of the military spouse as a young, uneducated mother or soon-to-be mother, supportive, immobile but highly moveable. I have been sent informational packets and have taken courses such as Lifestyle, Insights, Networking, Knowledge, and Skills (LINKS), and Wife Proficiency and Review (PAR) that have overwhelmingly assumed, among other things, that the spouse is a stay-at-home mother, has no job, is a heterosexual woman, is financially dependent on her spouse, has experienced multiple deployments, and has lived on base.

Many military spouses *do* embody many of these categories, and so it makes sense that the military and wider society through popular culture would engage with these representations. These representations align with what Smith (1993) calls the "standard American family," a "conceptions of the family as a legally married couple sharing a household. The adult male is in paid employment; his earnings provide the economic basis of the family-household. The adult female may also earn an income, but her primary responsibility is to the care of husband, household, and children" (p. 52). However, not *all* military families embody this standard, and further, such a conception of the American family, according to Foucault (1980), reinforces heteronormative ideals of family that perpetuate a capitalist model of the reproduction of new consumers and labor (p. 37). While many military families *do* consist of a nuclear, heterosexual family model, military spouses and members are only becoming more diverse in terms of gender and sexuality. The Williams Institute estimated in 2010 that 70,000 members of the U.S. military were gay, lesbian, or bisexual, and that there were 15,500 transgender military members serving (Gates, 2010, 2014). Many of those service members have partners and spouses who are a part of the military community as well.

My bisexuality and raw unadulterated feminism only grew stronger in graduate school, where I became equipped with scholarship to help support a sneaking suspicion that representation of military spouses by both the military and the wider world framed military spouses as heterosexual wives. That framing of wives also came with a further assumption that these wives would provide domestic services to their military husbands. For example, Enloe (2000) argues that generations of military leaders have worked tirelessly to find "militarized uses for those women who have married soldiers" (p. 157). This began in the 1950's, as military housing began in order to support the growing number of married military members. However, even as the military spousal population has grown more diverse, many representations have not, leading many programs in and outside of the military to focus on service and domesticity as ways for military spouses to help their military members. Thus, often military spouses are obliged to unquestioningly perform a supportive, traditionally "female" role, regardless of their initial identifications, desires, or intentions.

For example, figure 5.1 below is an example from the *4th MCD's Resource Guide to Recruiting for Marines & Families*,[1] sent to me in the mail after my husband's graduation from recruiter school. One section of the guide is "A Day in the Life of a Marine Corps Recruiter" timeline. In this timeline, the fictional Marine, "Hunter," interacts with his wife, "Ann," twice: at the beginning and end of the day. In both representations, Ann is marked as the sole care-provider of their children and the cook of the house, rising in the morning after caring for their child all night to cook breakfast for Hunter. Below is our introduction to Ann and Hunter:

"A DAY IN THE LIFE OF A MARINE CORPS RECRUITER"

Have you ever wondered what the day of a Recrutier looks like? The following article provides you with an example of what a typical day in the life of a recruiter might look like.

4:00 a.m. Hunter awoke to the sound of a local morning radio program as the disc jockey was telling his listeners about the rainy day outside. His wife Ann was already up and he could smell the aroma of frying bacon. Hunter shut off the clock radio (opportunity clock) and listened to the rain beating on the roof. Today would be tight, and he wanted to make the most of every minute.

4:10 a.m. "I hope the eggs aren't too hard," Ann said. She set the plate of bacon and eggs on the table and poured a cup of coffee. She yawned. "Do you feel like going back to bed?" Hunter asked. "You were up all night with the baby." Their two year-old-son had been awake all night, sick with the flu. "I may do just that," Ann responded. "I don't think he has a fever," she said, as if anticipating Hunter's next question. "I felt his forehead this morning and he is cool and sleeping peacefully."

Figure 5.1. *MCD's Resource Guide to Recruiting for Marines & Families*
Taken from *4th MCD's Resource Guide to Recruiting for Marines & Families*

This text offers a one-dimensional glimpse at Ann as a domestic caregiver, despite the fact that this text is created specifically *for* spouses and their families. In it, the implicit assumption is made that spouses should do traditionally feminized labor: cooking and childcare. As I read this manual, I thought about my own position as a spouse: I do not often cook and do not have children, and I do not wake up with my spouse because it is much earlier than I need to wake up for my own job. It appeared to me that Ann's portrayal was provided as an example and an expectation, published in a military-sanctioned document. What did it mean that my actions as a military spouse looked nothing like Ann? Did this make me a "bad" recruiter wife?

Beyond the representations from the military itself, media depictions of military spouses are often limited to the virgin/whore dichotomy: either the wife chastely pines away for her lover while he's on deployment, like Taya Kyle in *American Sniper*, or she's cheating on her husband and taking his money, like the nameless girlfriend in *Jarhead*. Television shows like *Army Wives* likely seek to capitalize on diversifying the understanding of the military spouse, but only end up adding more one-dimensional possibilities: the officer's wife obsessed with her husband's career, the dutiful and abused wife, the outcast paid surrogate mother, the gossips, the cheaters, the uneducated mother of illegitimate children. Beyond television and movies, websites, blogs, books and magazines further portray the military spouse in the supportive role, while Facebook groups like Just the Tip of the Spear (JT-TOTS) or Overly Sensitive Military Wives (OSMW), shaming sites run by Marines and military spouses, treat spouses with very little respect, referring to them as "dependas," or if they are overweight, as "dependapotamuses."

These representations rub off. What I began to notice through my interactions with other spouses in online support groups, is that we had all "learned" how to behave and act as good military spouses through these representations provided to us via military and popular culture. Sometimes, we enforced these behaviors on others through shaming or simple socialization. For instance, spouses would compete with each other on who made the cutest care package, or shame each other for breaking flag etiquette or wearing inappropriate attire to the ball. Over time, we enforced the "rules" of how to be a good military spouse, rules we had learned from popular culture, the military itself, and then from each other. I saw these behaviors and equated them to something I had learned in my queer theory courses: gender performativity.

These individual behaviors are small bits and pieces of repeated acts that make up a gender performativity of the "military wife." Butler (1994) asserts that gender or sex is not necessarily assigned at birth, but rather that gender is performed subconsciously through repetitions of behavior and enactments.

The performativity of the military wife similarly encapsulates multiple socialized, subconscious rituals that make up the archetype of the military spouse. Spouses who deviate from this performativity—through choice or because of gender or sexuality differences—may find themselves isolated because of that difference. Despite the military's increasing diversity, representation of the ideal military spouse from both inside and outside the military is still overwhelmingly female and heterosexual, which offers few alternatives for how to behave as a spouse and feel included in the military spouse community.

In essence, military wives' inculcation into the military system forces them through disciplinary practices (such as base dress codes, Lightfoot, 2017; Volkman, 2014), socialization, and military information, to perform their gender as always already in service to the military member, and therefore to the military itself. Bartky (1990) suggests "the disciplinary power that inscribes femininity on the female body is everywhere and it is nowhere; the disciplinarian is everyone and yet no one in particular" (p. 36). The concept of gender performativity already insinuates that no one is necessarily aware of the ways in which gender has been performed on or around a particular subject. Thus, often military spouses are obliged to unquestioningly perform a supportive female role, regardless of their initial desires or intentions.

Having learned about gender performativity and rhetorical representations of gender, I often felt as if I was at an impasse: I wanted to assert my difference from the one-dimensional representation of the military spouse I saw everywhere, so I would make my difference known to everyone, especially those in the military community. I was *not* a mom, I had a college education, I had a job, I wasn't all that interested in my husband's career, I was not right-leaning in my politics or even very religious. I thought asserting my difference would help to shift people's perceptions of military spouses, but instead I just shifted others' perceptions of *me*. I found myself isolated from those who did proudly identify as military spouses, or who embodied certain characteristics of what I felt was a limited representation. As I pushed others away with my defensiveness, I pushed deeper into my identity as an academic.

In some ways, this push toward my identity as an academic was perhaps an act of self-preservation. In order to maintain my focus on my academic career, I felt I needed to disconnect as much as possible from the military's ties to what I saw were traditional spousal roles. If I did not, I might end up feeling guilty for being unsupportive of my husband in terms of handling the domestic labor of a home and a marriage. Truthfully, this push for my separate identity as a scholar has often worked in my favor; my uncompromising focus on my work has allowed me to be very successful in graduate school.

However, it has also caused a strain on my husband's capacity to easily transition in his career. He has often chosen to wait on career moves—like becoming a career recruiter—until I finish my Ph.D. and procure a (hopefully) tenure-track position. Because of my choice to separate myself from the military, we've often found ourselves in an awkward tug-of-war between our two careers.[2]

SEEKING BALANCE

"Babe, I wish you were here. None of the guys at my station know if you exist. They're calling you Ghost Wife." I stared at the text message from my husband. I had skipped Family Day for the millionth time, mostly this time because it was 30 minutes away and started at 10 am—prime weekend writing time for me.

I received that text from Dave just a few months ago. Clearly, six years into my life as both a graduate student and military wife, I still struggle with finding balance between these two parts of my life. Graduate school has taught me a level of criticality that I love and appreciate, but it has also caused me to isolate myself from military life in order to avoid contending with that criticality. However, in the remaining part of this chapter, I will present some ways in which I am beginning to blend these two identities by finding the commonalities inherent in the military and academia.

When I began the proposal for this book chapter, I found myself visiting and revisiting the words I had written, searching for any of my own perceptions of events that Dave might disagree with. I didn't want to misrepresent his own experience of the military, and I didn't want him to see me as ungrateful. I also wanted to tell my—our—story from how I had experienced it, from a feminist perspective. Still, the possibility of all of this making it to print had higher stakes—what if someone from his unit discovered I was a scholar and Googled me, only to find me questioning and pushing back against the military industrial complex. Even now, I ask Dave to read all my drafts to make sure that he "approves" of what I have to say. He's never told me to change anything, except to provide more accurate military terms I might not know myself.

Last night, I asked him if he was ok if I used his first name, and he said he was fine with it. "Are you sure?" I asked, rolling over in bed to face him. "Sure." He said, "What are you worried about?" I paused. "Maybe that someone in the Marines will read it and confront you about it." He chuckled. "If someone confronts me about your chapter, I'll be like 'Hey! You have a wife in grad school too! We can be friends now!'" He, as usual, was completely unworried.

I know I am lucky to have a spouse who is both supportive of my career and of my desire to question and critique *his* career in my work. If it was the other way around, I'm not sure I would be able to handle it with as much grace as Dave. But, on the other hand, we often have discussions of the similarities of our lives: we both work within problematic, hegemonic institutions rooted in racism and sexism. We both hope to make a tiny dent in fixing those institutions for the better.

In some ways, my husband and I both feel resistance to the military system. While my resistance to the hegemony, sexism, and heteronormativity of the military is made explicit through my relatively public side-eye directed at the Marines, my husband's resistance is quieter. He stays in the military because he sees and hopes to help alleviate the bureaucratic failings of the top-down system on a daily basis: in missed wages, clerical errors that have impacted basic allotment of housing, higher-ups' lack of awareness around relocations, medical care, VA benefits, etc. I do not know a single enlisted Marine who could say they have not been "screwed" by the bureaucracy of the military in one way or another. Dave stays, both despite and because of the Marine's shortcomings; people who care about a community know it often can only be changed from within.

And yet, my husband is not the only person who works from within an often failing system. I have begun to marvel at the similarities between academia and the military: being rewarded for good work with more duties, being subject to tone policing, marveling at administrations and university presidential decisions extremely far removed from those working "on the ground." I have found that, while I have trouble identifying wholeheartedly with all the trappings of a military spouse, I have less trouble identifying with military members who find themselves frustrated with the military while continuing to stay loyal to it. I do it myself every day as an academic.

While it was easy for me to see how the military was perpetuated by ideological state apparatuses, it took me much longer to recognize that the university system is one as well (Althusser, 1968). Concepts like freedom and family drive people to go to college, to take out student loans they may never be able to afford to pay back, just as they drive people to join and support the military. Further, just as the military relies on surveillance and the development of "docile bodies" (Foucault, 1995) to perpetuate itself as a repressive state apparatus, so too does the American public school system. Just as the military suffers from bureaucratic failings, universities are experiencing an extreme increase of administrators who create more bureaucratic steps in the education process (McElroy, 2017). Just as the military sometimes relies on the feminized labor of women, so too does the academy (Bianco, 2016), especially in my field of writing and rhetoric (Holbrook, 1991; Spitzer-Hanks, 2016). Just as I have experienced unpleasant interactions with military members who disagree with my politics, so too has my husband experienced the same from my academic colleagues. In many ways, my experience of academia and the military are like two sides of the same coin: similar experiences, seemingly on opposite sides of a political spectrum.

TAKE-AWAYS

While I have aimed at providing personal and scholarly examples of the complexity of being both a military wife and graduate student in this chapter, I close with a more practical conclusion: a set of practices that have helped me in my own life as I theoretically and personally interact with the military daily. What follows are a few suggestions for other spouses who may be experiencing similar issues as I have outlined.

Communication with my spouse. I have never been afraid to be outspoken to my husband about my problems with the military—I communicated early on that my interest in him had very little to do with his military status, as I discussed in my first vignette. However, he has also never been afraid to tell me when he feels that I am being unfair in my representation or understanding of the military or military life, and I have been careful to listen. When I first began writing about military wives, my husband was skeptical, unsure of my claims that the military relied on military spouses for unpaid support and labor. However, over time and through our personal discussions, my arguments have become more nuanced and I have also found moments in which I could point out in real time the expectations of wives mandated by the military. Such communication has led to my husband's wholehearted support of my work, and even a transparency to other military members about my work. Once, over lunch with another recruiter and my husband, I began describing my research to my husband's coworker. When this co-worker began to express disbelief at my claims, Dave put his burger down and simply, quietly said, "It's true, dude. I've seen it."

Empathy with those in the system. Like the academy, the military is made up of a vast network of individuals. While it often feels like an impenetrable force, I have learned to recognize it as an organization of individual people. Just as in the academy, not all of those individuals are people I like or agree with; however, I can see them as people with only so much power within the system and over me. Just as within the academy, much of the most oppressive aspects of the military are beyond any one individual's capability for change;

furthermore, often that oppression points inward toward the individuals in the organization. Just as the academy does not adequately support adjunct instructors, neither does the military adequately support all of its veterans. To blame individual members of the system for the system's ills is likely beside the point and further ignores the ways in which the system oppresses those specific individuals who make up the system. I have come to learn in this work that much of my problems with the military are with it as a system, rather than with any individual people. Such an understanding has allowed me to nuance my arguments and work still within the community of which I am a part.

Developing empathy for me has meant trying to better understand the ways in which military spouses and members are just as caught up and sometimes powerless within the military system as I am. In addition, when I am feeling particularly defensive or judgmental about the military's connection to political issues I do not agree with (Donald Trump's trans military ban, for example) I try to remember that those political issues exist in my own home of academia in different ways (lack of resources for trans students, for example).

Recognition of ambivalence. Being a liberal academic who is married to a Marine often means I feel as if I am sacrificing my own radical liberal politics in order to live my life. I often become caught in an all-or-nothing, black-or-white thought loop in which the military is entirely bad and the academy is entirely good. However, as the above two practices would indicate, I have learned that such binary thinking does not represent my lived reality in either my connection to academia or the military. While I do still find myself remaining quiet about my husband's job in certain social circles, I also am careful to express my real, complicated, ambivalent feelings about the military when prompted. Similarly, such a nuanced understanding of the academy as also an oppressive system has allowed me to be humble about my graduate work with other military members. I do not claim to have all the answers.

Willingness to compromise. My husband spends more time talking about cultural rhetorics than he would ever prefer to, at parties and gatherings where all of my friends end up tailspinning into intellectual conversations that, frankly, barely anyone in the wider world cares about. I have also found myself at more than one barbeque where the main entertainment was a BB gun fight in the woods. Neither of these get-togethers bolster a shared sense of enjoyment between Dave and me. Once, as I complained about having no one to talk to at a party populated by mostly Marine families, my husband brought up the graduate school cocktail party in which I left him chatting with some professors he didn't know for nearly an hour. He is right; his identity as a Marine is complicated by my investment in graduate school as well. While we have nearly opposite taste in what makes a great party, we share an understanding in how much our careers matter to each other. Dave has always been good at biting the bullet and coming to my graduate functions. I am working to become better at going to his.

Being a military spouse while in a graduate program like mine is not without its troubles, as I hope to have indicated in this chapter. I am constantly shuttling back and forth between my desire to dismantle the complex oppressive powers of the military while I also benefit from the military in the form of my husband's pay, medical benefits, family programs, and built-in community. What might it mean if my criticisms of the military led to its destruction (an extremely unlikely case)? I would have no way to fund my life in graduate school, and the work I do would no longer be necessary or useful. In this way, my life as both a military spouse and academic are inherently tied; I am implicated in the "mutual camouflage and co-constitution of military and civilian" (Hyde, 2015, p. 108). I am also continually supportive of my husband's career, and in this sense, I have multiple roles enacted by the archetypal military wife. I am learning how to blend a life where my two identities are seemingly at odds. I am learning how to become whole.

NOTES

1. I am left with many questions about this manual: nowhere does it say when the original draft of this packet was created; the back page of the packet indicates at the time of publication, it was in its fifth edition, having been updated on August 9, 2012. I received the packet in the fall of 2013. While the content appeared to be outdated, I am unsure when the packet was originally created.

2. I'm unsure of whether this kind of tug-of-war would exist in the same way for a dual-military family. I know if I were also a Marine but still studying writing and rhetoric in the same program, my concerns about my connection to war might still be fraught, especially in terms of my social interactions with fellow graduate students. On the other hand, my husband and I might receive more dual support in our career choices if we were both military members, especially if the military were to fund my education and my intention was to return to the military after finishing my degree. In that case, my loyalties might align more strongly to the military rather than to the academy.

REFERENCES

Althusser, L. (1968). *On the reproduction of capitalism: Ideology and ideological state apparatuses.* London: Verso.

Bartky, S. L. (1990). *Femininity and domination: Studies in the phenomenology of oppression.* New York: Routledge.

Bianco, M. (2016, April 16). Academia is quietly and systemically keeping its women from succeeding. Retrieved from https://qz.com/670647/academia-is-quietly-and-systematically-keeping-its-women-from-succeeding/.

Butler, J. (1994). Gender as performance: An interview with Judith Butler by Peter Osborne and Lynne Segal. *Radical Philosophy, 67*(4), 32–39.

Butler, J. (2006). *Gender trouble: Feminism and the subversion of identity.* New York: Routledge.

Enloe, C. (2000). *Maneuvers: The international politics of militarizing women's lives.* Berkeley: University of California Press.

Enloe, C. (2014). *Bananas, beaches and bases: Making feminist sense of international politics.* Berkeley: University of California Press.

Foucault, M. (1980). *The history of sexuality.* 1st ed. New York: Vintage Books.

Foucault, M. (1995). *Discipline and punish: The birth of the prison.* 2nd ed. New York: Vintage Books.

Gates, G. J. (2010). *Lesbian, gay, and bisexual men and women in the US military: Updated estimates.* Williams Institute, UCLA School of Law.

Gates, G. J., & Herman, J. L. (2014). *Transgender military service in the United States.* Williams Institute, UCLA School of Law.

Holbrook, S. E. (1991). Women's work: The feminizing of composition. *Rhetoric Review, 9*(2), 201–229.

Hyde, A. (2015). *Inhabiting no-man's land: The military mobility of military wives.* Diss. Gender Institute of the London School of Economics and Political Science.

Lightfoot, L. (2017, May 9). These 7 dress code violations can get you thrown out of buildings on base. Retrieved from http://militaryoneclick.com/these-7-dress-code-violations-can-get-military-families-thrown-out-of-buildings-on-base/.

McElroy, W. (2017, June 16). Administrative bloat on campus: Academia shrinks, students suffer. Retrieved from https://www.jamesgmartin.center/2017/06/administrative-bloat-campus-academia-shrinks-students-suffer/.

Smith, D. (1993). The standard North American family: SNAF as an ideological code. *Journal of Family Issues, 14*(1), 50–65.

Spade, D., & Wilse, C. (2015). Norms and normalization. The Oxford Handbook on Feminist Theory. Oxford Handbooks Online.

Spitzer-Hanks, T. (2016, April 13). On 'feminized space' in the Writing Center. Web log post. Retrieved from http://www.praxisuwc.com/praxis-blog/2016/4/13/on-feminized-space-in-the-writing-center.

United States Marine Corps. (2012). *4th MCD's Resource Guide to Recruiting for Marines & Families,* 5th ed. Harrisburg: USMC, 17.

Volkman, M. (2014, June 16). Decoding the military commissary dress code. Retrieved from http://militaryshoppers.com/decoding-the-military-commissary-dress-code/.

Chapter Six

Military Spouses' Uncertainty Management

Navigating Academic Goals and Military Needs

Michael Sollitto and Catherine Cole

The stress, insecurity, and anxiety of military spouses is an overlooked source of struggle by academics and practitioners alike. Blue Star Families (2018) reported in their most recent Military Family Lifestyle Survey that 28% of military spouses are unemployed, yet actively seeking employment. Additionally, 51% of the military spouses who are employed earn less than $20,000 per year. As such, military spouse employment and military pay and benefits are two of the biggest issues that military families face (Blue Star Families, 2018). The stress associated with searching for gainful employment may lead military spouses to pursue college degrees to improve their professional standing and lend further financial support to their active-duty loved ones. Despite more military spouses pursuing higher education than civilian spouses (Harrell, Lim, Castaneda, & Golinelli, 2004), higher education can introduce new uncertainty for military spouses that they must manage.

For military spouses, like traditional college students, uncertainty could conceivably be triggered by ambiguity about where to pursue their degree, what subject to study, what programs provided by the military and/or the educational institution can assist them with tuition and emotional support, and how they can balance the strain of being both a military spouse and a college student. However, what distinguishes military spouses from traditional college students is that they may have more life experience and be older than traditional college students. Military spouses also face uncertainty about PCSs, deployments, and managing their families in the face of constant upheaval and change. Clearly, there is no easy answer for military spouses in their pursuit of personal and educational excellence (Mehta & Jorgenson, 2015). The strain of their educational pursuits, in combination with the strain of being a military spouse, may lead spouses to re-evaluate if pursuing a degree is worth the additional emotional, physical, and financial strain, and subsequently leave their academic programs. Therefore, to make our desired contribution we will use Uncertainty Management Theory (UMT; Kramer, 2004) to discover why uncertainty occurs for military spouses, how they manage it, and the result of their uncertainty management.

LITERATURE REVIEW

Uncertainty Management Theory

In their original development of Uncertainty Reduction Theory (URT), Berger and Calabrese (1975) argued that uncertainty is a key concern for individuals during their initial encounters with other people. Berger (1987) stated that uncertainty is "a function of both the ability to predict and the ability to explain actions of other and self" (p. 41). Similarly, Kramer (2004) defined uncertainty as "a lack of information related to the inability to predict some future behavior or outcome" (p. 8). Given individuals' uncertainty, Berger and Calabrese (1975) postulated that individuals would communicate to reduce the discomfort created by their uncertainty. However, as the years progressed, communication scholars questioned the assumption that uncertainty and communication were mutually inclusive (e.g., Kramer, 1999). In his critique of URT, Kramer (2004) stated that URT is limited because it failed to explain that seeking information may actually increase uncertainty, people may reduce uncertainty to ascertain the benefits of future interaction, and people may actually prefer uncertainty more than certainty in some situations.

Reasoning that individuals can experience uncertainty about themselves, others, the relationships they have with others, and various situations, Kramer (2004) proposed Uncertainty Management Theory (UMT) to account for the possibility that people can experience uncertainty and choose not to engage in communication to reduce their uncertainty. Specifically, Kramer conceptualized a model of uncertainty management in which individuals experience a phenomenon that is inconsistent with their mental scripts about how social behavior should unfold. Upon encountering uncertainty, Kramer (2004) contended that individuals use cognitive strategies to reduce their uncertainty. Individuals can deny that their uncertainty exists, tolerate the uncertainty, assimilate the uncertainty, accept the uncertainty, or engage in imagined information seeking, all of which may affect individuals' motivation to seek information. Kramer then asserted individuals' pursuit of information to reduce their uncertainty can be affected by competing motives. On the one hand, seeking information can be one means by which individuals manage uncertainty. On the other hand, people may be concerned about their image (e.g., that asking questions may make them appear foolish), that seeking information may be socially inappropriate, that the information may provide little utility, that they lack ability to gather information, or that seeking information may prompt unpleasant emotions, but they may feel the need to seek information "just because it is interesting to know" (Kramer, 2004, p. 102).

When individuals determine that their level of uncertainty outweighs the barriers to their information seeking, they choose to seek information through passive, active, interactive, or alternative communication strategies (Fetherston, Cherney, & Bunton, 2018; Kramer, 2009). Individuals using passive strategies receive information without actively pursuing it. Individuals using active strategies gain information "without assuming the sender role needed for interactive approaches" (Kramer, 2004, p. 106). Individuals using interactive strategies receive information by directly interacting with the source of their uncertainty. Individuals using alternative strategies engage in behaviors, such as conversing with others, to focus their mind on something other than their uncertainty. Individuals, after engaging in the various information strategies, may experience increased, decreased, or sustained levels of uncertainty (Kramer, 1999). UMT provides an effective framework to explore how military spouses manage their uncertainty about being simultaneously a college student and a military spouse.

Military Spouses' Uncertainty about Academic Programs

Although military spouses face uncertainty about their spouse's general military assignments and duties, it is the uncertainty stimulated by professional and personal aspirations that can compound the struggles facing military spouses in their marriages and with their families (Castaneda & Harrel, 2008; Lim & Schulker, 2010). In addition to concern about their service member's military career, military spouses must face the uncertainty of an academic program to enhance their skills and abilities to eventually join the workforce (Castaneda & Harrell, 2008). Given that college students tend to experience uncertainty about the specific requirements for their classes, discipline-specific terminology, the personal value of their classes, the structure of their classes, their classmates, and their own scholarly performance (Sollitto, Brott, Cole, Gil, & Selim, 2018), it seems likely that military spouses experience similar types of uncertainty upon enrolling in academic programs. However, given the added emotional, mental, and physical stressors experienced by military spouses (Wheeler & Stone, 2010) and their firm commitment to keep their families together (Castaneda & Harrell, 2008), it is conceivable that they face uncertainty about PCSs, deployments, and supporting their families in the face of constant upheaval and change that makes their experiences unique from traditional undergraduate college students. Therefore, using UMT as a guide, we proposed the following research question:

RQ1: What uncertainty do military spouses experience while navigating their academic programs?

Sources of Information and Information-Seeking Strategies

Despite most military spouses feeling that few people understand the hardships that they face (Davis, Ward, & Storm, 2011), military spouses often turn to a variety of sources to manage their uncertainty. For example, researchers have discovered that military spouses seek support from other spouses who share similar experiences (Davis et al., 2011), family and friends (Wheeler & Stone, 2010), and from family support groups provided through the military (Faber, Willerton, Clymer, MacDermid, & Weiss, 2008). Military spouses also seek support and information to calm their anxiety and manage their uncertainty about their service member's deployment from online support groups (High, Jennings-Kelsall, Solomon, & Marshall, 2015) and from the media (Faber et al., 2008).

Although the sources that military spouses turn to are often effective for helping them cope with the stressors of their service member's deployments and their own professional and personal endeavors (Padden, Connors, & Agazio, 2011), it is reasonable to expect that military spouses consult different sources regarding their uncertainty about their academic programs, and that they seek information with various communication behaviors. Undergraduate students seek information from their classmates by disclosing their level of uncertainty, inquiring about the level of uncertainty that their classmates are feeling, asking direct questions, and collaborating with their classmates (Sollitto et al., 2018). Additionally, undergraduate students tend to seek information from their instructors by asking overt questions, observing others, asking third-party questions (i.e., inquiries directed at people other than the source of their uncertainty), asking indirect questions, and testing their boundaries (Myers & Knox, 2001). Due to the uncertainty that military spouses experience regarding their service member's military situation and their own professional and personal aspirations, they may consult with a variety of sources by stating how they feel, asking questions, collaborating together, or possibly observing them to manage their uncertainty. Therefore, we proposed the following research questions:

RQ2: From whom do military spouses seek information about navigating military and academic life?

RQ3: What communication strategies do military spouses use to manage their uncertainty about military and academic life?

Outcomes of Uncertainty Management

Military spouses value the opportunity to find comfort, solace, and support from variety of individuals in their social networks (Davis et al., 2011; Wheeler & Stone, 2010). Specifically, military spouses have expressed that when they feel good about themselves and more positive about their service member's deployment, they experience positive marital changes, increased self-confidence, and self-discovery when they have friends, family members, and fellow military spouses to provide social support and information to them (Davis et al., 2011).

In a study of undergraduate students, Sollitto and colleagues (2018) discovered that after receiving information about their classes from their classmates, students experience increased knowledge and skills, affirmation that they are on the right track with their understanding, strengthened social bonds with their classmates, and new perspectives from their classmates. However, they also discovered that information seeking sometimes results in increased confusion. These experiences of undergraduate students aligns with Kramer's (2004) argument that information seeking can increase, maintain, or decrease an individual's level of uncertainty. In other words, receiving information may sometimes result in greater levels of confusion and uncertainty. Despite military spouses being distinct from traditional college students in the kinds of uncertainty that they may experience and the way they manage their uncertainty, it is conceivable that, given the additional burdens that military spouses encounter, they will experience a variety of outcomes from their information-seeking strategies. Therefore, using UMT as a guide, we proposed the following research question:

RQ4: What outcomes do military spouses experience from managing their uncertainty about military and academic life?

METHOD

We used a thematic analysis to proceed with our investigation about the uncertainty that military spouses face in their academic programs. Thematic analysis provides researchers a method for describing their data and discovering emergent patterns and themes about the phenomenon of interest (Braun & Clark, 2006). According to Boyatzis (1998), thematic analysis proceeds in three stages: making decisions about data collection, analyzing the data, and validating the results.

Data Collection

Upon IRB approval, we posted links to an online open-ended survey in several Facebook groups specifically devoted to military spouses. We provided potential participants a brief description of the investigation and told them that their participation would be voluntary, but greatly appreciated. Upon clicking on the survey link, participants were provided with a cover letter explaining the basic details of the study, their rights as participants, and the amount of time that the survey would take for them to complete. After consenting to participate, participants responded to four open-ended survey questions and seven brief demographic questions. The sample consisted of 68 military spouses and fiancés/fiancées (58 women, 1 man, and 9 who declined to identify their sex). We included fiancés in the study to achieve as much knowledge as possible about the experience of people experiencing military life. The average age of the participants was 26.9 years ($SD = 6.91$). The sample included first-year students ($n = 4$), sophomores ($n = 7$), juniors ($n = 5$), seniors ($n = 6$), graduate students ($n = 14$), no longer enrolled students ($n = 23$), and nine participants who declined to report their academic standing. The 23 participants who were no longer enrolled had completed some college ($n = 1$), a four-year degree ($n = 7$), and a graduate degree ($n = 15$). Participants were spouses of active-duty service members in the Army ($n = 42$), Navy ($n = 11$), Air Force ($n = 4$), Marine Corps ($n = 1$), and Coast Guard ($n = 1$). Nine participants declined to identify their spouses' military branch. The nine participants who declined to answer the demographic questions provided substantive answers to the study questions.

Participants responded to the following questions: (1) Explain the things about your academic program that you are/were sometimes unsure or uncertain about. (2) Describe who you talk(ed) to you when you are/were unsure or uncertain about your life as a military spouse and college student. Explain the relationship that you have/had with that person or those people. (3) Describe what you say/said or do/did to gain information from the people you talk to when you are unsure or uncertain about your life as a military spouse and college student. (4) What outcomes do you achieve from the information that you receive about the things you are sometimes unsure or uncertain about in your life as a military spouse and college student?

Data Analysis

We used thematic analysis to organize and search patterns in our data (Boyatzis, 1998; Braun & Clark, 2006) by following several steps. First, we identified our units of analysis as any words, phrases, sentences, or series of sentences that signified meaning for our study about military spouses. Second, the second author conducted a reading of all the data collected to gain preliminary understanding of how military spouses manage their uncertainty. During this step, the second author identified preliminary codes that best reflected the participants' responses and wrote them on a separate sheet of paper (Milliken, 2010).

Third, we assessed the similarities and differences between the initial codes to create emergent themes from our data (Glaser & Strauss, 1967) about the types of uncertainty that military spouses experienced (RQ1), the sources of their uncertainty management (RQ2), their information-seeking strategies (RQ3), and the outcomes they receive from their uncertainty management (RQ4). Following Patton's (2002) suggestions about coding qualitative data, we carefully read and re-read the responses to ensure that each of the codes used from the themes were internally homogeneous with one another and that they were heterogeneous from other themes. After we decided upon names that best reflected the emergent themes, we created definitions for each theme and identified exemplary quotes from our participants that best represented our themes. We then created a code book, complete with names and definitions, to code the remaining data.

Following our data analysis, we engaged in member checking, in which we asked a subset of participants within the larger population if our results reflected their experiences to ensure the validity and rigor of our data (Lincoln & Guba, 1985; Tompkins, 1994). The second author solicited the perspective of people who participated in the study and asked if the emergent themes aligned with their experiences. The participants agreed that the emergent themes did truly represent their experiences as military spouses pursuing their education.

RESULTS

Types of Uncertainty

Military spouses expressed three distinct kinds of uncertainty they had experienced in their lives as military spouses and college students: program logistics, academic/professional success, and family consideration. Military spouses encountered uncertainty about *program logistics* when they were unsure about how long their academic program would take them to complete, the assignments and types of exit requirements that they would have to complete (e.g., theses, dissertations, exams), the tuition for their program and the cost of their textbooks and materials, basic details about the tasks they would perform in their program, meeting with faculty and advisors, and location of the program (e.g., geographic proximity or if they could do online programs).

Each of the details military spouses mentioned included concern about important information they would need to ensure they made a good personal choice. As one military spouse articulated, "I was uncertain about what future courses would require in terms of workload, how long a master's thesis and doctoral dissertation would take to complete, location of clinical rotations, and yearly assistantships." Another military spouse noted, "I spent a lot of time searching for the right program so that I could be sure that it met my needs." As such, finding the best program may be more challenging for military spouses than for their civilian counterparts.

Military spouses experienced uncertainty about *academic/professional success* when they were anxious about their ability to handle the rigor and challenge of their academic programs, if the programs would help them acquire basic knowledge and skills necessary for succeeding professionally, and finding career opportunities that aligned with their academic expertise and life as a military spouse. The theme suggests that military spouses encountered questions about whether they possessed the intellectual and emotional skills needed to successfully combat the rigors of their academic programs and the rigors of being a military spouse.

Military spouses also pondered whether the classes they took and the assignments they completed would truly prepare them for a successful career in the field that they chose to study and if employers would be willing to hire a job candidate who needs to move frequently to accommodate their active-duty spouse's military orders. One military spouse commented, "I am unsure if getting my accredited MBA will actually result in a position which provides me appropriate compensation and quality of life . . . but I am still unsure at times about whether or not undertaking such a challenge will pay off financially." Another military spouse added, "I was curious about whether or not the program will help me excel in the job market or just put us into more debt." In discovering military spouses' uncertainty about academic/professional success, it is evident that they face questions about how well they will be able to use their knowledge and skills from their programs in their careers, and if they will be able to successfully use their knowledge and skills to find a satisfying career. Therefore, it appears that, although traditional college students face uncertainty about their academic/professional success, this kind of uncertainty might be heightened for military spouses due to the other stressors that they experience in their lives.

Military spouses experienced uncertainty about *family considerations* when they faced questions about when they will have to move from their current location to a new location, if they could manage their academic program in combination with their service member's schedule, and if they would be able to care for their children while being away for classes or accomplishing program-specific assignments. It appears that when military spouses experienced uncertainty about family considerations they became anxious about the possibility of relocating and what that relocation would mean for their academic progress and, subsequently, what it would mean for their opportunity to contribute financially in the future. This kind of uncertainty highlights the unpredictability and constant uncertainty surrounding military orders, almost to the point that certainty about family considerations is elusive.

Military spouses also questioned how they would care for and spend time with their children, despite the number of hours they would be away from their children during a given week. For example, one military spouse shared her experience being unable to assist her service member as much as she would like due to her class schedule and responsibilities, "My husband often had to work odd hours or go on random missions with little time to prepare, and having children made it difficult for me to assist him." Another military spouse voiced, "I am a spouse with children, so the most concern for me was the question of who was going to pick up my children from school every day?" Therefore, military spouses struggle with their desire to attend classes and complete their school work while also desiring to assist at home and with children as much as they desire. This tension, again, underscores how military spouses' experiences are distinct from traditional college students. Military spouses may be more likely to have children and, unlike their civilian counterparts, they may be less able to reliably depend on their partner for daily childcare responsibilities, due to the service member's military responsibilities. Overall, the thematic analysis revealed that military spouses experience uncertainty about their program logistics, academic/professional success, and family considerations.

Sources of Information

Military spouses reported that they seek information from three primary sources to help them navigate their lives as military spouses and college students: family, friends, and professionals. Military spouses sought information from *family*, which included their parents, siblings, grandparents, and their spouses, who were available to answer questions, provide support, and listen. For many military spouses, these familial relationships provided unique and firsthand experience about being a military spouse and pursuing professional or personal goals, which made their information and support particularly appealing and important. However, military spouses may actually have more difficulty reaching out to family for information and support than traditional college students because of the distance that often separates military spouses from their family.

For example, one military spouse remarked, "I spoke with my mother (who was an Army girlfriend, fiancée, wife, and widow). My mother is my best friend." Another military spouse offered, "The person that I talked to was my husband about the program. He explained to me that if I want to move forward with my academic [career] then I can always change my area later on in life." Yet another military spouse succinctly and enthusiastically remarked that she confided in and sought information from her parents, "I seek information from my mother!" Clearly, military spouses reach out to their family, people that they appear to have the closest bond with who are capable of offering useful and comforting support and information. Evidently, military spouses value the opportunity to discuss with their family members the stress, concerns, and anxiety they experience about their lives as military spouses and college students.

Military spouses also reached out to their *friends*. Their friends were people in their personal social networks that included classmates, fellow military spouses, and community members who were available to answer questions, provide support and information, and listen. For example, one military spouse expressed, "The person that gave me the most support is a friend that understood the importance of finishing college and understood the life of a military spouse. Her husband was active military in the past and she helped me." Another military spouse stated, "I would reach out to other military spouses. They experienced similar struggles."

Military spouses also sought information from *professionals*. Professionals included trained individuals who specialize in providing advice, council, and information. These professionals were comprised of academic counselors, instructors, Veterans Affairs (VA) coordinators, and behavioral therapists that helped military spouses sort through the stress and uncertainty of being a military spouse and being enrolled in an academic program. For example, one military spouse stated, "I talked to licensed counselors in order to understand the emotional and cognitive ramifications of how to support my husband's career and my own." Another military spouse expressed her relief from reaching out to her academic advisor, "I would also call my academic advisor and he would put my worries at ease." Finally, another military spouse noted her experience with the VA coordinator on campus, "The VA coordinator is the first person I spoke to on campus. I go to him for most of my educational needs and concerns." Overall, the thematic analysis revealed that military spouses seek information from family, friends, and professionals.

Information-Seeking Strategies

Military spouses reported that they use three distinct information-seeking strategies to manage their uncertainty about their lives as military spouses and college students: seek guidance, share concerns, and consult published sources. When military spouses *seek guidance* they asked questions to alleviate their uncertainty by requesting new perspectives, advice, and support from individuals in their social network. Seeking guidance appears to be a strategy that military spouses used to acquire new or unique insight about how to progress in their programs and manage their lives as military spouses. For example, one military spouse exclaimed, "I asked questions, a lot of question[s]! You can never ask too many. I asked what grants/scholarships were available to me. I asked them how they did it." Another military spouse commented, "My best friend moved away with her military spouse and I would talk to her about everything and question what she is doing, what her plans are, and what it took for her to get where she is."

When military spouses *share concerns* they expressed their level of uncertainty or anxiety about their lives as military spouses and students and shared experiences, frustrations, and insecurities. Essentially, when military spouses share concerns they initiate conversations with others to express their level of uncertainty. As one military spouse expressed regarding her uncertainty about education and their family finances, "I told him I wasn't certain I could afford to continue classes, financial aid wouldn't cover me, and the only units with my program were farther from the unit than I wanted him to have to drive." Another military spouse explained her uncertainty about beginning an academic program, given the unpredictability of military life, "I explained to other spouses that were in school that I was reluctant to go to school because of the lifestyle needed for classes and the lifestyle of being a military spouse." Although sharing concerns may be a less direct form of gathering information, it is conceivable that these strategies functioned as a way for military spouses to express themselves and generate conversation about their own experiences as a mechanism toward uncertainty reduction.

Military spouses who *consult published sources* read, research, and consume information from books (e.g., books about challenges of military life), brochures (e.g., pamphlets about academic programs), websites (e.g., information about programs, websites devoted to pursuing education while being a military spouse), and various social media accounts (e.g., Facebook groups related to military life) to find the information and support that they desire. By consulting published sources, military spouses were able to peruse various outlets and find information at a pace comfortable to them and retain that information for when they needed it the most. For example, one military spouse commented, "I read lots of articles and books about being a military spouse and a student." Another military spouse voiced, "I joined a support group page and that's where I get a lot of my information regarding the Army." Yet another military spouse intimated that she consulted media to gain information about which colleges best fit her needs, "I looked into colleges that offer my major and saw how many were near any military base." Overall, the thematic analysis revealed that military spouses seek guidance, share concerns, and consult published sources to manage their uncertainty.

Outcomes of Uncertainty Management

Military spouses reported achieving three distinct outcomes as a result of their uncertainty management: support, solutions, and increased uncertainty. Military spouses experienced *support* when they gained reassurance, affirmation, and assistance with overcoming the stress in their lives. Spouses noted that they gained confidence and comfort in knowing that they had made good and correct personal and professional decisions in their lives and that their lives will be fine. Regarding the relationship with her husband and her decisions about education, one spouse said, "Ultimately, my husband and I reaffirmed our mutual commitment to each other and I decided I would do an MBA and then job hunt at our next duty station." Another military spouse noted, "I've gained more confidence in my academic decision."

Military spouses achieved *solutions* when their concerns or inquiries resulted in additional clarity, new perspectives, or success working through their college curriculum, their family situations, and their concerns about employment. Military spouses expressed their belief that they solved the problems facing them by acquiring the requisite support and information to help them meet and overcome their challenges. For example, one military spouse stated, "My husband offered to transfer the unused portion of his GI Bill to me and helped me find an alternative program at a school in our city that would help me achieve the same goal." Another military spouse said, "My husband's solution to my childcare concern was to find a nanny. We ended up finding a teenage high school graduate. Her dad worked on base and would drop her off early in the morning and she would stay until I got home."

Military spouses encountered *increased uncertainty* when they actually became more confused or anxious about their academic career and their lives as military spouses. Ultimately, some military spouses expressed that their efforts to manage their uncertainty yielded only more uncertainty. As one military spouse decried about her inability to find employment, despite earning a degree, "I still have yet to find a job that will take someone for having the degree without the experience." Another military spouse stated that "No information was really that helpful." Evidently, while seeking information was beneficial for many military spouses, some still experienced ample confusion and anxiety despite their efforts to acquire comfort and information. Therefore, it seems that seeking information can often lead to more questions. Overall, military spouses experienced support, solutions, and increased uncertainty as a result of their uncertainty management efforts.

DISCUSSION

The purpose of this research study was to use UMT to develop richer knowledge about how military spouses manage their uncertainty about navigating their lives as military spouses and as college students. Results of our study extend the utility of UMT and reveal that military spouses face uncertainty about their programs and their ability to handle the adversity related to their military experiences. They seek comfort and assurances to manage their uncertainty. As a result, military spouses' uncertainty management results in support, solutions, and increased uncertainty. Therefore, although military spouses are similar to traditional college students in many ways, these results also reveal several ways that military spouses pursuing their education are distinct from traditional college students.

The first way that military spouses pursuing their education differ from traditional college students is in the prevailing nature of uncertainty. Although college students are able to gather information that calms them and helps them succeed academically (Sollitto et al., 2018), their uncertainty may be more easily managed because of the task-focused environment of college classrooms. However, military spouses constantly handle uncertainty in their military lives, and their academic programs simply add to that uncertainty. Military spouses constantly face the possibility of moving to a new location, wondering about their finances, and being away from their loved ones for variable periods of time (Blue Star Families, 2018). Although they may actively manage their uncertainty, the possibility exists that the more that they proactively seek information, the more that certainty will elude them, because the pursuit of information may reveal even more questions than answers (Kramer, 2004).

The second way that military spouses are distinct from traditional college students is from whom they seek information. Like traditional college students, military spouses seek information from classmates or people in their social network (Sollitto et al., 2018). However, military spouses also seek information from their family members and professionals. Collectively, it seems that military spouses seek comfort and information from people that they trust on a personal and intimate basis, such as their family and friends, and on a professional basis, such as their counselors, instructors, and VA coordinators. It appears that these sources provide military spouses with additional perspective and information because they have explicit experience and expertise to assist them with the logistics of their academic programs and in providing assistance with navigating family considerations and professional ambitions. Furthermore, the results suggest that military spouses specifically seek out these trusted individuals because they value their experience with military life and find their perspectives comforting and familiar (Davis et al., 2011; Lapp, Tollefson, Hoepner, Moore, & Divyak, 2010).

A third way that these results reveal that military spouses are distinct from traditional college students is in the prominent focus that military spouses place on their family. Family is a common focus in the way that military spouses experience uncertainty, and manage their uncertainty. Given that many military spouses are confined to a certain geographic area and face concerns about the possibility of moving and/or caring for children, it makes sense that military spouses want academic programs that challenge them academically and provide professional utility (Beebe & Frei, 2016) while also allowing them to care for and manage their families. Military spouses are fiercely committed to keeping their family intact as they consider their professional ambitions (Castaneda & Harrell, 2008). In so doing, they make decisions regarding their academic programs with their family as a key consideration. Similarly, whenever military spouses encounter uncertainty, they turn to their family members for consolation, support, and guidance. As a result of their uncertainty management, military spouses can gain assurance in knowing that they have made beneficial decisions for themselves and their families.

Limitations and Directions for Future Research

As with any study, this investigation contains limitations that future researchers could improve upon. First, our sample consisted mostly of women. It is conceivable that male military spouses may have unique experiences worthy of future investigations. Second, we were unable to account for the type of program in which our participants were enrolled. It is possible that some programs compound military spouses' uncertainty more than other programs. Third, we also were unable to account for how many participants were enrolled in online degree programs and how many were enrolled in face-to-face programs. We encourage future scholars to ascertain the unique experiences that military spouses may have in online vs. face-to-face degree programs.

Future scholars should also inquire about the strategies that military spouses use to gain information from particular sources, the content of that information, and what outcomes those strategies yield. Additionally, scholars could also inquire about whether military spouses' uncertainty fluctuates at different points in time. For example, it would be fruitful to explore if their uncertainty increases when they face major life decisions, when they experience major academic endeavors, or when they receive information about new military orders. Much of the research about uncertainty in military families tends to focus on deployment (e.g., Knobloch & Wilson, 2015). However, military spouses experience uncertainty about many other aspects of their life. Therefore, to complement our results, future scholars should explore military spouses' uncertainty about events other than deployment.

Practical Contributions for Military Spouses Pursuing Advanced Degrees

For military spouses pursuing advanced degrees, we offer several suggestions based on the results of our thematic analysis. First, in selecting a program, military spouses should search for as much information as possible about the length of the program, how it relates to their personal and professional goals, and how easily it is to transfer from one program to another. Second, we advise military spouses to seek information from fellow military spouses who are enrolled, or have been enrolled, in academic programs to select programs suitable to their family situation and educational interests. Third, upon enrolling in an advanced degree program, keep faculty members abreast of the volatile circumstances that military spouses often face. Fourth, we advise military spouses to share with their loved ones how personally meaningful and important their academic pursuits are. Military spouses often provide endless support and sacrifice to their active-duty spouses, and active-duty service members should reciprocate whenever possible. We encourage military spouses enrolled in online degree programs to involve themselves in the community of the online class. Take advantage of opportunities to connect with other students and the instructor. Specifically, we encourage military spouses to inform their instructors about their experiences as military spouses and the uncertainty that accompanies it, and use that opportunity to establish camaraderie.

Practical Contributions for Advisors, Instructors, and Administrators

Advisors and instructors can often assist military spouses in managing their uncertainty about the logistics and professional value or utility of their programs. Further, college administrators can recognize the uncertainty that military spouses experience and develop or enhance their VA programs to better assist military members and their families by offering classes at varying times to accommodate military spouses' schedules, using a blended classroom structure allowing students to meet one or two times a week in a physical classroom and then one or two times a week online, or accommodating military spouses with young children by offering childcare options. College administrators can also facilitate events on campus to assist military spouses in developing rapport and camaraderie with fellow military spouses and other professionals on campus. Further, these professionals (i.e., instructors, advisors, and VA coordinators) should realize that military spouses' uncertainty may be unique; therefore, they need to stay abreast of any information, opportunities, and programs to assist their military spouses and, perhaps more importantly, listen and provide comfort to military spouses in need of someone to understand their experiences and needs.

REFERENCES

Beebe, S. A., & Frei, S. S. (2016). Teaching communication to working adults. In P. L. Witt (Ed.), *Communication and Learning* (pp. 673–698). Boston: Walter de Gruyter.

Berger, C. R. (1987). Communicating under uncertainty. In M. E. Roloff & G. R. Miller (Eds.), *Interpersonal processes: New Directions in Communication Research* (pp. 38–62). Newbury Park, CA: Sage.

Berger, C. R., & Calabrese, R. J. (1975). Some explorations in initial interaction and beyond: Toward a developmental theory of interpersonal communication. *Human Communication Research*, *1*, 99–112. doi:10.1111/j.1468-2958.1975.tb00258.x.

Blue Star Families (2018). 2017 military family lifestyle survey. Retrieved from https://bluestarfam.org/survey/.

Boyatzis, R. E. (1998). *Transforming Qualitative Information: Thematic Analysis and Code Development*. Thousand Oaks, CA: Sage.

Braun, V., & Clark, V. (2006). Using thematic analysis in psychology. *Qualitative Research in Psychology*, *3*, 77–101. doi:10.1191/1478088706qp063oa.

Castaneda, L. W., & Harrell, M. C. (2008). Military spouse employment: A grounded theory approach to experiences and perceptions. *Armed Forces & Society*, *34*, 389–412. doi:10.1177/0095327x07307194.

Davis, J., Ward, D. B., & Storm, C. (2011). The unsilencing of military wives: Wartime deployment experiences and citizen responsibility. *Journal of Marital and Family Therapy*, *37*, 51–63. doi:10.1111/j.1752-0606.2009.00154.x.

Faber, A. J., Willerton, E., Clymer, S. R., MacDermid, S. M., & Weiss, H. M. (2008). Ambiguous absence, ambiguous presence: A qualitative study of military reserve families in wartime. *Journal of Family Psychology*, *22*, 222–230. doi:10.1037/0893-3200.22.2.222.

Fetherston, M., Cherney, M. R., & Bunton, T. E. (2018). Uncertainty, technology use, and career preparation self-efficacy. *Western Journal of Communication, 82*, 276–295. doi: 10.1080/10570314.2017.1294704.

Glaser, B., & Strauss, A. (1967). *The Discovery of Grounded Theory*. Chicago, IL: Aldine.

Harrell, M. C., Lim, N., Castaneda, L. W., & Golinelli, D. (2004). Working around the military: Challenges to military spouse employment and education. Retrieved from http://www.dtic.mil/docs/citations/ADA452563.

High, A. C., Jennings-Kelsall, V., Solomon, D. H., & Marshall, A. D. (2015). Military families online: Seeking and providing support through internet discussion boards. In E. S. Parcell & L. M. Webb (Eds.), *A Communication Perspective on the Military: Interactions, Messages, and Discourses* (pp. 101–120). New York: Peter Lang.

Knobloch, L. K., & Wilson, S. R. (2015). Communication in military families across the deployment cycle. In L. H. Turner & R. West (Eds.), *The Sage Handbook of Family Communication* (pp. 370–385). Thousand Oaks, CA: Sage.

Kramer, M. W. (1999). Motivation to reduce uncertainty: A reconceptualization of uncertainty reduction theory. *Management Communication Quarterly, 13*, 305–316. doi:10.1177/0893318999132007.

Kramer, M. W. (2004). *Managing Uncertainty in Organizational Communication*. Mahwah, NJ: Lawrence Erlbaum.

Kramer, M. W. (2009). Managing uncertainty in work interactions. In T. D. Afifi & W. Afifi (Eds.), *Uncertainty, Information Management, and Disclosure Decisions: Theories and Applications*. (pp. 164–181). London: Routledge.

Lapp, C. A., Tollefson, T., Hoepner, A., Moore, K., & Divyak, K. (2010). Stress and coping on the home front: Guard and reserve spouses searching for a new normal. *Journal of Family Nursing, 16*, 45–67. doi:10.1177/1074840709357347.

Lim, N., & Schulker, D. (2010). Measuring underemployment among military spouses. Retrieved from http://www.dtic.mil/dtic/tr/fulltext/u2/a515809.pdf.

Lincoln, Y. S., & Guba, E. G. (1985). *Naturalistic Inquiry*. Beverly Hills, CA: Sage.

Mehta, M. S., & Jorgenson, J. (2015). Work-family predicaments of Air Force wives: A sensemaking perspective. In E. S. Parcell & L. M. Webb (Eds.), *A Communication Perspective on the Military: Interactions, Messages, and Discourses* (pp. 121–138). New York: Peter Lang.

Milliken, P. J. (2010). Grounded theory. In. N. J. Salkind (Ed.), *Encyclopedia of Research Design* (pp. 548–552). Thousand Oaks, CA: Sage.

Myers, S. A., & Knox, R. L. (2001). The relationship between college student information-seeking behaviors and perceived instructor verbal behaviors. *Communication Education, 50*, 343–356. doi:10.1080/03634520109379260.

Padden, D. L., Connors, R. A., & Agazio, J. G. (2011). Stress, coping, and well-being in military spouses during deployment separation. *Western Journal of Nursing Research, 33*, 247–267. doi:10.1177/0193945910371319.

Patton, M. Q. (2002). *Qualitative Research & Evaluation Methods*. 3rd ed. Thousand Oaks, CA: Sage.

Sollitto, M., Brott, J., Cole C., Gil, E., & Selim, H. (2018). Students' uncertainty management in the college classroom. *Communication Education, 67*, 73–87. doi: 10.1080/03634523.2017.1372586.

Tompkins, P. K. (1994). Principles of rigor for assessing evidence in "qualitative" communication research. *Western Journal of Communication, 58*, 44–50. doi:10.1080/10570319409374483.

Wheeler, A. R., & Stone, T. R. A. (2010). Exploring stress and coping strategies among National Guard spouses during times of deployment: A research note. *Armed Forces & Society, 36*, 545–557. doi:10.1177/0095327x09344066.

Chapter Seven

Military Spouses, Advanced Degrees, and the Myth of Keeping Busy

Abby E. Murray

> Give me a task to do each day,
> To fill the time when he's away.
>
> —Army Wife's Prayer

I feel strongly that military spouses should discuss mortality and the politics of war openly, since many of us are faced with the realities of the body, of death, from the time we first feel committed to a service member. Advanced degrees, which can prompt more open dialogue and engaged critical thinking, are not encouraged enough in military spouse communities, and war is not a part of our human history to be taken lightly. I realize a proposal to speak more openly about war and trauma is also a request to make ourselves uncomfortable, and it is human instinct to seek comfort in times of crisis. But avoiding discomfort is a luxury we simply cannot afford—not if we are hoping to foster healthy communication between service members and spouses, or between military and civilian communities.

In marrying a service member in 2004, I accepted a new reality into my everyday life: the person I loved was consciously and professionally risking his life. His friends were dying. Strangers around him were dying. His mortality seemed, to me, more tenuous. As a civilian in a country that fought its wars in faraway homes, streets, backyards, and places of worship, I was more likely to die from a traffic accident than war wounds.

Audre Lorde (2007) wrote, "In becoming forcibly and essentially aware of my mortality, and of what I wished and wanted for my life, however short it might be, priorities and omissions became strongly etched in a merciless light, and what I most regretted were my silences" (p. 47). I wish I'd found Audre Lorde's writing when I was 20 and overwhelmed and new to military life, when I had yet to understand what a shocking privilege it would be to stay silent. I have only begun to write my silence. The following poem (2017b) is from a recent issue of *Prairie Schooner*:

When I Tell You I Love You

When I tell you I love you what I mean is
I've seen your body in pieces
as recently as last night, on the couch,
the BBC needling through our longest day
like light through a keyhole. I said, *oh God*.
You said *there's going to be a war*
and each word was a metal coil
small as a finger, hot enough to cook teeth,
each word was a sheet used to lift you into a truck.
When I say I love you what I mean is
you're too old to love a rifle like a brother
and I'm too old for false comfort
but even now, on the couch, with the TV
showing us the closed front door
of a well-dressed leader, we feel
what I think is love fumbling for the generator,
lights blinking on in the city of us,
and there are people with suitcases lined up
on the streets of our marriage like memories,
and when I tell you I love you what I mean is
our memories travel in times of upheaval
from the mind toward the rib cage, crossing
that treacherous, tender river of throat.
When I tell you I love you what I want you to hear is
that each remembrance is a family
and when war comes, you and I will sleep
on the shore of ourselves. We'll watch
the horizon for incoming rafts. (Murray, 2017b, p. 187)

This poem was written at the beginning of Brexit, but the fear remains more and more palpable with each subsequent scandal and tragedy that unfolds on our newsfeeds daily. Every time I drive past a disabled weapon parked and propped up on display on post, I feel this way. At every ceremony where rifles are carried, armed, or fired. Every wives' coffee.

* * *

When I applied to MFA programs in early 2007, I wasn't looking for something to do so much as a way to survive my intellectual and emotional responses to military life. I had no desire to stay busy as I moved from state to state. I wanted to stay alive. My husband's experiences in combat were following him home, where all I could do was help carry them.

I knew the only way I could pull off a master's degree was through a low-residency program, a structure I found out about after searching brokenheartedly through traditional school programs I thought were out of reach; they all seemed to require their students to live in a single place (typically the university's hometown) for years at a stretch. But Pacific University, located in Forest Grove, Oregon, offered a two-year program during which most of the written work was completed, reviewed, and revised through the mail, while students returned to Oregon for two two-week residencies of intensive workshops, craft talks, and readings. I was accepted, and I traveled to each residency from a different duty station, graduating in 2009.

Poetry became a belonging I could carry wherever my husband was transferred. In fact, once I began to value my writing—recognizing my identity in its ability to connect me to others and keep me awake—I saw it as an asset I couldn't leave behind if I wanted to. Poetry was my most effective method of communication in city after city that felt indifferent to my coming and going.

In 2011, I was teaching writing at the community college just outside Fort Carson, Colorado, but my wheels were spinning. I established a local reading series at the art gallery. I taught violin lessons on the side. I published my poems in chapbooks and journals. I enjoyed all this, but staring down the barrel of my husband's third deployment made me feel as if I was putting most my energy into projects framed by his career rather than my own, simply because I had yet to start mine. None of my projects were long-term and had a pop-up-tent feel to them; after Tom's assignment changed, the reading series would end, my writing students would study with my colleagues, and my violin students would find new instructors. I could submit my poetry from anyplace. The way I lived—how I chose to spend my time—felt non-essential in a way that was unsettling. It was too easy to wrap up my own work while my husband's training seemed crucial and woven into every decision we made.

I contacted the local university to see about collaborating on a larger community engagement project, and when I mentioned I was here with my active-duty husband, they suggested I get involved by setting up chairs for their events. I couldn't help wondering, is this all that is expected of me? Contributing only what is easily taken down when I'm done? What was I doing? When I was an undergraduate volunteering for literacy projects and studying the impact of art on communities, I didn't picture myself landing here, where my daily life seemed more like free time I had the option of filling than precious time I needed to prioritize.

I wanted to write more often and live near a community *I'd* chosen. I wanted to stay married, too. So, while my husband packed his duffels for Afghanistan, I packed my applications to Ph.D. programs. Years later, my husband would admit (with some embarrassment) that it didn't bother him at the time. He didn't think I'd be accepted; there was nothing to worry about.

* * *

I wanted to get out of Colorado as soon as possible once my husband was gone. When orders were received, the Family Readiness Group (FRG) would ramp up its required meetings to help spouses "cope." Town hall sessions would abound, complete with PowerPoint slides attempting to explain how phones work overseas and why spouses shouldn't expect to talk to "their boys" at all hours. When we did have opportunities to communicate, spouses were encouraged to avoid giving deployed service members too many details about stressful situations at home, and to reassure them on all fronts. *Remember to be brave.*

When orders were received, I'd begin scolding myself for the way I felt about reintegration classes we'd have to take when we were lucky enough to be reunited, both of us alive. We would be encouraged for several hours to avoid co-dependence, excessive alcohol, difficult questions and/or post-deployment isolation. Attendance at reintegration workshops and group meetings would be mandatory. We would receive tiny cards and flyers with phone numbers to report domestic violence. The advice would be contradictory and constant. Get involved, take a break, be patient, trust your instincts, take action, give it time, plan ahead, let it be. I wasn't confused; I was annoyed. So I wrote.

When He Receives Orders to Afghanistan and a Parking Ticket: How to Respond

What you say matters,
each word tagged
and monitored
like an eaglet.
Make your voice
a small bird,
the kind he can hold
in the palm of his hand:
chickadee, sparrow, canary.
Use words that behave
in the corridors of memory.
Don't say *Fuck*.
Don't be a blue jay.

Don't crack your head
on the window
or rifle through his duffel.
Don't ask where he parked.
When he hands you
the ticket, its charges
printed in dark red script,
let the checkbook
fly from your purse
like a finch.
Post payment immediately
and sing, sing, sing.
Don't hoard bits of paper,
don't shred his orders.
Don't bark, don't pick.
You are not a magpie,
you are not a crow.
Your voice is a long, sweet song.
Build a nest on his shoulder
and rest your head there.
Fill his ears with feathers
so downy and slight
they can stuff a canal
and never weigh more
than an ounce. (Murray, 2017a)

The imagery reveals how I am taught to respond to my husband's military career. I am told to be supportive, comforting, and sweet. To an extent, I am. I love my husband and am afraid of his death. The poem's voice, however, is where I wield my bitterness. The way I am taught to respond to trauma and grief leaves me even more unsatisfied and angry.

* * *

The military life has been difficult for me to navigate. When I think of the roadblocks I've encountered as I've explored and established my own identity (feminist, student, teacher, mentor, wife, mother, activist, writer) in several communities, traditions surrounding the military spouse come to mind.

When I tell civilian friends my husband's job requires my presence and uncompensated contributions to fundraisers, frequent ceremonies, and socials, they are shocked. "But it's 2018!" they say, as if more should have changed in the past 70 years. These traditions aren't passed directly from my husband's workplace to me, either; they are often transmitted through him, and his attitude about spousal involvement is influenced by the nature of these expectations. He loves me, but he makes mistakes. He is surrounded by peers accustomed to working in an environment where spouses, most of them women, adapt quickly (albeit sometimes reluctantly) and remain available for constant support, even when service members cannot reciprocate. Spouses are honored for "holding down the fort" and playing the part of therapist, parent, reintegration specialist, career support office, professional mover, fundraising expert, administrative assistant and more—all of them time-consuming roles that service members lean on heavily.

More than once, my husband has reaped the consequences of my losing a game I refuse to play. He has been told he is not a *power couple* and I am not a *multiplier*. I am absent, I am unfriendly, I am unsupportive—these are the kinder terms. I never know what to say. So I write.

At the Wives' Coffee

You should know
   there is no coffee
      at the Wives' Coffee

There's prosciutto
   and cream puffs
      and conversation starters
         printed on glossy paper

And here's a tip
   from the commander's wife:

Wives who forget
   to wear the crest pin
      will be fined a dollar
         because *these pins*
            aren't free ladies

and immediately
   I'm a stump
      rolled into the river
         before a flood
            I am uncooperative

a hollow log sheltering rebel fish
   a disruption of roots

But the conversation starters

are required and my question is

What discussion topic bores you to sleep every time?

and I want sleep to come to me
    now like a shovel arrives in dirt
        but instead I blurt BABIES
            and one of the wives
                Danielle, I think

hugs her eight-month bump
    so I grasp for more words
        as if they're ropes
            that might tow me ashore

PRESCHOOL
    I mean PINTEREST
        I mean WHO SAID WHAT

And the air is stiff
    with some wrong
        that smells like burning

and I know it's me—
    I recognize the flavor
        of my own smoke

which I wear heavy in my hair,
    the emblem of defeat no other wife has earned

sinking in now like a hammered crown

And you should know
    every Wives' Coffee
        is actually my coronation (Murray, 2018a)

In this poem, the near-constant miscommunication between myself and other spouses is evident, as well as—to an extent—the traditions surrounding how and why service members' wives must gather. We are brought together to build a community that is pleasant, positive, and in my experience, superficial.

* * *

I was accepted to several Ph.D. programs in 2012 and chose the one at Binghamton University, where I was offered full tuition coverage and a stipend. My husband was surprised but distracted, embedded somewhere near the Pakistan-Afghanistan border. While he was gone, I packed up our house and pets near Fort Carson and paid out of pocket to U-Haul our life from Colorado to New York.

At the end of my first semester, deployment ended. My husband returned to Colorado and lived with a buddy for a couple months until he was reassigned—our good luck—to an ROTC teaching position at the University of Scranton, Pennsylvania, just 65 miles south of Binghamton. I was happy. I was teaching for the Binghamton Poetry Project, a nonprofit organization that brings free poetry workshops into schools, libraries, and Boys & Girls Clubs. I was taking grad courses, writing and publishing my poetry. I was the poetry editor for *Harpur Palate*. I was teaching and running my fastest miles. I was living with my husband for the first time in two years. Then I was pregnant.

I took over as director of the Poetry Project in my second trimester while continuing to teach, expanding the workshops into the veterans' center downtown. On my due date, I attended a 12-hour poetry workshop. Two weeks after delivering my daughter, I taught a poetry workshop for first graders and set up internships for Binghamton undergraduates interested in literary nonprofit work.

I can do this, I thought. I *was* doing it. My proximity to military life was simultaneously distant and intimate in a way I could manage without feeling guilty or ignorant. I had few required ceremonies and no wives' coffees to attend. I worked with veterans and recently separated service members on a regular basis, writing with them and talking about the power of language and story.

That's not to say I was entirely removed from military life. On a frigid winter Tuesday, my husband and I traveled to Scranton for a hail and farewell near the university where he taught. Before the ceremony, a cheerful spouse found me munching celery by the snack table. To be honest, I had a lot of reading to do and my email inbox was mushrooming into a giant mass of untended tasks. I wanted to leave. I didn't want to chat or eat celery.

"So!" she chirped, addressing me by my husband's last name. I tried not to bristle. "Getting a Ph.D., wow! Will you be a real doctor, or just the kind that writes?" She tipped her head to the side a bit, curious.

I don't remember what I said. Her conscious meaning was clear; she wanted to know if I would become a medical doctor or a decorated thinker. But the question smoldered in my mind. What was I doing, here but not here, physically present at a hail and farewell when my mind was stretched thin as a bookmark between poetry and war? I was asking myself why I sacrificed time I could have been devoting to my own work; meanwhile, I felt that other spouses were, in veiled terms, asking why I diverted time from supporting my husband's career at all. Couldn't I slow down?

The answer seemed clear but not entirely kind. I was succeeding in academia and nonprofit work in spite of the expectations placed on me as a service member's spouse: the expectation that, if I did work, my job would primarily serve as a way to keep busy; it would be easy to put down whenever my husband was home. In reality, I was fully present in all my accomplishments at the university even when I was off campus, and I was surrounded by people who never asked how I kept myself busy.

* * *

My husband's redeployment in 2013 was unlike the previous ones. PTSD was apparent to me but not to him, and even if he did admit feeling it, there was no chance he'd ask for help to confront it. He became fiercely protective of his career and the way I spent my time. His stress responses were out of control. He seemed vulnerable and tender one moment, then withdrawn or furious the next, and he developed a paranoia that we were being followed. He would sporadically confide in me about brutal combat experiences (next to the bagels in the grocery store, or at the end of what seemed like a quick phone call about dinner plans, etc.). I handled every story like the narrative it was: I made space for it by hearing it, but I found myself able to more effectively process the details in writing than discussion.

By this point, I was about to finish my first year of courses in my doctoral program and was immersed in German war poetry, having audited a few German courses after fulfilling my language requirement. Writing poetry *auf Deutsch* set my blood on fire. I felt capable of not only raising my voice but hearing it, identifying it. In Bertolt Brecht, Nelly Sachs, Else Laske-Schüler, Georg Trakl, Paul Celán, and Günter Eich I found familiar music, as if I'd been trying to sing in the same key all along. These were the voices that said *look, look at this war*. They didn't moralize or treat language like some panacea for brutality, and they certainly didn't spare the energy it might've taken to ignore it. I wrote my truth of the wars in Iraq and Afghanistan as they were carried home by my husband:

Calling Rats
translated from German

In the desert, in a concrete hut
behind a door made of cloth,
a rat gives birth in the filing cabinet

between your last two t-shirts.
She shreds the collars for comfort,
surrounds her brood with the scent
of your neck torn to ribbons.
Into a bucket of water they go.
When you tell the story a year later
you slump at our kitchen table,
a houseplant bloomed with blame.
War brought the rats to me, you say,
they stole the last bit of cotton
between my body and the burn pit.
At night I open your eyelids and see the rat,
her children asleep in your skull.
When I coax them out they do not trust me.
I offer them some paper, a piece of apple.
They want the hem of your sleeve. (Murray, 2018b, p. 24)

[Die Berufung der Ratten]

In der Wüste, in einer Hütte
hinter einer Tür aus Stoff,
gebar eine Ratte ihre Jungen
in der Schublade eines Büroschranks
zwischen deinen letzten beiden T-Shirts.
Sie zerfetzte aus Behaglichkeit die Kragen,
bettete ihre Brut in die abgenagten Fasern deiner Sachen,
umgibt sie mit dem Duft deines zerrissenen Nackens.
Sie gehen in einen Eimer aus Wasser.
Als du die Geschichte ein Jahr später erzählst,
sackst du an unserem Küchentisch zusammen,
eine Zimmerpflanze erblüht aus Schuld.
Der Krieg hat mir die Ratten gebracht, sagst du,
sie haben das letzte Stück Baumwolle
zwischen meinem Körper
und der brennenden Feuergrube gestohlen.
Nachts öffne ich deine Augenlider
und sehe die Ratte, ihre Kinder
schlafend in deinem Schädel.
Wenn ich versuche sie zu überreden herauszukommen
sehe ich, dass sie mir nicht trauen.
Ich biete ihnen etwas Papier an, ein Apfelstück.
Sie wollen den Saum deines Ärmels.

In the poetry of witness, I find more truthful and intimate ways of acknowledging the repercussions of war—my own complicity and the lasting effects of violence and loss and trauma. In poetry, keeping busy is a myth; speaking the truth is reality. I cannot ignore the consequences of America's war, particularly as they manifest in my husband's behavior and our marriage.

The German poetry of post-WWI and WWII looks hard at the devastation of war simply by speaking it. Günter Eich (1997), a German soldier captured by Americans in WWII (and later a member of Grüppe 47, a collective of German writers whose work was instrumental in rebuilding the German language after its appropriation by the Nazi regime) says the goal of writing poetry is to orient himself in reality. Writing is the act of naming, of calling out what is there to the reader. This permits understanding—the ability to return to a feeling or experience and find familiarity. It is language that connects us to our past.

Paul Celan (2001), too, addresses poetry in this way, saying he writes poems "to orient myself, to find out where I was and where I was meant to go, to sketch out reality for myself."

Poetry is where I've built my home, as I've moved from post to post. I can see so much of my life from here.

* * *

In "Poetry, Injury, and the Ethics of Reading," Elaine Scarry (2014) writes about poems as platforms for deliberation—places wherein two or more arguments can be comprehended and acknowledged. While Scarry points to Greek epics as examples, I wonder if there is such a thing as poetry *without* dispute, even now.

In all my poems I am speaking to be heard. The willing audience is one that needs to comprehend my argument and compare it somehow to what is not my argument. Celan (2001) said poetry is essentially dialogue, and as I hear it, the conversation is either harmonic or discordant.

Poetry is the meeting of experiences. My life as a military spouse—or, more specifically, my life as a person very close to trauma—is lived in a space where it is confronted by a reader's similar or dissimilar experience.

* * *

In 2015, my husband's luck in finding assignments in the northeast finally ran out. He was reassigned to Joint Base Lewis-McChord in Washington State, where we'd actually hoped to be assigned for years. My family lives in the Pacific Northwest. I was born there.

But I was doing so well in New York. I was mostly parenting solo with Tom in Scranton, then Rhode Island to attend the War College, but I was loving all aspects of my work, writing my dissertation, teaching, running the Poetry Project, publishing poems. I didn't want to leave, so I didn't plan to. I figured my daughter and I could catch up with my husband the following year after I graduated, which would put off my going into a cutthroat job market. I wasn't set to complete my degree until June 2016.

My husband's the one who found a creative writing job at University of Washington, Tacoma, near JBLM, and I submitted my application warily. Other grad students at Binghamton were constantly talking about rigged, "fake" searches, where internal candidates were all but guaranteed the position even though the school had to go through a national search process. I wasn't hopeful.

I was surprised but skeptical when they asked for a phone interview. I was floored when I got a campus visit and forgot to breathe when I was offered a position.

The unexpected thrill of joining the academic community beyond graduation was intense, and I held on to it as I finished my work with the Poetry Project and made arrangements to complete my dissertation out of state.

My husband was excited too, reassured that we'd move west as a family.

* * *

Moving from a town whose military presence is mostly retired to a town where active-duty service members were everywhere raised old challenges in how I was expected to prioritize my time. I hadn't had to go to a ball in years and suddenly I was being asked to cut my evening classes short in order to make cocktail hour on time in a gown. I didn't even own a gown. I still don't.

On nights when I was slammed with grading or writing projects or research, I was warned not to miss mandatory town hall sessions on post or FRG meetings or battalion fundraisers or luncheons for officers' wives. Socializing with other wives was required though no one liked to say so. It made it sound as if the wives were unpleasant by nature, which they weren't. They were friendly. But my husband did his job well and looked forward to promotion; I was told, for the first time in years, to "play nice" when I had no time for games in the first place.

My anger returned and I acknowledged it through poetry. "Asking for a Friend" (Murray, 2018a) won the Founders' Prize for *Rhino*, a literary journal based in Illinois.

Asking for a Friend

Is there a way to tell
the commander's wife

Military Spouses, Advanced Degrees, and the Myth of Keeping Busy

you're a pacifist
and it's possible
to trust your spouse
but mourn his work
because the death
he's delivered
through the cracks
of thatched rooftops
is more than a fracture
beneath his skin
and the flag is a reminder
and gravel is a reminder
and pins and ribbons
and coins and the smell
of diesel and buildings
without doors are a reminder
and you won't secure
the gold battalion crest
over your left breast
no matter how many
times she tells you
it's like a sweetheart pin
and the last thing
you want when
your father is found
dead in his duplex
is an email asking when
she can drop off some
meatballs in sauce
and you can't stop
swaddling your brain
in yesterday's *Times*
to see what city has fallen
as if they topple
rather than burn
and you refuse to stop
reading and doubting
until no one makes sense
and every deployment
is a Talking Heads song
and every morning
is an invitation to dance
in a pill bottle
and you're not interested
in keeping busy

and you don't want
more group texts
and you don't want
your daughter learning
to shoot a rifle
with the other kids
who aim at a silhouette
of someone's son
tied to a haystack
and you don't want
to host a dress swap
before the gala
and you don't want
a souvenir photo
with the bald eagle
and every time
the commander says
let's thank our ladies
you want to toss the table
champagne flutes and all
and watch the favors
you've done to prompt
his gratitude go flying
because you've tried to say
war is necessary
but the words are like
spiders in the shower
they have every right
to be there and yet
you are crawling up
the side of yourself
trying to get clean
without howling
and you don't want
to call them *our boys*
and you don't want
to be called *household 6*
or a rock or a pillar
and the only commanders
you trust are the ones
who seem pained
by the movement
of their own bones
given to them
by their mothers

freely and without
any mental reservation
and it's against your beliefs
to say things are fine
when the satellites
click and blink above us
unwilling to share
which target needs water
and which needs bread
and if anyone knows
a way to say this
without provoking
the commander's wife
to roll a wide stone
over your spouse
and his career
let's meet soon
I'll buy you a beer (Murray, 2018c)

I'd like to say that framing this poem's meaning as a question is merely poetic technique, but that wouldn't be honest. Military relationships and interactions are ripe with problematic terminology, symbols, and practices. I recently attended the promotion ceremony of a former student and, in his short speech, he thanked me for my critical eye and academic support, then he thanked his wife for being beautiful, for being a rock. He's a good man. But no one even blinked. I couldn't help feeling like the spouse—who may have sacrificed more than any of us—wasn't truly acknowledged, and that bit of silence was actually built into our expectations.

* * *

I've spent some time over the past year thinking about what it means to be a military spouse in an academic community. I've only come up with answers that constantly shift and contradict themselves.

I have seen and heard individuals representing academic institutions speak dismissively of military-affiliated students and faculty. (One colleague of mine confided in me—with good intentions—that she found it difficult to sympathize with combat veterans. "They signed up," she said. "They knew what they were getting themselves into.") Universities value all too often the financial gains of offering educational and professional opportunities to service members, veterans, and their families, but it isn't difficult to argue that there is a lack of assistance in addressing veterans' social and psychological needs as they transition from military to academic communities. I find this to be true. While individual faculty are personally and professionally committed to serving military-affiliated students, the majority seem unfamiliar, undecided, or uncomfortable acknowledging their needs.

By the same token, I have experienced isolation in military communities because of my academic affiliation. Spouses and service members I've never met have dubbed me *snob* and *elitist* after hearing I teach college writing (which is terribly ironic, considering the status of lecturers on most academic ladders). I have been called a *poor sport* and *detriment* to my husband's career because my own professional goals demand most of my time, and I've never been interested in or able to take on official FRG roles.

In the free creative writing workshops I offer in Tacoma, across the street from campus, I work at a table crowded with military spouses, significant others, siblings, and children of veterans. They write poetry, essays, and short stories, then they talk about what it means to experience combat indirectly through their loved ones, or to survive assault, or witness sexism, racism, and hatred on post and off.

No one calls deployment an "adventure" in these workshops, though I suppose it could happen. They don't speak about their creative or academic accomplishments as techniques to kill time and they don't seem interested in "keeping busy" as a way to cope with military life.

I suppose, as a military spouse *and* poet, I have simply not felt compelled to see any of my passions or interests as tools to look away from what is painful, uncomfortable, or urgent. They are methods of accomplishing quite the opposite. I don't expect all spouses to feel this way, but I do wish more literature and common conversations surrounding the military spouse experience acknowledged our complex identities.

* * *

Overwhelmingly, I find near constant encouragement for military spouses to cope, and to find pleasure and camaraderie in the process as often as possible. Every direction I turn, online and on post and in libraries, I find the promise of survival tips for those married to veterans and service members. Most of them approach the "adventures" of military life in a light-hearted way that makes me question whether my struggling with military life is really as universal as it seems.

It's true that the military life is difficult, but I am married to a service member; I am not one. I spend a great deal of time focused on achieving my goals as a writer and citizen, and, for the most part, my husband has been happy to honor that. I may have spent more time than some civilian spouses thinking about my partner's mortality during my twenties, but not all.

The military influences my poetry, activism, and the way I choose to teach. But military life is not the primary catalyst for my pursuing advanced degrees; I earned my master's and doctorate because I wanted to read and write and surround myself with other readers and writers. One could say that I earned my advanced degrees in spite of military life.

I should say, however, that I am more interested in working with veterans, service members, and military families and loved ones than I might have been had I not married my husband. I am drawn to the history of violence and the way it is portrayed and complicated in art because art is historically linked to the expression of injustice and survival. I care deeply about the hundreds of service members and families I've met. I support student veterans not only because they deserve human kindness but because, often, by the time they reach my classes, they too are thinking critically about what influence the military has on their current relationships and goals.

But the traditions and expectations of a military lifestyle do not consume my hours or my thinking. That's not to say I have no cause to cope; I do. I engage with my trauma and loss and conflict by writing essays and poetry, by seeing a therapist via Skype (God bless him and his medical biller), by seeing my doctor and working constantly to know and listen to myself. I have as much reason to cope as anyone else, but if the military lifestyle has afforded me one obligation, it has been the need to think critically about human history and behavior, to question authority and suspect any person or practice that appears to dismiss this need as superfluous or threatening. I do not need to be okay, or convince others that I am okay, during deployments or reintegration or these seemingly unending periods of time when our country teeters on the brink of war.

I need to remain in conversation with my husband and myself. I need to not lose sight of our history as Americans and the purpose of our military. I can do this by reading and questioning, over and over. Recently, after reviewing a great deal of popular blogs written by and for military spouses, I realized I also needed to consider carefully how I define the practice of coping.

The top 100 military wife blogs (collected on Feedspot and updated weekly) are ranked based on Google searches/reputation, popularity on social media, quality and consistency of posts, and Feedspot's "expert review" (Agarwal, 2018). This list is interesting to me, as I reflect on my own experience as a military spouse. The majority of the ranked blogs are centered around activities and practices that are often enjoyable and healthy but require little to no critical thinking or questioning, such as physical exercise, cooking & baking, home decorating & organization, bargain hunting, tips on motherhood and finding jobs that are as readily available as they are temporary. (This is not to say the blogs listed encourage hobbies as a method of avoiding critical thinking. All of them, in some way, acknowledge the difficulty of military life, but they do so in ways that are appealing to newcomers, which is to say they would rather call military life an "adventure" than acknowledge its relationship to violence and death.)

Indeed, of the first 50 blogs ranked, #36, *The Military Spouse Book Review*, is the only one that proudly describes itself as a place for military spouses to "share ideas about books, writing, military life and more." I'm drawn to the site for its promise of dialogue, and I am also intrigued by two other blogs that confront less commonly discussed subjects, including PTSD and military life from the perspective of a lesbian spouse. Overwhelmingly, however, I am saddened (and not surprised) by the wealth of blogs (Myers, 2018) that encourage spouses to keep busy by watching TV, shopping, or celebrating the fun aspects of solitude. Employment is often addressed in these blogs but only conceptually; finding and landing jobs is difficult—I agree—but what is the content of these jobs? How do they connect us to what we want to create, what we want to see in ourselves? Are jobs a means to understanding the world around us, or are they merely tools for keeping busy?

I have always thought of coping as a form of consciously struggling, of seeing and understanding an issue even if it is unresolvable. If coping is the act of finding pleasure outside of confronting my real fears and identity, then I have no interest in it. I will write instead.

I see writing and coping as different practices, and while the effects of writing can be healing, it is not inherently therapeutic. I remember, as a young poet, when my husband was in Iraq for the second time, hearing Kay Ryan (2011) speak in Washington D.C. about poetry as anything but a "healing art." I was shocked to understand that poetry could be seen outside of its perceived effects, but I agreed. Empathy may be fundamental to literature, yes, because it is created and acted by humans (Scarry, 2014). But the pursuit of healing and the pursuit of writing are two distinct endeavors.

Coping, not in its literal definition but in the way it is addressed in popular literature for military spouses, is perceived as a way of getting through some experience or way of thought, of making it to a safe end, of successfully experiencing some event or time without feeling irreparably harmed by it. Is this survival, or a means to putting it off? How do I cope with my husband's combat experiences and all their ethical dilemmas? How do I cope with the perception that I've been "left behind" or the assumptions and expectations the Army places on me through him? There is no way through military life without enduring harm—the kind of harm that scars and lingers and influences the way you act, think, and speak.

In writing (and in studying writing) I acknowledge the harm that war, politics, tradition, and trauma have caused me. I try to acknowledge the harm it has brought to my family, my country, and millions of people. My husband is committed to his job and to the safety of his country, and he has the right to be. But there is no just war, and his work is intertwined with the loss of many lives that count as both means and end to conflict.

REFERENCES

Agarwal, A. (2018, June 20). The top 100 military wife blogs and websites for military wives [Web log post]. Retrieved from https://blog.feedspot.com/military_wife_blogs/.

Celan, P. (2001). *Selected poems and prose of Paul Celan*. (John Felstiner, Trans.). New York: Norton. (Original work published in 1958)

Eich, G. (1997). Some remarks on "literature and reality." (Stuart Friebert, Trans.). In Stuart Friebert, David Walker, & David Young (Eds.), *A Field Guide to Contemporary Poetry and Poetics* (pp. 115–116). Oberlin: Oberlin College. (Original work published in 1956)

Lorde, A. (2007). The transformation of silence into language and action. In *Sister outsider: Essays and speeches*. Berkeley: Crossing Press.

Murray, A. E. (2017a). When he receives orders to Afghanistan and a parking ticket: how to respond. *Dialogist, 4*. Retrieved from https://dialogist.org/v4i1-abby-e-murray/.

Murray, A. E. (2017b). When I tell you I love you. *Prairie Schooner* 91:4 (p. 187). Lincoln: University of Nebraska Press.

Murray, A. E. (2018a). At the Wives' Coffee. *New Ohio Review, 24*.

Murray, A. E. (2018b). Calling rats. *How to be married after Iraq* (p. 24). Georgetown: Finishing Line.

Murray, A. E. (2018c). Asking for a friend. *Rhino, 2018*. Retrieved from https://rhinopoetry.org/poems/asking-for-a-friend-abby-e-murray.

Myers, A. (2018) 9 reasons why it's okay when he deploys [Web log post]. Retrieved from https://themilitarywifeandmom.com/coping-with-deployment-separation/.

Ryan, K. (2011). A reading and conversation with Kay Ryan. Presented at the AWP conference, Washington, D.C.

Scarry, E. (2014). Poetry, injury, and the ethics of reading. In Peter Brooks and Hilary Jewett (Eds.) *The humanities and public life* (41–48). New York: Fordham University.

Chapter Eight

Counsel for the Military Spouse
Law School, the Bar Exam, and Beyond
Katherine Lee Goyette

Friday, September 9, 2016, was a terrible day in my life as a career-minded military spouse. I had rushed to court that morning and was on my own with a double caseload because my docket partner had taken the morning off. I dropped half that caseload off of counsel's table onto the floor just as Judge entered the courtroom, and then later opened up my email to the news that another attorney had been promoted. This was the second attorney that had bypassed me, and I immediately knew it was because of my status as a military spouse attorney. We had been stationed at Fort Carson since February 2014, and my supervisors saw the writing on the wall. I was told later that day that if I was promoted and PCSed (Permanent Change of Station) six months later, it would be a bad "management decision." In the alternative, if my husband deployed instead, they would be able to promote me.

Employment barriers such as this due to my husband's military service was not unusual, but I was particularly appalled at what was supposed to be a merit-based promotion had instead been based on the federal government's decision as to where to place my husband. Employment prospects are already grim for people that are married to active-duty service members, as active-duty service carries with it the realities of PCS-ing every three to four years to a new duty station. As a military spouse attorney, employment barriers are twice as strong: law licensure is required in each individual state, and bar rules with respect to law licensure are not generally accommodating to the geographically insecure reality of military life; then, even with a law license, employment is not guaranteed.

This essay will review statistics of military spouse education and employment, examine military spouses in the context of regulated professions, present an autoethnographic reflection of my law school experiences and navigating the bar examination after graduate school as a military spouse, discuss issues facing military spouse attorneys, and finally, give personal recommendations for military spouse attorneys seeking to maintain their legal career through multiple military moves.

MILITARY SPOUSES, EDUCATION, AND EMPLOYMENT

In 2010, the RAND National Defense Research Institute, sponsored by the Office of the Secretary of Defense, the Joint Staff, the Unified Combatant Commands, the Department of the Navy, the Marine Corps, defense agencies and the defense Intelligence Community, published a report (Measuring Unemployment among Military Spouses, 2010) that measured underemployment among military spouses. It found that 22% of military spouses have high levels of education and had a tendency to have an "educational mismatch" to their current employment. A 2017 survey released by the Hiring Our Heroes U.S. Chamber of Commerce Foundation (2017) found that 88% of military spouses have post–high school education, 34% held a college degree, and 15% held postgraduate degrees. While the unemployment rate within the military spouse community has dropped from 23% in 2015 to 16% in 2017, the 16% unemployment rate is four times the unemployment rate for adult women and three times the rate for women between the ages of 20 and 25. Of the military spouses that are employed, 25% are working more than one job, 70% do not believe that their education or past work experience is being fully utilized in their current job, and almost two-thirds indicated that they had held previous positions that required greater skills and responsibilities. The survey also found that increased challenges existed for spouses with degrees, as the transient nature of military life created a higher probability of unemployment and underemployment (Hiring Our Heroes U.S. Chamber of Commerce Foundation, 2017).

The Council of Economic Advisors, an agency within the federal executive branch, published a report (Military Spouses in the Labor Market, 2018) that found that despite higher educational levels, military spouses are less likely to be labor force participants when compared to the general working population (57% to 76% in 2016). Military spouses in the workforce were also found to earn less than would otherwise be expected; when compared to other labor participants with similar characteristics, military spouses earned 26.8% less in wage and salary income. Finally, the Council confirmed how military spouses continue to face higher rates of unemployment and be disproportionally affected by occupational licensing requirements in state-regulated professions (Military Spouses in the Labor Market, 2018).

Military Spouses in Regulated Professions

A report by the U.S. Congress Joint Economic Committee Chairman's Staff to Senator Bob Casey (Strengthening Military Households by Decreasing the Barriers to Work, 2012) revealed that barriers to military spouse employment included frequent relocations and licensure portability. The top three occupations for military spouses at the time included teachers, childcare workers, and registered nurses, which all require licenses or certifications. Five years later, the Department of Defense (DoD) State Liaison Office released a report conducted by the University of Minnesota (Military Spouse Licensure Portability Examination, 2017) that examined states' efforts in supporting the portability of six military spouse career fields (cosmetology, dental hygiene, massage therapy, mental health counseling, occupational therapy, and real estate commission). This DoD report found that 23 states and the District of Columbia had legislation specifically addressing military spouse licensure that included licensure by endorsement (no examination requirements in order to transfer licensure), temporary licensure (provisional licensure allowing practice within the state subject to submission of supplemental application documents or meeting additional requirements), and expedited licensure processing (prioritization of a military spouse licensure application so that employment can begin as soon as possible after submission of a licensing application). A quarter of states had enacted legislation for only licensure by endorsement and temporary licensure; and a minority of states had enacted legislation that provided for only licensure by endorsement, or only temporary licensure accommodations (Military Spouse Licensure Portability Examination, 2017).

My Law School Experience

During the summer between my first and second years of law school, I clerked at a local law firm until it downsized and I was laid off. The following school year, I obtained school credit by clerking for a Kansas House Representative, clerking for legal counsel for the Kansas Department for Aging and Disability Services, interning with the local pro bono legal services agency, and participating in my law school's legal clinic. Many law schools offer legal clinics, where students can obtain temporary law clinic law licenses and take a variety of different cases for low income or pro bono clients. In participating in my school's law clinic, I was able to take my few years of legal education and finally apply it in a courtroom setting; it also gave me insight into the areas of law that I was in interested in. In other words, I learned early that contested divorces can be emotionally draining, both for the clients and the attorneys on both sides. I spent a substantial amount of time talking with my first divorce client, who finally ended up taking money in exchange for a dirty, aged, marital couch that the parties spent countless hours disputing over. Law clinic was a wonderful experience for me in my final year of law school, and it also served as a résumé builder after graduation. Other opportunities that are available to law students that help bolster a résumé include moot court or mock trial participation and extracurricular law school student organizations, which are generally based on practice area (e.g., Labor and Employment Law Society), culture (e.g., Asian-Pacific American Law Student Association), or advocacy and politics (e.g., Women Law Students Association, Law Students for Veterans Affairs). If a student has strong legal writing skills, they can consider applying for a position on the law school's various legal publications, such as a law review or law journal, as the competitiveness of such positions are considered by employers.

In addition to extracurricular law school student organizations, it is beneficial to formally join the American Bar Association, which recently launched a Law Student Division in 2016 and is free for all law students attending American Bar Association–accredited law schools. This legal community provides law school exams and class study tips, career resources, bar exam resources, division events and competitions, leadership opportunities, and publication opportunities on its blog, student lawyer magazine, and podcast (American Bar Association for Law Students, 2018). I also joined my local state bar association, which may or may not be mandatory in your jurisdiction upon passing the bar and may also provide free membership for students. Early on, I utilized these bar membership opportunities to network for job prospects and get published in order to add a new section on my résumé. To this day, I continue to serve on a Kansas Bar Association committee and write columns for the Bar's magazine that is printed and published online.

The Bar Examination

Upon graduation from law school, it is important to consider whether the state where bar admission is sought has adopted the Uniform Bar Examination (UBE). Currently, more than half of U.S. jurisdictions have adopted the UBE, which can be accommodating for purposes of transferring a score from one jurisdiction to another (Comprehensive Guide to Bar Admission Requirements, 2018). It may behoove law school graduates in non-UBE states to consider sitting for the bar examination in a UBE jurisdiction so that a comity application may be sought following years in practice and a PCS move.

The decision on where to sit for the exam should be considered early in a military spouse's final year of law school because bar applications are tedious and often require multiple years of prior residential addresses, employment history, criminal and traffic history. Bar examination applications are typically submitted early in the final semester of law school in advance of the July exam. Military spouses can gauge where to sit for the bar examination based upon their service member's military occupational specialty (MOS), as well as determine whether the application is worth the expense based on the estimated amount of time left in the jurisdiction after an application is processed. Further, bar exam applicants should note that a number of jurisdictions have unique provisions, such as residency requirements for licensing, allowances for sitting for the bar examination prior to graduation from law school, conditional admission rules, deferred admission rules, ABA-accredited law school graduation requirements, and additional courses or skills training prior to admission (Comprehensive Guide to Bar Examination Requirements, 2018).

As a military spouse, keeping an electronic and paper record of submitted bar exam applications is crucial, due to lack of recollection of residential history and other information due to frequent PCS military moves. Further, if a jurisdiction requires registration with the NCBE (Gunderson & Guback, 2018) for purposes of completing a bar application background check, login information should be saved for future NCBE web-based bar applications. Prior to the application, ensure that driver's license and other information is up-to-date, and try not to make any major life changes requiring notification of the jurisdiction's board of bar examiners (and in the case of an NCBE jurisdiction, the board of bar examiners *and* the NCBE). While a bar application is pending, applicants have an ethical obligation imposed to keep the board apprised of traffic citations or other criminal history and life changes (e.g., residential addresses, employment changes), which can be tedious to submit. For NCBE-based bar applications, it is helpful to call the NCBE directly to inquire the name of the analyst assigned the submitted application, as receipt of an email address is helpful to address any issues with processing. Finally, depending on the jurisdiction, consider application practice pending admission so that a client base can be established and a résumé gap avoided.

Military Spouse Attorney Licensing Accommodations

Military families move approximately every two to three years, in addition to undertaking temporary or extended unaccompanied deployments (Sahl, 2014). Such frequent relocations, regular absences of their service member, and extended periods of single-parenting creates challenging circumstances that can be mitigated or magnified by a military spouse's employment (U.S. Department of the Treasury, U.S. Department of Defense 2012). Military spouse attorneys face unique challenges with military moves, as bar admission must be obtained after each move, a process that can only be described as "expensive, time-consuming, and sometimes an exercise in futility due to the difficulty many military spouses face when finding a job" (Loyd, 2014). A service member's refusal to move can result in criminal prosecution (Findley, 2016), so spouses may choose to live apart from their active-duty service member—often separating children from the other parent for long periods of time to maintain employment (Loyd, 2014).

In 2012, the American Bar Association's House of Delegates adopted a resolution urging state bar authorities to "accommodate the unique needs of military spouse attorneys who move frequently in support of the nation's defense" by enacting admission by endorsement policies, reviewing existing bar application and admission procedures to ensure they are not unduly burdensome upon military spouses, encouraging mentorship programs that connect spouses with local bar members, and offering reduced bar admission and membership fees (American Bar Association, 2012). That same year, the Conference of Chief Justices adopted Resolution 15, also urging state bar admission authorities to consider the development of rules allowing for bar admission without examination by military spouse attorneys (Conference of Chief Justices, 2012).

For a military spouse attorney, the ideal type of bar admission is admission by endorsement—based upon current law licensure in good standing in another jurisdiction, lack of disciplinary history, and a service member's active-duty orders to the jurisdiction. This is the broadest type of military spouse bar admission, which has been adopted in states such as Colorado (Supreme Court of Colorado, 2014), Illinois (Supreme Court of Illinois, 2013), and Oklahoma (Supreme Court of Oklahoma, 2014).

As of September 2018, 32 jurisdictions (including D.C. and the U.S. Virgin Islands) have adopted law licensure accommodations for military spouse attorneys (Military Spouse JD Network, 2018). In general, an attorney would have to sit for the bar exam or have a certain amount of law practice experience in order to waive the bar exam requirement and obtain a state law license (Comprehensive Guide to Bar Admission Requirements, 2018). These jurisdictions have generally made accommodations for military spouse attorneys, acknowledging the difficulty of the military lifestyle; the majority of such jurisdictions with military spouse attorney law licensing accommodations generally require licensure in another jurisdiction, no prior law license disciplinary action, and active-duty orders in the state seeking law license admission (Military Spouse JD Network, 2018). Others impose additional requirements, such as mentorship requirements (Supreme Court of Florida, 2018).

However, a number of jurisdictions have adopted provisional licensing procedure, imposing the requirement that the military spouse attorney work under the supervision of a licensed attorney (Loyd, 2014; Supreme Court of Virginia, 2015). This supervision requirement is particularly burdensome for a military spouse interested in solo practice, or who is unable to find employment in a larger legal setting, such as a large private practice firm or government employment (Loyd, 2014). An application to the bar of Idaho, for example, requires a military spouse to identify local counsel that consents to supervision of the military spouse, namely, personally appearing with the attorney on all matters before the court and taking responsibility to the court, Bar, Supreme Court, and the client for all services rendered by the military spouse (Supreme Court of Idaho, 2012). While this type of military spouse law licensing accommodation benefits military spouses by not imposing a prior practice requirement, for spouses interested in positions requiring many court appearances, finding a locally licensed attorney willing to take on the large responsibility of supervision may prove to be rather challenging (Lloyd, 2014).

A final type of military spouse law licensing accommodation is a waiver policy in lieu of a formal rule or law license. These policies differ from other states' rules in that it requires the applicant to establish a case for a waiver of prior practice requirements (Sahl, 2014). New York has a general waiver policy applicable to anyone applying for licensure; it is not specific toward military spouses (New York Court of Appeals, 2014). Alternatively, Massachusetts published on its state website a message to military spouses:

"The [Board of Bar Examiners] welcomes inquiries and petitions for Admission by Motion from attorneys spouses of service members. . . . The BBE understands the unique circumstances faced by those military spouse attorneys who must move frequently . . . where the needs of the Service result in the necessary relocation of a military spouse attorney to Massachusetts, the BBE is committed to working with the petitioner to accommodate their unique circumstances and to expedite the bar application process to the extent appropriate." (Commonwealth of Massachusetts, 2014)

While the availability of a waiver policy serves as acknowledgement that military spouse attorneys require accommodation with licensing, it can provide challenges for state bar authorities: waiver policies require the subjective consideration of each military spouse's circumstances, as compared to the uniform application of a rule to all military spouses' applications.

However, not all waivers and policies are effective. The Supreme Court of Georgia adopted a Military Spouse JD Waiver Process and Policy in 2016, and this policy received media attention after the Supreme Court issued a decision reversing the Georgia Board of Bar Examiners' denial of military spouse attorney Harriet O'Neal's application (Supreme Court of Georgia, 2018). Ms. O'Neal's application was denied without a clear rationale and the Supreme Court aptly noted that "the benchmarks employed by the Board to assess the waiver request of a military spouse are uncertain. . . . The policy makes it difficult to ascertain what criteria the Board consider in its determination of whether a military spouse has shown good cause for a waiver" (Supreme Court of Georgia, 2018). Ms. O'Neal's waiver petition was reversed and remanded back to the Board. Ms. O'Neal has been in Georgia for two years and still has yet to receive a licensing decision under Georgia's policy mechanism.

My own personal experience has been different when we lived in different states. Fortunately, my service member has been stationed in jurisdictions with established military spouse law licensure rules instead of vague waiver policies. The timing of Colorado's adoption of its rule coincided well with the timing of my service member's return from his Kuwait and Iraq deployment; my application processed in less than three weeks during the holiday season (Supreme Court of Colorado, 2014). In Tennessee, on the other hand, it took approximately six months and a substantial amount of following up with the NCBE analyst; I was ultimately able to separately apply for a temporary law license while awaiting full military spouse law licensure.

Recommendations for Military Spouse Attorneys

Challenges with licensing aside, military spouse attorneys also face difficulty obtaining employment due to the transient nature of the military lifestyle (Sahl, 2014). According to a 2016 military spouse attorney survey conducted by the Military Spouse JD Network (MSJDN, a military spouse bar association), 61% of respondents reported being asked by a prospective employer about their status as a military spouse. Respondents also indicated that their military affiliation was a major reason why an employer chose not to hire them, specifically due to frequent military moves, concern that deployments would interfere with work performance, employment gap periods in résumés, and the perception that the military spouse was looking for a job instead of a career. In a study by RAND Corporation prepared for the Office of the Secretary of Defense, a thorough analysis of military spouse employment compared to their civilian "look-a-like" counterparts was conducted, including how "observed" (e.g., education level) and "unobserved" (e.g., employer bias) factors influence military spouses (Harrell, Lim, Castaneda, & Golinelli, 2004). A tenth of spouses interviewed for the study mentioned employer stigma toward military spouses. These spouses reported being perceived as less likely to be promoted and less likely to be sent to supplemental trainings compared to their civilian coworkers (RAND, 2004). My experience at the DA's office while stationed at Fort Carson, Colorado, involved employer stigma toward my military spouse status, as I was declined a promotion—twice. Ultimately,

I was promoted, but only because my husband later deployed to Eastern Europe, not solely based on the merits of my job performance.

As I moved from state to state, I attended job fairs, bar association events, and sat in court to observe application of district rules and become familiar with local jurisdictional procedure and verbiage (e.g., "trial" in lower criminal court actually means a "preliminary hearing" in Tennessee). I found that networking within the military spouse attorney community can be helpful for finding out about local bar resources (and free local CLEs), bar application processing times, and jobs available in the local job market. The Military Spouse JD Network (MSJDN), a military spouse bar association, has a Homefront to Hired program that partners with employers nationwide to encourage the hiring of military spouse attorneys, often offering virtual or teleworking positions that can survive multiple military moves (Homefront to Hired 2018). MSJDN also hosts a Making the Right Moves event, a military spouse attorney professional development conference held annually in Washington D.C. A few weeks after settling into Fort Campbell, I contacted the local Fort Campbell MSJDN chapter and was able to meet with local attorneys to get a feel for which firms to associate with, idiosyncrasies with the state's bar application, and which bar events in the area were beneficial to attend.

For both traditional and non-traditional legal jobs, networking with military spouse organizations can help navigate employment in the community near a spouse's assigned duty station. There is a large U.S. Chamber of Commerce Foundation Hiring Our Heroes Military Spouse Professional Network nationwide, assisting military spouses with professional development and career networking within local military communities (U.S. Chamber of Commerce Foundation 2018). The organization holds regular events, including LinkedIn tutorials and salary negotiation techniques, and has established "Military Spouse Economic Empowerment Zones," or areas within the United States that the organization has established relationships with local employers, educational institutions, and community resources to encourage hiring of professional spouses (U.S. Chamber of Commerce Foundation 2018). Military OneSource hosts "MySECO," or the "Spouse Education & Career Opportunities" portal, which provides career coaching, résumé toolkits, entrepreneur and self-employment resources, a job portal, and other useful information to help navigate a career with a mobile military lifestyle (Military OneSource, 2018).

While Military OneSource's MySECO website provides information about the U.S. Department of Defense military spouse federal hiring preference, the USAJobs.gov HelpCenter is also informative about whether eligibility is applicable to certain positions (Military One Source 2018; USAJOBS Help Center 2018). In addition, the Army's Office of the Judge Advocate General

(OTJAG) also maintains a special military spouse attorney hiring policy that allows military spouses to be placed in federal civilian attorney positions in U.S. Army Office of the Staff Judge Advocate (OSJA) offices without applying through the traditional USAJobs.gov portal (Department of the Army, 2017). Civilian attorney positions open on Army posts do not require a law license in the jurisdiction where the Army post is located; any law license will suffice because it is federal employment.

Pro bono work can help a military spouse attorney develop rapport with the local offices, especially if there are future position openings. In addition, pro bono work can help fill a résumé gap while waiting for a licensure application to process, or allow spouses to continue utilizing their legal skillset if in circumstances where part-time work is preferred (e.g., when children are very young, during short-term duty assignments, or where law licensure accommodations aren't available).

Finally, it is best to maintain the mantra that the worst a potential legal employer can do is opt not to hire—so it is worth the time to inquire. As a former prosecutor from Colorado, I attempted to seek employment at my local Tennessee District Attorney's Office, but was aggressively rejected. After a three-hour interview that same day at a criminal defense law firm down the street, I was employed as an associate the following week. That being said, it isn't always this easy; when was I was trying to transition from Kansas City to Fort Carson, Colorado, it took me countless hours of filling out job applications and multiple interviews before snagging a job over six months later.

For all military spouses, PCS-proofing a professional career proves to be difficult. Add in specific state-by-state law licensing requirements, and the career path of a military spouse attorney appears bleak. Yet, with the majority of jurisdictions' adoption of military spouse law licensing accommodations, hiring preferences, networking opportunities within the military spouse and military spouse attorney communities, recognition by the larger legal community of the difficulties with following a service member throughout a military career while maintaining one's own legal career makes the prospect of continuing down a legal career path as a military spouse promising.

As a military spouse attorney, I completely understand how a career in law and supporting a service member spouse can seem like a complete impossibility. I have skipped two PCS moves with my husband in order to maintain my legal career. Between multiple deployments, National Training Center rotations, Joint Readiness Training Center rotations, and countless weeks in the field, and I've probably lived apart from my husband longer than we've been married. But, I am determined to not give up on my legal career solely because I'm a military spouse. The military spouse attorney community has motivated me to network hard, take advantage of professional development opportunities, and keep all my legal job opportunities open—no matter where the Army sends us.

REFERENCES

American Bar Association (2012). Resolution 108. Retrieved from http://www.americanbar.org/content/dam/aba/administrative/house_of_delegates/2012_hod_midyear_meeting_daily_journal.pdf.

American Bar Association for Law Students (2018). Why Join? Retrieved from https://abaforlawstudents.com/why-join/.

American Bar Association (2018). ABA Free CLE Series. Retrieved from https://www.americanbar.org/cle/free_cle.html.

American Bar Association (2018). The Bar Examination: Comprehensive Guide to Bar Admission Requirements. Retrieved from https://www.americanbar.org/content/dam/aba/administrative/legal_education_and_admissions_to_the_bar/2018_ncbe_comp_guide.authcheckdam.pdf.

The Center for Research and Outreach (REACH) (2017). Military Spouse Licensure Portability Examination. Retrieved from https://reachfamilies.umn.edu/sites/default/files/Reports/Complete_Report_8-18.pdf.

Commonwealth of Massachusetts (2014). Military Spouses Seeking Admission on Motion. Retrieved from https://www.mass.gov/service-details/learn-about-admission-by-motion-in-massachusetts.

Conference of Chief Justices (2012). *Resolution 15: Encouraging Adoption of Rules Regarding Admission of Attorneys Who Are Dependents of Service Members*. Retrieved from https://ccj.ncsc.org/~/media/Microsites/Files/CCJ/Resolutions/07252012-Encouraging-Adoption-of-Rules.ashx.

Department of the Army, Office of the Judge Advocate General. (2017). Memorandum for All JALS Legal Assistance Practitioners. *Acceptance of Voluntary Legal Assistance Services—Volunteer Attorneys*. Retrieved from https://www.msjdn.org/wp-content/uploads/2018/01/Acceptance-of-Vol.-Leg.-Svcs-Nov-2017-1.pdf.

Findley, Bridget (2016). Operation Amendment: Military Spouse Attorneys for Legal Licensing Accommodations. *The Federal Lawyer*, *63*(35).

Gunderson, J. A., & Guback, C. J. (2018). *Comprehensive Guide to Bar Admission Requirements*. National Conference of Bar Examiners and American Bar Association Section of Legal Education and Admissions to the Bar. Retrieved from http://www.ncbex.org/pubs/bar-admissions-guide/2018/mobile/index.html.

Harrell, M. C., Lim, N., Castaneda, L. W., & Golinelli, D. (2004). Working around the military: Challenges to military spouse employment and education. RAND National Defense Research Institute, Santa Monica, CA. Retrieved from http://www.dtic.mil/dtic/tr/fulltext/u2/a452563.pdf.

Hiring Our Heroes U.S. Chamber of Commerce Foundation (2017). *Military Spouses in the Workplace: Understanding the Impacts of Spouse Unemployment on Military Recruitment, Retention and Readiness*. Retrieved from https://www

.uschamberfoundation.org/sites/default/files/Military%20Spouses%20in%20 the%20Workplace.pdf.

Homefront to Hired (2018). *Military Spouse JD Network*. Retrieved from https://www.msjdn.org/homefront-to-hired/.

Lim, N., & Schulker, D. (2010). Measuring Underemployment among Military Spouses. RAND National Defense Research Institute, Santa Monica, CA. Retrieved from https://www.rand.org/content/dam/rand/pubs/monographs/2010/RAND_MG918.pdf.

Loyd, J. (2014). Barred from service: Support our troops by supporting their attorney spouses with uniform license portability. *McGeorge Law Review, 46*(3), 573–604.

Military OneSource (2018). *Spouse Education & Career Opportunities*. Retrieved from https://myseco.militaryonesource.mil/portal/.

Military Spouse JD Network. (2018). *State Licensing Efforts*. Retrieved from https://www.msjdn.org/rule-change/.

Military Spouse JD Network (2017). *2016 Annual Military Spouse Attorney Survey Report of Findings*. Retrieved from https://www.msjdn.org/wp-content/uploads/2012/12/2016AnnualMilitarySpouseAttorneySurvey.pdf.

New York Court of Appeals (2014). *Rules for the Court of Appeals for Admission of Attorneys and Counselors at Law, Rule 520.14: Application for Waiver of Rules*. Retrieved from http://www.nybarexam.org/Rules/Rules.htm#520.14.

Sahl, J. P. (2014). Cracks in the profession's monopoly armor. *Fordham Law Review, 82*(6), 2635–2663.

Supreme Court of Colorado (2014). Rule 204.4 Military Spouse Certification. *Rules Governing Admission to the Practice of Law in Colorado*. Retrieved from http://www.coloradosupremecourt.com/PDF/BLE/Rules%20Governing%20Admission%20to%20Practice%20Law%20in%20Colorado.pdf.

Supreme Court of Florida (2018). *In Re Amendments to the Rules Regulating the Florida Bar and the Rules of the Supreme Court Relating to Admissions to the Bar-Military Spouse Rules*. Retrieved from http://www.floridasupremecourt.org/decisions/2018/sc18-158.pdf.

Supreme Court of Georgia (2016). *Military Spouse JD Waiver Process and Policy*. Retrieved https://www.gabaradmissions.org/news.action?id=740.

Supreme Court of Georgia (2018). In the Matter of Harriet O'Neal. Retrieved from https://www.gasupreme.us/wp-content/uploads/2018/09/s18z0774.pdf.

Supreme Court of Idaho (2012). *Idaho Bar Commission Rules, Rule 229: Military Spouse Provisional Admission*. Retrieved from https://isb.idaho.gov/wp-content/uploads/ibcr.pdf.

Supreme Court of Illinois (2013). *Rule 719: Admission of Military Spouse Attorneys from Other Jurisdictions*. Retrieved from http://www.illinoiscourts.gov/supremecourt/rules/Art_VII/artVII.htm#Rule719.

Supreme Court of Oklahoma (2014). *In Re New Rule Granting Special Temporary Permit to Current Military Spouse,* 2014 OK 114. Retrieved from https://law.justia.com/cases/oklahoma/supreme-court/2014/scbd-6167.html.

Supreme Court of Virginia (2015). *Rules of the Supreme Court, Rule 1A:8. Military Spouse Provisional Admission.* Retrieved from http://www.courts.state.va.us/courts/scv/rulesofcourt.pdf.

The Council of Economic Advisors, the Executive Office of the President of the United States (2018). *Military Spouses in the Labor Market.* Retrieved from https://www.whitehouse.gov/wp-content/uploads/2018/05/Military-Spouses-in-the-Labor-Market.pdf.

The U.S. Congress Joint Economic Committee Chairman Senator Bob Casey's Staff. (2012). *Strengthening Military Households by Decreasing the Barriers to Work.* Retrieved from https://www.jec.senate.gov/public/_cache/files/961dd14b-9cee4110-ba83-ddd171210985/strengthening-military-households-by-decreasing-the-barriers-to-work.pdf.

The White House. (2018). *Executive Order Enhancing Noncompetitive Civil Service Appointments of Military Spouses.* Retrieved from https://www.whitehouse.gov/presidential-actions/executive-order-enhancing-noncompetitive-civil-service-appointments-military-spouses/.

USAJOBS Help Center (2018). Military Spouses. Retrieved from https://www.usajobs.gov/Help/working-in-government/unique-hiring-paths/military-spouses/.

U.S. Chamber of Commerce Foundation (2018). Hiring Our Heroes Military Spouse Professional Network. Retrieved from https://www.hiringourheroes.org/programs-events-military-spouses/.

U.S. Department of the Treasury, United States Department of Defense (2012). *Supporting Our Military Families: Best Practices for Streamlining Occupational Licensing Across State Lines.* Retrieved from http://archive.defense.gov/home/pdf/Occupational_Licensing_and_Military_Spouses_Report_vFINAL.PDF.

Part III

STRATEGIES FOR ENHANCING ACADEMIC, MILITARY, AND PROFESSIONAL LIFE

Chapter Nine

Joining the Ranks

Considering Military Spouse Life as a Lesbian Graduate Student

Karen Tannenbaum

I am a lesbian social psychology Ph.D. student in a committed, long-term, monogamous relationship with Jen, an enlisted active-duty service member in the United States Navy. I am employed as a researcher, and I conduct research with a focus on examining interpersonal challenges and social issues among active-duty service members and veterans. I met my military partner well after starting graduate school and about a year after working full-time on research involving military participants. Though my academic and professional interests center on romantic relationship research and include the impact of military transitions on service members and their romantic relationships, I never personally considered life as a prospective military spouse, much less the implications of being a lesbian military spouse currently in the process of attaining an advanced degree. Through research in social psychology, consistent self-inquiry, and reflecting on my romantic relationship, I initiated a personal journey to gain a better understanding of important considerations related to becoming a military spouse with intersecting identities using an autoethnographic approach. By utilizing an autoethnographic method, I will demonstrate that the paucity of research on combined identities of military and same-sex romantic partnership falls short of providing an explanation for distinctive experiences faced by non-heterosexual, non-cisgender, and non-monogamous military romantic relationships.

Romantic relationships have been empirically studied over decades, and an expansive program of research examines romantic relationships in the military and the complexity of uncertainty and unique stressors facing military couples. For example, current findings suggest, perhaps not surprisingly, that post-traumatic stress disorder (PTSD) is linked to relationship distress among military members (Taft, Watkins, Stafford, Street, & Monson, 2011) and spouses (Lambert, Engh, Hasbun, & Holzer, 2012). Military deployments are linked to partner distress (e.g., Allen, Rhoades, Stanley, & Markman, 2011), and reintegration following deployments is also related to negative romantic relationship outcomes (Sayers, Farrow, Ross, & Oslin, 2009). Civilian research on same-sex couples, on the other hand, also identifies unique stressors that impact relationship outcomes, including social disapproval, rejection by family members, relationship concealment, and invalidation (Meyer, 2003). Neither body of literature, however, empirically examines the compounded effects of intersecting military spouse and queer identities.

My aim with this chapter is to expand my personal understanding of life as a queer military partner pursuing an advanced degree through autoethnography. In this chapter, I will systematically explore my intersecting identities as a military partner, a gay woman, and a Ph.D. student through using social psychological theories related to minority stress, love, and intersectionality. By using an autoethnographic method, I will specifically review several considerations of life as a prospective military spouse with intersecting identities through hindsight (Bruner, 1993; Denzin, 1989, Freeman, 2004) and epiphanies (Bochner & Ellis, 1992; Couser, 1997; Denzin, 1989) that delineate my experiences as a military partner and what I expect in a same-sex military relationship.

This chapter begins with a brief outline of the theoretical framework and a description of my methodology. I analyze my experiences in the context of romantic relationships research and present specific concerns and corresponding strategies to address three themes related to intersecting identities: considerations for military partners, considerations for lesbian military partners, and considerations for military partners with advanced degrees or who are in the process of pursuing advanced degrees. With each theme, I begin with a personal experience and reflect on the broader significance to concerns one may have when thinking about "joining the ranks" as a military spouse and suggested strategies to mitigate such concerns. I conclude each section by reviewing the saliency of my experience, how it contributes to the field of military romantic relationships, and my ultimate decision to "join the ranks" in order to be with Jen.

THEORETICAL FRAMEWORK

I will be applying several constructs outlined in Sternberg's (1986) Triangular Theory of Love and Meyer's (1995; 2003) Minority Stress Theory. Sternberg's (1986) theory of love suggests that love can be explained with varying combinations of three separate components in relationships—intimacy, passion, and commitment. Intimacy encompasses experiences of closeness, connectedness, and bonding among relationship partners. Passion comprises the excitement and energy around physical attraction in relationships, as well as processes that influence the desire and motivation for sex and romance with relationship partners. Commitment refers to the decision to stay in the relationship and maintain love in that relationship. Combinations of each of the three elements produce several different types of love and can change with time. For example, companionate love stems from a presence of commitment and intimacy without passion and is characterized as a committed long-term friendship-type of love. In this example of companionate love, passion may have faded over time, leaving a committed relationship without the physical attraction motive for sex and romance, or it may not have existed from the relationship's start. Consummate love consists of all three love theory components and, according to Sternberg, is easier to reach than to preserve. That is, people ought to consider relationship maintenance strategies to sustain intimacy, passion, and commitment in their relationships over time, assuming attaining and supporting consummate love is the ultimate relationship goal.

In contrast, Minority Stress Theory (Meyer, 1995; 2003) indicates that sexual minorities and gender diverse populations (see Testa, Habarth, Peta, Balsam, & Bockting, 2015) experience stressors unique to sexual and gender identity, including expectations of rejection, internalized homophobia, and sexual or gender identity concealment, which ultimately impact health and well-being. Specifically, social stigmatization and prejudice aimed at sexual minorities leads to distinct stressors that in turn instigate insidious adverse health outcomes among this population. The Minority Stress Model assumes that these stressors are unique to marginalized groups, are rooted in social processes, and are chronically experienced by minority populations (Meyer, 2003).

In this autoethnography, I focus on my experiences related to varying intersecting identities: lesbian, graduate student, and military partner. Using these two theories, I critically examine my previous experiences with my partner that are relevant to my decision on whether or not to become a military spouse. Specifically, I use Sternberg's love theory to provide a framework to understand how our relationship may change over time as a function of Jen's military service and relationship maintenance strategies directly relevant to distinctive experiences as a lesbian military partner pursuing an advanced degree. I also apply the tenets of the Minority Stress Model to frame specific experiences linked to social disapproval in the context of romantic relationships and navigating romantic relationships with a military partner that may be unique to non-heterosexual military romantic relationships.

METHOD

Autoethnographic research methods allow researchers to use critical self-reflection and analyze their experiences in relation to broader cultural experience (Ellis, 2004). One objective in autoethnographic qualitative methods is generalizability—not to the population, but to readers (Ellis & Bochner, 2000; Ellis & Ellingson, 2000). It is my hope that readers can identify with my processes themselves or bear in mind people in their social networks that may be contemplating life as a military spouse. It is also my hope to show that military relationships are more than just heterosexual-presenting monogamous dyads with female spouses and their military husbands. I want to encourage conversation about experiences and supports for other forms of queer relationships—including consensual non-monogamous relationships with service members, relationships with gender queer partners, and other non-heteronormative relationships.

When reading this chapter, keep in mind that military partner life is very new to me. I have not yet become a spouse, though my partner and I are moving in that direction. As such, one critical element of this autoethnography is a deep examination of whether I am interested in "joining the ranks." The prospect of military-related transitions is remarkably abstract and I have yet to actually experience them with Jen. I can, however, speak to my experience as a lesbian and a Ph.D. student when describing my concerns along with corresponding strategies to address such concerns. However, as with most autoethnographies, this study is limited to my experiences as a feminine cisgender gay civilian woman in a same-sex relationship with a masculine cisgender woman in the military. It is important to highlight that my experiences do not represent experiences of all other queer military couples. I will address the following questions in the remainder of this chapter:

1. What do I expect life as a military partner to be like, should I decide to join the ranks?
2. How will my identity as a lesbian cisgender woman influence my life as a military partner and vice versa?
3. How will my identity as a doctoral-level social psychologist influence my life as a military partner and vice versa?

ROMANTIC RELATIONSHIPS IN THE MILITARY—LIFE AS A MILITARY PARTNER

In order to get a sense of what my life would be like as a military spouse, I will first provide some context highlighting key elements of my relationship.

I met Jen, an enlisted service member in the United States Navy, about one year after I finished coursework for my Ph.D. program, though I have not yet completed my candidacy exam. Jen and I are in a committed long-term monogamous relationship, and we cohabitate; we are not yet engaged or married.

Jen was slated to end her contract with the military about two years after we met and was not expecting to move to another duty station prior to her end of active service. As most service members do, she questioned her next steps in the military and considered re-enlisting to pursue a military career and ultimately opted to extend her contract by several years. During this process, it was clearly important to her to keep me looped in and involved in her decision. She asked how I would feel if she were to re-enlist, knowing that it would mean an impending Permanent Change of Station (PCS) and eventual deployment. At first, I was resistant to weigh in. I firmly believed that re-enlisting was a personal decision that Jen needed to make on her own, and I did not feel as though I had jurisdiction to contribute to her decision. She said, "I wanted you to weigh in on whether or not I should re-enlist, because your views on this decision directly affect me and directly affect our lives together."

I knew that we were in a committed relationship, but realizing that Jen wanted my input in order to take my opinions into account for her career and her future made me feel closer to her than I had felt before. Although my response was nothing but encouraging, she asked me to take more time to think and share my thought process with her. She was concerned that I was not thoroughly marinating on how her military life would impact mine, and she was absolutely correct. She wanted to make sure that I knew what I was signing up for. I told Jen that, as long as I am in my Ph.D. program, I cannot move more than a two-hour radius from my university's campus. I am still, after all, working on my degree with a full-time job—moving to another state could delay my degree (and budding career) progress at this point.

Abuzz with thoughts of long distance, uncertainty, and communication strains, Jen and I spent several hours discussing "what ifs" involved in re-enlistment. I zeroed in on the prospect of a PCS. It could mean up to four years apart and we did not know where she might end up. I grew more and more concerned with how to keep our relationship strong in the face of long distance, but also with respect to pressures and limitations unique to military life (e.g., inability to take last-minute leave or long weekends, unpredictable work hours, not communicating for months at a time during deployments). I wondered how Jen's impending military transition would impact our relationship. Specifically, how would Jen and I maintain communication long distance? How would we maintain passion in our relationship?

As a researcher, I turned next to the scientific literature about military life. Extant research suggests that military transitions (deployments, training assignments, PCSs) have salient negative effects on military spouses. For example, deployments are linked to higher reports of symptoms of depression and anxiety among military spouses (Lester et al., 2010; Mansfield et al., 2010) and secondary traumatization following the service member's return from deployment (Dirkzwager, Bramsen, Adèr, & Van der Ploeg, 2005). Moving as a function of permanent changes of station induces stress and thins or severs connections with support networks, including friends, family, and community ties (Ender, 2006; Lincoln, Swift, & Shorteno-Fraser, 2008). Additionally, anecdotal evidence suggests that military spouses struggle with limited or lacking sexual communication and satisfaction, though no peer-reviewed scientific literature on the topic exists to date.

However, mobility in military life may also lead to some positive outcomes, including self-expansive experiences living around the country or around the world (Sheppard, Malatras, & Israel, 2010). In the event that civilian partners cannot move with their service members, military transitions offer an opportunity for people in military romantic relationships to connect from a distance in a variety of ways, including social media and associated applications and video camera. Though limited or infrequent communication between couples during deployment has an active role in relationship conflict, increased communication during deployments is associated with marital satisfaction (Lewis, Lamson, & Leseur, 2012) and lower symptoms of PTSD among service members (Carter et al., 2011). Additionally, showing support enhances relational maintenance under stressful circumstances (Merolla, 2010). Social media can be used as a conduit to facilitate connectedness and improve overall well-being in military couples and also serves to provide resources to military spouses while their service members are on deployment (Rea, Behnke, Huff, & Allen, 2015), though care must always be taken to protect operational and personal security.

Armed with information about the potential pitfalls and benefits of being married to someone in the military, I then turned to Sternberg's (1986) triangular love theory to develop an understanding of how my relationship with Jen might change as a function of her military service. As previously identified, Sternberg's triangular theory of love suggests that love is based on three components: intimacy, passion, and commitment. Baumeister and Bratslavsky (1999) suggest that passion is essentially a function of changes in intimacy. When intimacy is unchanging (albeit high or low), passion will decrease or remain low (Baumeister & Bratslavsky, 1999). Consider couples in long-term relationships who may pick up a routine (e.g., come home from work, eat dinner, watch a television show, go to sleep, repeat). In support of this assertion, daily diary research shows that daily changes in intimacy (e.g., frequency of sex) predicts passion and sexual satisfaction (Rubin & Campbell, 2011). Taken together, if novelty is not consistently introduced in the relationship somehow, passion will likely dwindle.

If I were to become a military spouse and communication with Jen was inconsistent, what strategies could I use to maintain our intimacy, passion, and commitment? Perhaps we will need to carve out time to discuss strategies to maintain passion during military transitions that work for us. For example, some couples may keep journals of sexual thoughts and periodically mail them to each other. Others may feel comfortable using web cameras as part of an erotic scene. Some may also choose to assign each other sex-related "missions" to feel more sexually engaged in provision and receipt of pleasure. Yet other couples could consider venturing into novel sex toys that use Bluetooth technology to connect people from a distance. Even solo sexual pleasure and fantasizing can spice up routines and can, if desired, be a topic of conversation between couples during military transitions. Perhaps if I am to become a military spouse, my partner and I will use some of these strategies to maintain our relationship.

Another strategy that we could use to allow us to achieve and maintain consummate love is to collaboratively develop a relationship agreement prior to important military transitions. A relationship agreement can serve as a channel for facilitating discussion among partners about important relationship aspects and, if adhered to, can be used to maintain relationship quality (Hosking, 2013). This could involve setting communication goals (e.g., we use video chat at least once a week), methods for communicating even if schedules do not align (e.g., writing letters, sharing e-calendars), and, for some partners, standards for extra-dyadic relationships as part of maintaining sexual satisfaction. Certain arrangements may allow and sometimes even promote consensual non-monogamy in general or under specific circumstances. For example, some relationship partners adopt agreements for open relationships involving extra-dyadic sexual intercourse (Hosking, 2013). The decisions outlined in a relationship agreement are inherently personal and may require a considerable amount of creativity and openness for military couples. Before committing to being a military spouse, I ought to discuss these ideas with my partner and ensure that we're on the same page.

I expect that life as a military spouse will be both worthwhile and difficult. As long as Jen and I are open to maintaining intimacy, passion, and commitment in our relationship, I am open to joining the ranks as a military spouse. However, my decision to pursue this relationship ought to involve an evaluation of what life would be like as a same-sex couple in an institution that is historically intolerant of lesbian and gay people.

LIFE AS A LESBIAN MILITARY PARTNER

The U.S. military is no stranger to anti-LGBT sentiment, with a documented history of discrimination that is being rectified only in recent years. In line with general population attitudes toward LGBT people at the time, the military has used sexual orientation as grounds for dismissal as early as 1778 (U.S. Naval Institute, 2016). Lesbian and gay service members were forbidden from joining the military between 1959 and 1982. In 1993, President Clinton revised this policy and introduced "Don't Ask, Don't Tell" (DADT), which was a compromise to allow lesbians and gay service members to serve in silence (US Congress, 1993). Under President Obama's leadership, DADT was repealed, allowing gays, lesbians and bisexuals to join and serve in the military (United States Congress, 2010). However, the longevity of these newly accepting policies has yet to be determined, and they could be revised yet again at any time.

It is unclear how my sexual orientation may influence my lifestyle as a military spouse. To investigate this research question, I began by critically reviewing my experiences with acquaintances, friends, and partners who have served in the military. One truly profound experience that I will never forget occurred within a year of the repeal of DADT. I was dating a Marine who lived in the barracks at a Marine Corps base. Before the repeal of DADT, I would never have dreamed of holding her hand in public, or even sharing with others that I was in a relationship with an active-duty service member. I was reasonably cautious, and she and I would only spend time together in cities at least an hour outside of her base.

After the repeal of DADT, I began visiting her at her home in the barracks. Whenever I drove through gate and the military security guard asked about my business on base, I told him that I was there to see my friend. I intentionally used the term "friend" rather than "girlfriend." At some point, I casually mentioned my base entry routine to my girlfriend who responded, "We are not in the era of DADT anymore. You can tell the security guard that you are here to see your girlfriend. It's okay." The following day, I did as she said, and told a very stern military security guard that I was entering base to visit my girlfriend. He looked at me—at first with some confusion, then turned extremely serious. "You meant to say 'friend,' right? You're here to see your friend." I responded politely and agreed. "Yes, sir, I am here to see my friend." I was and still am shaken by this encounter. I never took that risk again and have since avoided using terms to imply that she and I were in a romantic relationship. If I were to become a military spouse, how would I handle situations like these? If we marry, will I feel comfortable walking openly with my spouse? Will I find a supportive environment? I am not sure.

To understand how I expect my identity as a lesbian cisgender woman to influence my life as a military partner, I again turned to the scientific literature related to the topic. As I previously explained, romantic relationships involving service members encounter numerous obstacles, including deployment and PCS-related stress (Andres, 2014; Meadows et al., 2016; Greene, Buckman, Dandeker, & Greenberg, 2010; Newby et al., 2005; Turner & Chessor, 2015). Studies demonstrate that generating and maintaining social support may be even more difficult for individuals in LGBT communities relative to our cisgender heterosexual counterparts. Given that an undeniable reality of military service is deployment and PCS, it is important to assess or at least discuss how same-gender or non-heteronormative couples may be exceptionally affected by changes in social support. As mentioned previously, the Minority Stress Theory (Meyer, 1995; 2003) indicates that sexual minorities experience stressors unique to sexual identity including expectations of rejection and sexual identity concealment, which impacts health and well-being. As a result, these partners may experience even more difficulties in building and maintaining social support in the face of military-related transitions and maintaining a strong relationship.

Though same-gender and heterosexual relationships are vastly similar in many ways (Kurdek, 2005), there are also undeniable differences between the two. Specifically, same-gender relationships have the burden of supporting romantic ties in a not-always-so-supportive environment (Lehmiller & Agnew, 2006; Mohr & Fassinger, 2006). For example, same-sex marriage is still illegal in many countries and anti-LGBT attitudes are prevalent even in states where same-sex marriage is permitted. Additionally, members of the LGBT community experience common milestones with respect to sexual identity development, which may include publicly declaring one's sexual identity, responding to reactions from one's family or religious community, and experiencing homophobia and discrimination (Levitt & Horne, 2002; Maki, 2017).

Thus, merely assuming that my experiences as a military spouse will be similar to heterosexual cisgender spouses may be limited. As such, it is important to critically evaluate how my experiences may be influenced by being lesbian. To answer this question, I thoughtfully and critically examined my experiences thus far with Jen in both civilian and military contexts. Again, I draw on one particularly salient experience.

Jen and I spent one of our earliest dates at a local zoo. We live in a relatively liberal area (our town is even affectionately referred to as the "gayborhood") and I have never felt uncomfortable holding hands or being affectionate with Jen in public. After admiring the statuesque giraffes and rugged rhinoceroses, Jen and I took a quick bathroom break. "Here we go . . ." Jen said, with thinly veiled sarcasm. Confused, I prompted her for more explanation. She continued, "I'm going to get a hard time for using the women's bathroom." I was baffled. It's the 21st century, and we were in the gayborhood! Although I've had plenty of negative experiences walking hand in hand with romantic partners in public, these experiences only happened in certain counties, states, and countries where same-gender relationships were not accepted or tolerated. In this case, I was certain nobody would give her grief, and I flippantly brushed off her concerns with a peck on the cheek. Sure enough, not even three steps later, a woman washing her hands made a very loud and remarkably insensitive gender-based remark about Jen's appearance. My jaw dropped and I was left speechless. I hesitated to say anything to the woman, not knowing how Jen would want me to respond. We ignored the woman and continued about our day without bringing it up. Later that evening, Jen and I processed the event together and talked through how to handle similar situations in the future.

Experiences of LGBT discrimination are not limited to sexual identity, but also include discrimination based on gender expression. Gender expression can vary among sexual minorities, and includes emotional presentation, physical presentation, and expression of gender roles (Lehavot, King, & Simoni, 2011). Jen presents as relatively masculine, and though she will get mis-gendered on occasion by seemingly harmless oversights, sometimes these experiences are indicative of a greater issue with relevance to safety.

To this day, I worry about how Jen would be treated and if her safety would be at risk if she were to PCS to a less-than-queer-friendly location. Furthermore, how will I be treated if we marry and I move with her? Living in an LGBT-friendly location is imperative for sexual minority and gender diverse communities, and is linked to various health outcomes. For example, LGBT individuals report better health outcomes in states where same-sex marriage is supported, suggesting that local attitudes have an impact on LGBT well-being (Hatzenbuehler, Flores, & Gates, 2017). Non-heterosexual military couples must take into consideration the impact of PCS location on their abilities to safely navigate public space together. Thus, my intersectionality as a military spouse and gay woman means I may experience more challenges than heterosexual military spouses. Nonetheless, I am still open to becoming a military spouse and will proactively seek out sources of support and LGBT communities.

MILITARY PARTNERS WITH ADVANCED DEGREES

In addition to being a gay woman, I am also a graduate student, and my desire to earn and use my Ph.D. is an essential part of my identity. As such, it is important to consider how being a military spouse will affect my ability to earn my degree and maintain gainful employment. I begin by summarizing my current degree progress and conversations Jen and I have had to date. Then, I articulate the questions I still have that science has yet to address.

As I mentioned at the beginning of this chapter, I have earned my Master's degree and am actively pursuing my Ph.D. My experience in graduate school has been stressful, which appears to be the norm. Among working with advisors, writing on deadlines, and making consistent degree progress, I have put a great deal of time and effort into my degree and I still have several degree milestones left to complete. I am in the process of completing requirements prior to taking my qualifying exam, followed by writing and defending my dissertation. As such, I still have a few years to go, and becoming a military spouse has the potential to derail my path.

However, as discussed at length in the previous sections, being a military spouse will also introduce challenges that may compound common graduate school stressors. A key predictor of resilience and psychological well-being in military spouses is establishing community support (Wang, Nyutu, Tran, & Spears, 2015). A robust body of literature links social support to other positive health outcomes (e.g., Albrecht, Goldsmith, & Thompson, 2003; Emmanuel, St John, & Sun, 2012; Lindsey & Yates, 2004; Shakespeare-Finch & Obst, 2011), and establishing social support from friends and family is particularly important for military partners in terms of overall life satisfaction and reducing stress (Klein, Tatone, & Lindsay, 1989). Social support refers to provision and receipt of emotional and instrumental guidance or assistance (Shakespeare-Finch & Obst, 2011) and can be transient due to military transitions. Essentially, even if military families unearth community and social support among other military families when moving to new locations, the consistency of this support network is never guaranteed.

The negative effect of graduate programs on marriages has been documented both anecdotally (there were several divorces among students in my program in my first few years of graduate school) and empirically (e.g., Houseknecht & Spanier, 1980; Scheinkman, 1988). I can imagine that marrying an active-duty service member does not necessarily reduce any of the stressors of graduate school beyond having a supportive spouse, but no empirical research has been published to date validating these assertions. However, given the unique topic of my research involving service members and their families, being a military spouse may actually provide additional insight relevant to my degree progress.

Although I am confident that I will complete my graduate school career, even if it requires living apart from my partner for an extended period of time, it remains unclear how being a military spouse with an advanced degree will affect my future beyond graduate school. How will it affect my employment?

While I have discussed continuing my current position with my employer once I graduate and my current employer allows several of my colleagues to telecommute, there is no guarantee that I will remain gainfully employed if I choose to PCS with Jen in the future. The research on this topic is reviewed at length in other chapters of this volume, but it is bleak. It is also unclear how my experiences as a military spouse will affect the trajectory of my research long-term. Will I still want to study military relationships, or will my research interests dwindle or be redirected, especially when Jen and I experience inevitable rough patches? Taken together, although I am committed to both my degree and my partner, it is unclear how my life will unfold as a military spouse with an advanced degree.

CONCLUSION

To reiterate, I am not yet a military spouse, and I am in the process of attaining my advanced degree. Although I am in a serious, committed relationship with my same-sex partner who is serving on active duty in the United States Navy, I have not yet agreed to become a military spouse, but I am seriously considering the option. This is a complex and life-changing decision. As such, it warrants careful thinking and a comprehensive evaluation of all considerations. In this chapter, I have used autoethnographic methodologies to report the factors I have considered in my decision to become a military spouse. Autoethnography is unique in that it is "both process and product" (Ellis et al., 2010, p. 1). In Ellis et al.'s (2010) overview of autoethnography, writing is described as a therapeutic outlet for authors to gain clarity and better understand their experiences and self-growth (Kliesinger, 2002; Poulos, 2008) and also as a medium through which they can better understand their relationships (Adams, 2006; Wyatt, 2008).

In this autoethnography, I used personal experience and relevant empirical support to understand a broader cultural experience of same-sex military partners. This chapter was more to me than just describing my experiences. When I was asked to contribute a chapter to this book, I was excited, yet I had some hesitation. I did not want to "jinx" my relationship with Jen by writing about what I should expect as a military spouse even though we are not married.[1] I approached Jen with the idea of writing this chapter and she was very supportive. Jen had a very important role in my writing process and we both gained a new understanding of our relationship. We spent hours talking through what her re-enlistment would mean for her, for us, and for me. We got to know each other even better through this process and became closer as a result.

Throughout this autoethnography, I have considered my intersecting identities as a potential military spouse, lesbian cisgender woman, and future doctoral-level researcher. Military culture is unique, but the military community includes representatives that mimic the American population at large. In addition to racial, ethnic, and religious diversity, the military includes both cisgender and transgender service members as well as heterosexual, lesbian, gay, and bisexual service members. The military spouse community is similarly diverse. Connectedness is an important facet of well-being and I am an active member of both the LGBT community and my graduate school community of high-achieving students. Will either of these communities have representation in military settings? Even if they do, will there be others who share similar intersectionality as me? I expect that, as a lesbian military spouse with an advanced degree, I will be relatively unique within this community.

All told, I have no idea what to expect as a military spouse. Nonetheless, I concluded my autoethnographic investigation by recognizing that Jen and I, in all of our consummate love, will be together for the long haul. I am not sure what the future will hold, but I am confident that we will support each other as I join the ranks of military spouses. I have faith in myself and my partner to succeed as a lesbian military spouse with an advanced degree.

NOTE

1. It is important to note that marriage is not necessarily an end goal for everyone nor is it necessarily representative of relationship closeness or commitment. Marriage may be viewed as a heteronormative developmental milestone that represents conforming to hegemony, particularly within the queer community, and as such may not be desired even if one is in a committed relationship.

REFERENCES

Adams, T. E. (2006). Seeking father: Relationally reframing a troubled love story. *Qualitative Inquiry*, *12*(4), 704–723.

Albrecht, T. L., Goldsmith, D. J., & Thompson, T. (2003). Social support, social networks, and health. *Handbook of Health Communication*, 263–284.

Allen, E. S., Rhoades, G. K., Stanley, S. M., & Markman, H. J. (2011). On the home front: Stress for recently deployed Army couples. *Family Process*, *50*(2), 235–247.

Andres, M. (2014). Distress, support, and relationship satisfaction during military-induced separations: A longitudinal study among spouses of Dutch deployed military personnel. *Psychological Services*, *11*(1), 22–30.

Baumeister, R. F., & Bratslavsky, E. (1999). Passion, intimacy, and time: Passionate love as a function of change in intimacy. *Personality and Social Psychology Review*, *3*(1), 49–67.

Bochner, A. P., & Ellis, C. (1992). Personal narrative as a social approach to interpersonal communication. *Communication Theory*, *2*(2), 165–172.

Bruner, J. (1993). The autobiographical process. In Robert Folkenflik (Ed.), *The culture of autobiography: Constructions of self-representation* (pp. 38–56). Stanford, CA: Stanford University Press.

Carter, S., Loew, B., Allen, E., Stanley, S., Rhoades, G., & Markman, H. (2011). Relationships between soldiers' PTSD symptoms and spousal communication during deployment. *Journal of Traumatic Stress*, *24*(3), 352–355.

Couser, G. T. (1997). *Recovering bodies: Illness, disability, and life writing*. Madison: University of Wisconsin Press.

Denzin, N. K. (1989). *Interpretive biography*. Newbury Park, CA: Sage.

Dirkzwager, A. J., Bramsen, I., Adèr, H., & van der Ploeg, H. M. (2005). Secondary traumatization in partners and parents of Dutch peacekeeping soldiers. *Journal of Family Psychology*, *19*(2), 217–226.

Ellis, C. (2004). *The ethnographic I: A methodological novel about autoethnography*. Walnut Creek, CA: AltaMira Press.

Ellis, C., Adams, T. E., & Bochner, A. P. (2010). Autoethnography: An Overview [40 paragraphs]. *Forum Qualitative Sozialforschung / Forum: Qualitative Social Research*, *12*(1), Art. 10, http://nbn-resolving.de/urn:nbn:de:0114-fqs1101108.

Ellis, C., & Bochner, A. P. (2000). Autoethnography, personal narrative, reflexivity. In Norman K. Denzin & Yvonna S. Lincoln (Eds.), *Handbook of Qualitative Research* (2nd ed., pp. 733–768). Thousand Oaks, CA: Sage.

Ellis, C., & Ellingson, L. (2000). Qualitative methods. In Edgar Borgatta & Rhonda Montgomery (Eds.), *Encyclopedia of Sociology* (pp. 2287–2296). New York: Macmillan.

Emmanuel, E., St John, W., & Sun, J. (2012). Relationship between social support and quality of life in childbearing women during the perinatal period. *Journal of Obstetric, Gynecologic & Neonatal Nursing*, *41*(6), E62–E70.

Ender, M. G. (2006). Voices from the backseat: Demands of growing up in military families. In C. A. Castro, A. B. Adler, & T. W. Britt (Eds.), *Military life: The psychology of serving in peace and combat* (pp. 138–166). Westport, CT: Praeger Security International.

Freeman, M. (2004). Data are everywhere: Narrative criticism in the literature of experience. In Colette Daiute & Cynthia Lightfoot (Eds.), *Narrative analysis: Studying the development of individuals in society* (pp. 63–81). Thousand Oaks, CA: Sage.

Greene, T., Buckman, J., Dandeker, C., & Greenberg, N. (2010). How communication with families can both help and hinder service members' mental health and occupational effectiveness on deployment. *Military Medicine*, *175*(10), 745–749.

Hatzenbuehler, M. L., Flores, A. R., & Gates, G. J. (2017). Social attitudes regarding same-sex marriage and LGBT health disparities: Results from a national probability sample. *Journal of Social Issues*, *73*(3), 508–528.

Hosking, W. (2013). Agreements about extra-dyadic sex in gay men's relationships: Exploring differences in relationship quality by agreement type and rule-breaking behavior. *Journal of Homosexuality, 60*(5), 711–733.

Houseknecht, S. K., & Spanier, G. B. (1980). Marital disruption and higher education among women in the United States. *Sociological Quarterly, 21*(3), 375–389.

Kiesinger, C. E. (2002). My father's shoes: The therapeutic value of narrative reframing. In Arthur P. Bochner & Carolyn Ellis (Eds.), *Ethnographically speaking: Autoethnography, literature, and aesthetics* (pp. 95–114). Walnut Creek, CA: AltaMira.

Klein, H. A., Tatone, C. L., & Lindsay, N. B. (1989). Correlates of life satisfaction among military wives. *The Journal of Psychology, 123*(5), 465–475.

Kurdek, L. A. (2005). What do we know about gay and lesbian couples? *Current directions in psychological science, 14*(5), 251–254.

Lambert, J. E., Engh, R., Hasbun, A., & Holzer, J. (2012). Impact of posttraumatic stress disorder on the relationship quality and psychological distress of intimate partners: A meta-analytic review. *Journal of Family Psychology, 26*(5), 729.

Lehavot, K., King, K. M., & Simoni, J. M. (2011). Development and validation of a gender expression measure among sexual minority women. *Psychology of Women Quarterly, 35*(3), 381–400.

Lehmiller, J. J., & Agnew, C. R. (2006). Marginalized relationships: The impact of social disapproval on romantic relationship commitment. *Personality and Social Psychology Bulletin, 32*(1), 40–51.

Lester, P., Peterson, K., Reeves, J., Knauss, L., Glover, D., Mogil, C., Duan, N., Saltzman, W., Pynoos, R., Wilt, K., & Beardslee, W. (2010). The long war and parental combat deployment: Effects on military children and at-home spouses. *Journal of the American Academy of Child & Adolescent Psychiatry, 49*(4), 310–320.

Levitt, H. M., & Horne, S. G. (2002). Explorations of lesbian-queer genders: Butch, femme, androgynous or "other." *Journal of Lesbian Studies, 6*(2), 25–39.

Lewis, M., Lamson, A., and Leseur, B. (2012). Health dynamics of military and veteran couples: A biopsychorelational overview. *Contemporary Family Therapy 34*(2), 259–276.

Lincoln, A., Swift, E., & Shorteno-Fraser, M. (2008). Psychological adjustment and treatment of children and families with parents deployed in military combat. *Journal of Clinical Psychology, 64*(8), 984–992.

Lindsey, A. M., & Yates, B. C. (2004). Social Support: Conceptualization. *Instruments for Clinical Health-care Research*, 164–199.

Maki, J. L. (2017). Gay subculture identification: Training counselors to work with gay men. Vistas Online.

Mansfield, A. J., Kaufman, J. S., Marshall, S. W., Gaynes, B. N., Morrissey, J. P., & Engel, C. C. (2010). Deployment and the use of mental health services among US Army wives. *New England Journal of Medicine, 362*(2), 101–109.

Meadows, S. O., Beckett, M. K., Bowling, K., Golinelli, D., Fisher, M. P., Martin, L. T., Meredith, L.S., and Osilla, K. C. (2016). Family Resilience in the Military: Definitions, Models, and Policies. *Rand Health Quarterly, 5*(3), 12.

Merolla, A. J. (2010). Relational maintenance during military deployment: Perspectives of wives of deployed US soldiers. *Journal of Applied Communication Research, 38*(1), 4–26.

Meyer, I. H. (1995). Minority stress and mental health in gay men. *Journal of Health and Social Behavior,* 38–56.

Meyer, I. H. (2003). Prejudice, social stress, and mental health in lesbian, gay, and bisexual populations: conceptual issues and research evidence. *Psychological Bulletin, 129*(5), 674.

Mohr, J. J., & Fassinger, R. E. (2006). Sexual orientation identity and romantic relationship quality in same-sex couples. *Personality and Social Psychology Bulletin, 32*(8), 1085–1099.

Newby, J. H., McCarroll, J. E., Ursano, R. J., Zizhong, F., Shigemura, J., & Tucker-Harris, Y. (2005). Positive and negative consequences of a military deployment. *Military Medicine 170,* 815–819.

Poulos, C. N. (2008). *Accidental ethnography: An inquiry into family secrecy.* Walnut Creek, CA: Left Coast Press.

Rea, J., Behnke, A., Huff, N., & Allen, K. (2015). The role of online communication in the lives of military spouses. *Contemporary Family Therapy, 37*(3), 329–339.

Rubin, H., & Campbell, L. (2011). Day-to-day changes in intimacy predict heightened relationship passion, sexual occurrence, and sexual satisfaction: A dyadic diary analysis. *Social Psychological and Personality Science, 3*(2), 224–231.

Sayers, S. L., Farrow, V. A., Ross, J., & Oslin, D. W. (2009). Family problems among recently returned military veterans referred for a mental health evaluation. *Journal of Clinical Psychiatry, 70*(2), 163.

Scheinkman, M. (1988). Graduate student marriages: An organizational/interactional view. *Family Process, 27*(3), 351–368.

Shakespeare-Finch, J., & Obst, P. L. (2011). The development of the 2-way social support scale: A measure of giving and receiving emotional and instrumental support. *Journal of Personality Assessment, 93*(5), 483–490.

Sheppard, S. C., Malatras, J. W., & Israel, A. C. (2010). The impact of deployment on US military families. *American Psychologist, 65*(6), 599–609.

Sternberg, R. J. (1986). A triangular theory of love. *Psychological Review, 93*(2), 119–135.

Taft, C. T., Watkins, L. E., Stafford, J., Street, A. E., & Monson, C. M. (2011). Posttraumatic stress disorder and intimate relationship problems: a meta-analysis. *Journal of Consulting and Clinical Psychology, 79*(1), 22.

Testa, R. J., Habarth, J., Peta, J., Balsam, K., & Bockting, W. (2015). Development of the gender minority stress and resilience measure. *Psychology of Sexual Orientation and Gender Diversity, 2*(1), 65–77.

Turner, J., & Chessor, D. (2015). Relationship satisfaction, conflict and psychological distress: The impact of combat deployment to Afghanistan on the romantic partners of Australian army personnel. *Journal of Relationships Research, 6,* E2.

United States Congress. (1993). Policy concerning homosexuality in the Armed Forces. 10 USC 654—Sec 654. U.S. Government Publishing Office. Re-

trieved from https://www.gpo.gov/fdsys/granule/USCODE-2010-title10/USCODE-2010-title10-subtitleA-partII-chap37-sec654.
United States Congress. (2010). Don't ask, don't tell repeal act of 2010. 10 USC 654—Sec. 654. U.S. Government Publishing Office. Retrieved from https://www.gpo.gov/fdsys/pkg/BILLS-111s4023pcs/content-detail.html.
United States Naval Institute. (2016). Key dates in US policy on gay men and women in military service. U.S. Naval Institute. Retrieved from http://www.usni.org/news-and-features/dont-ask-dont-tell/timeline.
Wang, M. C., Nyutu, P., Tran, K., & Spears, A. (2015). Finding resilience: The mediation effect of sense of community on the psychological well-being of military spouses. *Journal of Mental Health Counseling, 37*(2), 164–174.
Wyatt, J. (2008). No longer loss: Autoethnographic stammering. *Qualitative Inquiry, 14*(6), 955–967.

Chapter Ten

Overcoming Obstacles
A Practical Guide to Meaningful Employment as a Military Spouse

Georgia K. Jones and Lindsey Lee

Being a military spouse is tough. Deployments, relocating, childcare struggles, and everything else that comes with serving in the United States Armed Forces make being a spouse difficult. Obtaining an advanced degree under these circumstances is a heroic feat in and of itself! What most people (let's call them "civilians") don't know is just how hard it can be to find employment as a military spouse. One would think that having an advanced degree would make finding a job easier, but it can create a set of barriers not experienced by spouses with undergraduate degrees or no degree at all.

The objective of this chapter is to provide an overview of the challenges military spouses face when navigating higher education and employment and to provide practical advice on how to overcome those challenges and succeed in the workforce. The authors have both research and practical, personal experience in this area and strongly believe that while being a military spouse can be challenging when it comes to careers, it can also be leveraged as an advantage.

HISTORICAL BACKGROUND

The United States military has been assessing the needs of military families since the Revolutionary War. During the Civil War through World War II, military spouses participated in the workforce mainly by volunteering with the military units their husbands served in. Prior to 1847, Congress prohibited married men from enlisting in the military, and this prohibition continued until 1942 (Albano, 1994). By 1960, military family members outnumbered military members for the first time in history. However, from 1970–1979, the employment rate of military spouses more than doubled due to pressure to contribute income to the household because of inflation and meager military salaries. By 1981, the unemployment rate for military spouses (12%) was more than double that of civilian spouses (5%) due to frequent relocation, being offered entry-level jobs despite experience, and even being denied interviews when employers discovered they were military spouses (Grossman, 1981).

As military spouses entered the workforce, it became clear that they experienced a set of barriers different from the general civilian population. Grossman (1981) reported barriers to employment such as: being stationed in remote areas, frequent relocation, and extended separations from their spouses. A decade later, research showed that military spouses who had to leave their jobs to relocate due to military orders lost nearly an entire year's worth of earnings due to long periods of unemployment prior to and after a move and often accepted positions with lower wages and hours than they had prior to the move (Payne, Warner, & Little, 1992).

Fast-forward another decade, and military spouse employment was still a hot topic. Using data from the 2000 U.S. Census, Little, & Hisnanick (2007) compared military spouse earnings with that of their civilian counterparts. They found that male military spouses earned 70% of what male civilians earned and that female military spouses earned 50% of what female civilians earned. In 2005, based on past research on tied migration, Cooke & Speirs examined the effect of tied migration on the economic status of military spouses. They found that military spouses who relocated experienced a 10% decline in employment status and a four-hour reduction in hours worked per week. When military spouses relocate and seek employment in a new location, they are often forced to accept positions with lower pay, hours, or status than at their previous location. Oftentimes this is due to starting over at a new location where they have no professional network, therefore having to start on the bottom rung of the corporate ladder.

Around this same time period (1999–2010), the Department of Defense began studying retention in the United States military. Bourg & Segal (1999) found that military family support programs affect the commitment of military members and their spouses to the military. Drummet, Coleman, & Cable (2003) found that some service members decide not to re-enlist due to lack of support for their spouses' careers, and in 2009, the Department of Defense determined that spousal support for re-enlistment is a top factor in the member's decision to stay in the military. In order to address military spouse employment issues and boost retention, the Department of Defense began implementing various military spouse education and employment initiatives.

In 2008, the Department of Defense began allowing military members to transfer all or portions of their post-9/11 GI Bill to their dependents. In addition, the DoD founded the Military Spouse Career Advancement Accounts (MyCAA) and Spouse Education and Career Opportunities (MySECO), which provide career counseling, employment resources, and funding for eligible military spouses' education. All three of these benefits provide significant opportunity for military spouses to earn advanced degrees. Despite these programs, military spouses continued to face significant barriers to employment, specifically following relocation. The DoD (2009) reported that 60% of military spouses attempted to obtain employment after their most recent move. Of those 60%, only two-thirds found work and 11% gave up looking altogether. The DoD attempts to mitigate some of the relocation burden by offering the Military Spouse Preference Program (Program S) under the Priority Placement Program for federal DoD positions. This program allows spouses who have relocated due to military orders to receive priority hiring in government positions (Drummet et al., 2003). While these programs are certainly beneficial, more recent research shows that military spouses are still facing significant barriers to employment.

RECENT RESEARCH

Some of the most comprehensive research on military spouse employment has been conducted by the RAND Corporation for the Department of Defense. The two most consistent findings in these studies are that military spouse unemployment rates are significantly higher than their civilian counterparts (Lim & Schulker, 2010), and that military spouses believe that being a military spouse has negatively affected their work opportunities in some way (Castaneda & Harrell, 2008). In nearly all the recent research, almost all the barriers to employment for military spouses stem from frequent relocation. According to Trougakos, Bull, Green, MacDermid, & Weiss (2007), nearly one-third of military spouses must change jobs each year due to relocation. These frequent moves disrupt spouses' careers and force them to look for new jobs in new locations, often causing problems for their career development. Castaneda and Harrell (2008) found that military spouses who had higher levels of education were also more likely to perceive relocation as having a negative effect on their employment.

In addition to the large difference in unemployment rates between military spouses and their civilian counterparts, there is also the problem of underemployment. Lim & Schulker (2010) examined unemployment and underemployment among military spouses. They found that the average military spouse tends to be slightly more educated and younger than their civilian counterparts in the workforce. Because of their younger median age, they have less potential for work experience, leading to a high potential for underemployment due to educational mismatch (22% compared to 5% of civilian counterparts; Lim & Schulker, 2010). In this author's own research, all of the military spouses interviewed had a college education, yet all of them were working in a position that did not require their current level of education. Several were even working in positions that only required a high school diploma (Jones, 2013). In short, the combination of military spouse education initiatives and barriers to employment have led to underemployment among highly educated military spouses.

In addition to the RAND Corporation's research on military spouse employment, RAND also studied military spouses' knowledge of programs and initiatives designed to assist with education and employment. They found that many of the spouses interviewed lacked awareness of the programs currently offered by the Department of Defense to help them with employment (Castaneda & Harrell, 2008). When the spouses in the study were asked what the DoD could do to help them with employment, two-thirds of the recommended programs were already in place, suggesting that these programs either lack efficacy or need to be better promoted to make an impact (Jones, 2013).

In the most recent Military Family Lifestyle Survey conducted by Blue Star Families, Schiffer et al. (2017) set out to determine what military families report as their top challenges. Not surprisingly, military spouse employment was the second highest rated challenge with 43% of spouses stating it was their top issue, just under amount of time away from family (46%) and just above military pay/benefits (40%). In addition, 28% of military spouse respondents reported that they were unemployed, which was a 33% increase from the year before. One reason cited by Schiffer et al. (2017) for this increase in unemployment is participation in the labor force. Although the percentage of military spouses reporting that they were employed remained the same as previous years (47% employed full- or part-time), the number of spouses who were voluntarily not participating in the labor force decreased from 31% in 2016 to 26% in 2017. This means that more spouses want to work but cannot find jobs. This same survey found that 55% of military spouses report that they are underemployed, meaning they were working in jobs where they were overqualified, underpaid, or underutilized.

FINANCIAL IMPACT

As you can imagine, the financial impact of unemployment and underemployment for military spouses can be devastating. In 2009, it was estimated that 10.2% of enlisted military families were receiving some type of government assistance such as food stamps, WIC, or housing assistance (Savitsky, Illingworth, & DuLaney, 2009). Most military spouses state that they need to work in order to maintain financial stability. When the military member receives orders to relocate, the spouse's income is almost always eliminated until they are able to find work in their new location. Despite findings that 77% of military spouses feel that having two incomes is required for financial stability, Schiffer et al. (2017) found that only 47% of military spouses were employed. Of those employed spouses, 51% earned less than $20,000 annually, with 39% earning less than $10,000. Schiffer et al. (2017) go on to explain that this pay reduction is caused by the disruption of frequent relocation leading to periods of unemployment, interrupted employment, and underemployment. In addition, they posit that the compounding issues of relocation and heavy childcare and household burdens when the service member is deployed or unavailable, can have long-term effects such as lack of advancement and earnings growth and loss of seniority.

A recent study attempted to quantify the cost of military spouse unemployment and underemployment by aggregating data from recent surveys conducted by RAND Corporation, the Institute for Veterans and Military Families, U.S. Bureau of Labor Statistics, and the Department of Defense (Blue Star Families, 2016), and the results are simply staggering. Their research into unemployment of military spouses found rates ranging from 7% to 18%, compared to more similar civilian counterpart unemployment rates ranging from 4% to 6%. Similarly, and possibly more significantly, Blue Star Families (2016) also found large differences in the underemployment rates of military spouses compared to their civilian counterparts. Their research revealed underemployment estimates ranging from 35 to 40% compared to about 6% in civilian counterparts. They also found that military spouses tend to earn an average of 30% less than their civilian counterparts.

Using the data from multiple studies, Blue Star Families (2016) developed a financial model to determine the societal cost of both unemployment and underemployment of military spouses. Since their methodology allows for a range of potential values, they offer a conservative or low cost estimate and a high cost estimate. The cost components used in the comparison (e.g., income tax lost, unemployment benefits, etc.) are based on existing links between the item and its societal cost.

Low Cost Scenario

Using the more conservative estimates, Blue Star Families (2016) estimated that the total annual societal cost of military spouse unemployment and underemployment is approximately $710,344,000. This cost can be broken down into employment categories or into functional cost. Employment category refers to where the cost comes from (reduced labor force, underemployment, and unemployment), while functional cost refers to what money is actually lost (lost income tax, unemployment benefits paid, and health costs incurred).

Table 10.1

Employment Category Cost Analysis	Functional Cost Analysis
Reduced Labor Force Participation: $352,825,000	Total Lost Income Tax: $578,430,000
Underemployment: $266,255,000	Unemployment Benefits: $72,161,000
Unemployment: $131,264,000	Total Health Costs: $59,753,000
Total: $710,344,000	**Total: $710,344,000**

High Cost Scenario

Using the highest estimates, Blue Star Families (2016) estimated that the total annual societal cost of unemployment and underemployment is approximately $1,068,508,000. Again, they broke this estimate into employment categories and functional cost:

Table 10.2

Employment Category Cost Analysis	Functional Cost Analysis
Reduced Labor Force Participation: $352,825,000	Total Lost Income Tax: $762,775,000
Underemployment: $389,880,000	Unemployment Benefits: $228,232,000
Unemployment: $325,803,000	Total Health Costs: $77,501,000
Total: $1,068,508,000	**Total: $1,068,508,000**

In essence, Blue Star Families (2016) found that unemployment and underemployment cost society anywhere from 710 million to over 1 billion dollars each year.

SO WHY BOTHER?

After reading this information about the employment situation of military spouses, it is probably unclear why they bother at all to earn an advanced degree, especially when research shows that military spouses with master's and professional degrees earn 47 and 45% less than their civilian counterparts, respectively (Blue Star Families, 2016). Despite these statistics, Schiffer et al. (2017) reported that 51% of non-working spouses want to be employed. If childcare was available, this number jumps to 69%, and if a flexible job opportunity was available in their field it jumps to 79%. Military spouses want to work, and they want to work in fields that require advanced degrees. Ott, Morgan, and Akroyd (2018) found that the top career fields military spouses desired were medical, business, mental health and behavioral science, and education. They also found that military spouses have a high regard for education, with 73.7% of spouses stating that they believed they needed a graduate or professional degree to achieve their ultimate career goals. Military spouses are mainly pursuing these degrees out of personal interest and a desire to have meaningful employment, independent of their military spouse identity (Ott et al., 2018). Similarly, one of the authors of this chapter found that military spouses' main motivation for working was personal fulfillment and wanting to be an active member of the labor force (Jones, 2013).

OVERCOMING THE BARRIERS

In the course of pursuing employment, most military spouses seeking employment have encountered at least one of the many challenges previously discussed. Many will contend with them repeatedly upon relocation due to their spouses' military orders. Therefore, the belief may be that military spouses are adept at confronting and overcoming the barriers before them. However, the discouraging statistics presented paint a wholly different reality for most military spouses who desire to pursue employment, particularly those with advanced degrees. What, then, can military spouses do to ease employment transitions and reduce the stress associated with them? Little systematic research exists to map a clear path for the unique circumstances of the highly educated military spouse. However, we have compiled a catalog of best practices to guide military spouses who are seeking employment in industry rather than academia through the pitfalls and perils of frequent job searches and periods of unemployment.

Tip #1: Maintain Readiness

A key responsibility of military members is to maintain ongoing readiness to enact their given mission. Members engage in daily activities to ensure they are always ready to confront the defense challenges of our country.

Career-minded military spouses would be well advised to employ a similar readiness mind-set that informs their job search activities, even during periods of employment. For military spouses who wish to stay in the labor force and minimize periods of unemployment, even through military transitions, preparedness will be the key to success. Creating and maintaining a job search toolkit will serve spouses well and ensure job search activity can begin promptly when circumstances dictate it. At minimum, for spouses seeking non-academic industry positions, the job search toolkit should include the following:

- An updated résumé that is ready to be targeted
- Current social media profiles (especially LinkedIn)
- Business cards

It is beyond the scope of this chapter to detail résumé-writing best practices. However, having an updated résumé that contains the full breadth of employment and educational experiences (referred to as a "master résumé") will make the job application process much more efficient.

Social media has become an indispensable job search tool for all job seekers, but most especially for military spouses who frequently relocate. Tools like LinkedIn enable military spouses to connect with colleagues and other professional contacts and to build and maintain those networks over time. LinkedIn allows for direct connections with known colleagues and friends; users then become additionally connected to the networks of their direct connections, which exponentially expands the size of a job seekers' professional network. These circumstances enable job seekers to more readily make contact with hiring managers through referrals. Research has demonstrated that connecting with hiring managers through a referral gives them a sense of trust and confidence in the job seekers' qualifications and fitness for the job (Granovetter, 2005). Referrals increase a candidate's likelihood of being hired (Brown, Setren, & Topa, 2014), underscoring the importance of maintaining a professional network. Effectively utilizing social media may be the most efficient method for mobilizing professional networks when the job search begins. For example, in their study investigating the effectiveness of LinkedIn as a job search tool, Garg and Telang (2017) found that leveraging "strong ties" through LinkedIn increases job seekers' job leads, interviews, and job offers. That is, utilizing established relationships that are maintained via LinkedIn results in positive job search outcomes.

Given the findings described above, military spouses, at minimum, should establish a free LinkedIn profile, make connections, and keep their profiles current. Military spouses should make network connections aware of periods of active employment pursuit by publishing status updates and sending direct correspondence. Absent any direct connections elsewhere, LinkedIn may also be the best place to connect with industry-specific recruiters since as many as 94% of recruiters use the platform for building candidate pipelines (Lockhart-Durkee, 2014). LinkedIn has search tools such that contacts can be made within organizations targeted during the job search so that spouses can make themselves known to prospective employers. Like many social media platforms, LinkedIn provides the ability to post profession-related status updates/messages, share content of interest, and socially engage with professional connections. The platform's capabilities can be optimized by posting helpful industry-related tips or writing blog posts on current events impacting the field, which is an excellent mechanism for demonstrating expertise. Lastly, LinkedIn recently expanded its Military and Veterans Program to include military spouses. Through a partnership with the U.S. Department of Defense's Spouse Education and Career Opportunities (SECO) program, LinkedIn now offers military spouses one free year of LinkedIn Premium. Premium access includes access to thousands of LinkedIn Learning courses and a military spouse LinkedIn group, rated in the LinkedIn community as a source of top talent.

In addition to social media platforms like LinkedIn discussed above, in order to distinguish themselves from other job candidates, military spouses could consider further establishing an online presence by creating a personal website, where work samples or a portfolio of work can be posted. Website content should reflect currency in the field and must be maintained in order to avoid leaving a dated impression. Consider the "personal brand" you intend to convey and ensure content aligns with it (Philbrick & Cleveland, 2015). Employers are very likely to conduct an internet search of candidates they are considering for hire. In fact, a 2017 CareerBuilder survey found that 70% of employers are screening candidates via social media, a percentage that has been reportedly rising in recent years ("Number of employers using social media," 2017). Furthermore, the same survey revealed that 57% of employers are less likely to invite candidates for an interview who they cannot find online. Therefore, taking measures to control your online reputation constitutes an important job search activity.

Business cards are an essential networking tool (networking activities to be discussed in further detail later in this chapter). Many people overlook the need for them when unemployed. After all, what goes on a business card if not the business for which one works? In fact, business cards can be the most effective way to exchange contact information in any professional networking situation (and even in social situations in which surprising professional connections can be made). Therefore, military spouses should consider printing business cards identifying (1) what type of professional you are (e.g., Industrial/Organizational Psychologist), (2) email address, (3) phone number, (4) links to social media profiles, and (5) personal website (if applicable). For spouses who frequently relocate, avoid placing any location-specific information (e.g., mailing address) on the card so that your business cards will easily transfer across locations.

Tip #2: Cast a Wide Net

Perhaps the single most important piece of job search advice we will discuss here concerns specific job search strategies. The advent of the internet has simplified the job search process in many ways. Job boards are robust online repositories of job postings that can easily be searched by a variety of parameters including position, keywords, and location. In addition to housing job postings, job applicants have the ability to create a profile and upload a résumé so they become searchable by employers and recruiters using the job boards to source candidates.

Tens of thousands of jobs can be found on job boards and they are updated by the minute. The vast possibilities presented by job boards, as well as the relative ease of applying, make job boards a particularly alluring job search activity. Job seekers can feel very productive in a relatively short amount of time by searching for and applying for jobs through job boards. The problem with using the job boards is that employers often receive hundreds of job applications for a single position (Glassdoor for Employers, n.d.) and many candidates will never get a response to their application, much less an invitation for an interview. To improve the odds of receiving a response, job seekers should first attempt to leverage their professional networks to identify a contact within the organization with whom they can build a relationship. In addition, the résumé and other application materials must be highly customized for the specific position described in the job posting. That means the posting should be evaluated for keywords and those keywords should be integrated into the language used in the résumé in order to successfully pass through the screening performed by applicant tracking systems.

Given the limited chances of securing employment through responses to online job postings on job boards, job seekers must broaden their job search activity. First and foremost, spend time researching the organizations of interest. Understand their core business in order to develop a theory of their "pain": What is driving their need to fill the particular position of interest? On the basis of that theory, formulate a description of experience and qualifications that specifically address the pain. Attempt to identify a direct contact within the organization (leverage your professional network to do this; see more in the next section) and address your correspondence directly to him or her. Consider placing a fact-finding call to the organization to clarify any questions you may have about the position and inform your new connection of your intent to apply for the position. Use these initial steps as a springboard for developing a relationship with the organization, which will help you distinguish yourself from others in the applicant pool. After applying for the job, be sure you follow up with the organization to confirm they received your application. Use this connection as an opportunity to clarify their timeline for scheduling interviews and ask permission to follow up within a reasonable time if you hear nothing further.

The key takeaways are two-fold in this section. First, because so many jobs can be found through online job boards, it is worth exploring the opportunities there. However, those efforts should be coupled with a variety of other strategies, including research, networking, and fact-finding calls, to attempt to close the distance between yourself as the applicant and the prospective employer.

Tip #3: Network, Network, Network

Most employers prefer to hire on the basis of "word of mouth" (Maurer, 2017); therefore, a hidden job market of sorts exists that can only be accessed by networking and establishing professional relationships. Organizational research has consistently found that professional networking is associated with a variety of career benefits, including career satisfaction, salary growth over time, and greater likelihood of re-employment (Forret & Dougherty, 2004; Wanberg, Kanfer, & Banas, 2000; Wolff & Moser, 2009). The literature defines networking as, ". . . behaviors that are aimed at building, maintaining, and using informal relationships that possess the (potential) benefit of facilitating work-related activities of individuals by voluntarily granting access to resources and maximizing common advantages" (Wolff & Moser, 2009, pp. 196–197). Social media platforms, like LinkedIn, can make maintaining these relationships easier, but job seekers must routinely look for and attend in-person events at which professional networking opportunities will be available. There are many sources for such events: conferences or meetings of professional organizations, job fairs, local Chamber of Commerce events, etc. Job-seeking spouses can also consider volunteering, interning, or job sharing as longer-term networking opportunities in addition to the obvious skill-building and experience such work provides. When spouses are new to a community, anywhere new relationships can be built is an opportunity for networking.

Many people find networking among unfamiliar audiences intimidating and anxiety-provoking (Wanberg et al., 2000). The key to success at networking events is preparation. Preparedness includes being ready with printed résumés on résumé-quality paper, current business cards, and professional dress. Spend some time preparing an "elevator pitch" describing your skills and professional experiences to utilize as a conversation starter. Initially schedule yourself for events at which you will be most comfortable—where you will know someone, in an environment you are already familiar with, engaging in an activity you know you will enjoy. These "low stakes" situations provide an opportunity to practice and develop networking skills, making more difficult situations less intimidating. During the events, collect business cards and quickly connect with new contacts on LinkedIn.

Many job seekers find networking to be frustrating because networking activities are unlikely to turn into a tangible job opportunity immediately. At its core, the key objective of networking is to develop relationships, which take time and concerted effort to build and maintain. These circumstances place military spouses at a particular disadvantage since delayed hiring often leads to less time on the job due to the next inevitable PCS (Permanent Change of Station). However, possibly no one understands efficient relationship-building more than military spouses. Among the many challenges of frequent relocation, military spouses face the need to develop new social networks at each new assignment. These skills should prove useful for professional purposes as well. Perhaps another secondary benefit of frequent relocation is that military spouses have the ability to establish connections all over the country (and overseas in some cases). Ultimately, the goal of engaging in networking activities is to ensure that members of your professional network understand your professional experiences, know what you are capable of, and think of you first when they become aware of an opportunity for which you will be a good fit. Therefore, networking must be frequent and ongoing, certainly during periods of active job seeking, but also on an ongoing basis so those relationships can be leveraged when needed.

Tip #4: Understand, Develop, & Market Transferable Skills

For a variety of reasons, military spouses may find themselves accepting positions throughout their careers that are only loosely connected to each other in terms of job responsibilities or even industry. They may work in many different industries in a variety of different roles simply based on job availability in the local economies in which they live. While many spouses may find this frustrating and upward advancement may be elusive, the benefit is that they are likely developing a diversity of skills their civilian counterparts do not necessarily have.

Job-seeking spouses can capitalize on these circumstances by first fully understanding their skills and abilities and recognizing how these skills can transfer across a spectrum of positions. The next challenge becomes marketing that diversity of skills and experiences to prospective employers in a cohesive manner. Job seekers market themselves in many ways, with the résumé being the most obvious of marketing tools. Résumés, however, leave out a lot of a job-seeker's professional story. Therefore, cover letters are an essential, first opportunity to explain how a candidate's particular constellation of skills not only meets the employer's need (addresses their "pain"), but how the candidate will also bring additional value to the organization's operations. A cohesive statement of skills and abilities should be incorporated into the "elevator pitch" that can be used to spark conversation while networking. This pitch can also be effectively modified for use in interviewing. If job-seeking spouses effectively bring together seemingly disparate experiences on the basis of transferable skills, prospective employers will more readily see how they are distinguished as a leading candidate and how they can bring value to the organization.

Frequent relocations due to military orders may also give spouses unique educational opportunities. Periods of unemployment, although often not desirable, can give military spouses an opportunity they may not otherwise have to develop new skills. Spouses may be able to utilize periods of unemployment to pursue professional certifications or licenses, take additional specialized courses or workshops, or even pursue advanced degrees. All of these educational efforts will ultimately strengthen existing skills, close skill gaps, and enhance a career-minded spouse's ability to compete when job searching. Relatedly, activities such as volunteering or participating in an internship program can not only serve the purposes of keeping spouses busy and giving them an opportunity to network in what may be a new local community, but can also be valuable for developing new or strengthening existing skills.

Tip #5: Pursue Telework Opportunities

There does not appear to be any published research examining the prevalence rates of telework among military spouses. A recent report based on U.S. Census and Bureau of Labor Statistics data, however, suggests that remote work opportunities have been significantly rising for at least the past 10 years (Global Workplace Analytics & FlexJobs, 2017). Anecdotally, interest in telework among military spouses certainly appears to follow these trends. It is not difficult to imagine the benefits such arrangements offer military spouses. Perhaps most obviously, a "portable" career can significantly reduce the financial strain associated with relocation and eliminate the time between jobs that military spouses typically experience. Maintaining employment through telework may also mean that military spouses have many of the same opportunities for career growth and advancement that civilians enjoy in traditional workplace settings. Furthermore, teleworking often gives employees increased flexibility in their schedules (Gajendran & Harrison, 2007). Many military spouses may need such flexibility to accommodate the often-unpredictable work schedules, temporary duty assignments, and deployments of their active-duty spouses.

Of course, not all jobs are conducive to telework arrangements. However, for military spouses in occupations that lend themselves to work-at-home situations, there are a couple of strategies for consideration:

1. If you are currently employed and facing a military relocation, discuss the possibility of converting your job into a telework position with your employer. Not all employers will be able to accommodate such requests, but it is worth having the conversation.
2. Consider independent contracting and entrepreneurship. Not everyone is well suited to pursuing this avenue as it requires the ability to build and operate a business. However, securing contract work can be lucrative and would give military spouses complete control over their worklife.
3. Connect with one of the several organizations that advertise legitimate work-at-home opportunities. Those listed below specifically serve military spouses:

- Mad Skills
- HirePurpose
- VirtForce (public Facebook group)

Of course, there are other telework recruiting organizations that do not specifically target military spouses, but may also be fruitful pursuits. Some of these include:

- FlexJobs
- Virtual Vocations

We would be remiss if we did not issue a caution about the abundance of scams that military spouses will encounter in their search for virtual work. Bypass "opportunities" that require payments up front or promise big paychecks in little time with little experience required. However, the prudent search for teleworking opportunities may provide career-minded military spouses a viable long-term employment path.

Tip #6: Know the Available Resources

While military spouses find themselves in unique and challenging circumstances as it relates to building a meaningful career, the military spouse status also comes with a variety of job search resources that are not available to civilian job seekers. Maintaining awareness of these resources and how to access them may ultimately help military spouses expedite the job search process, minimize downtime between jobs, and build relevant job skills.

One of your first stops at your new location following a PCS should be the duty station's family support center (e.g., the Airman and Family Readiness Center [AFRC], the Army Community Service Center, the Navy's Family and Fleet Support Centers). Family readiness centers commonly have advisors who specialize in assisting spouses with employment. As part of this role, they typically build and maintain relationships with employers in the local economy and distribute job postings from employers recruiting military spouses and transitioning service members. In addition, they often host job search–related workshops and provide one-on-one guidance related to résumé writing and interview preparation. All of these services are usually free of charge to spouses.

There are also a multitude of organizations who support a range of military family needs, including spouse employment, which can be found online, but most will also have a social media presence via tools such as Facebook, LinkedIn, and Twitter. The following is a brief catalog of various resources that military spouses may find useful for job search purposes:

- America's Career Force
- Blue Star Families
- Department of Defense Spouse Education and Career Opportunities program (SECO)
- Hire Heroes USA
- Hiring Our Heroes Military Spouse Professional Network
- Military OneSource
- Military Spouse Advocacy Network (MSAN)
- Military Spouse Career Advancement Accounts (MyCAA)
- Military Spouse Corporate Career Network (MSCCN)
- Military Spouse Employment Partnership (MSEP)
- National Military Family Association (NMFA)
- National Military Spouse Network
- Paradigm Switch
- United Services Organization (USO) Pathfinder
- Veterati Mentoring Program

There are many employers that recognize the unique value that veterans and military spouses offer and, therefore, make concerted efforts to recruit them. Often that will mean they have personnel dedicated to administering veteran and military spouse recruitment programs. Consider targeting employers who advertise themselves as military-friendly and reach out to them to determine if they have in-house resources to assist military spouse applicants. These will prove to be essential connections in these targeted circumstances.

Spouses interested in federal employment should make use of all available resources via the USA Jobs website, including the federal spousal preference program for those who are eligible. This program matches spouses with federal job opportunities and allows them to be given preference in the hiring process to improve spouses' competitiveness for positions for which they are qualified. Installation civilian employment offices will have personnel with expertise in the spousal preference program and can provide assistance navigating the complicated federal hiring process.

Tip #7: To Disclose or Not to Disclose

Military spouses seeking employment will frequently encounter the challenge of deciding whether or not to disclose their status to prospective employers during the hiring process. As a military spouse, you should be aware of your legal rights. It is illegal for employers to discriminate on the basis of marital status; therefore, any questions relating to such during the hiring process, particularly during interviews, are inappropriate and possibly illegal. However, that will not necessarily stop employers from asking questions related to your marital status, so you should have a response prepared. Even if they do not ask direct questions related to your status as a military spouse, some employers may persist in asking tangentially related questions, such as your reason for relocating to their area or to explore the reason for short-tenure positions in various locations. There are basically two approaches to these questions: (1) decide to disclose your military spouse status as the explanation, or (2) pointedly ask them how the questions relate to your qualifications for the position. Your level of comfort with this mild confrontation and your assessment of the risk it poses in terms of potentially compromising your competitiveness for the position should inform your approach. Ultimately, as a military spouse, you will have to determine the approach that works best for you in your particular circumstances.

OUTLOOK FOR THE FUTURE

As previously identified, there are a multitude of military spouse employment initiatives, from federal hiring preferences to local initiatives. Despite the myriad resources available to assist military spouses with employment, the recent research shows that unemployment and underemployment continues to rise. There are ongoing efforts at the local and federal levels to mitigate the employment burden for military spouses, and there are scores of organizations, programs, and resources dedicated to assisting military spouses with continuing education and employment.

In addition to national programs and local initiatives, there are currently three legislative bills proposed to ease military spouse employment concerns. Although none of the these bills have yet become law, it is encouraging that there has been recent recognition of the special challenges military spouses face relating to employment by individuals who are in a position to improve these circumstances. While we await continued progress, the best strategy for military spouses who wish to maintain ongoing employment during the time they spend as a dependent of a service member is to engage in job seeking and professional development activities on an ongoing basis, even while stably employed. That is, employment prospects will be broadened to the extent that spouses: (1) nurture their professional networks by continually making and maintaining connections, (2) actively pursue continuing education for the purpose of developing skills and remaining current in the industry in order to increase competitiveness, and (3) persist in pursuit of their educational and professional goals in spite of the barriers. After all, military spouses are nothing if not resilient.

REFERENCES

Albano, S. (1994). Military spouse recognition of family concerns: Revolutionary War to 1993. *Armed Forces & Society*, *20*(2), 283–302.

Blue Star Families. (2016). Social cost analysis of the unemployment and underemployment of military spouses. Sorensen Impact Center and University of Utah. Retrieved from https://bluestarfam.org/milspouse-employment/.

Bourg, C., & Segal, M. W. (1999). The impact of family supportive policies and practices on organizational commitment to the Army. *Armed Forces & Society*, *25*(4), 633–652. doi:10.1177/0095327X9902500406.

Brown, M., Setren, E., & Topa, G. (2014). Do informal referrals lead to better matches? Evidence from a firm's employee referral system. IZA Discussion Paper No. 8175. Available at SSRN: https://ssrn.com/abstract=2441471.

Castaneda, L. W., & Harrell, M. C. (2008). Military spouse employment: A grounded theory approach to experiences and perceptions. *Armed Forces & Society, 34*(3), 389–412. doi:10.1177/0095327X307194.

Cooke, T. J., & Speirs, K. (2005). Migrations and employment among the civilian spouses of military personnel. *Social Science Quarterly, 86*(2), 342–355. doi:10.1111/j.0038-4941.2005.00306.x.

Department of Defense. (2009). Report of the 2nd quadrennial quality of life review. Department of Defense. Retrieved from http://www.militaryhomefront.dod.mil/12038/Project%20Documents/MilitaryHOMEFRONT/QOL%20Resouces/Reports/Quadrennial%20Quality%20of%20Life%20Review%202009.pdf.

Drummet, A. R., Coleman, M., & Cable, S. (2003). Military families under stress: Implications for family life education. *Family Relations, 52*(3), 279–287.

Forret, M. L., & Dougherty, T. W. (2004). Networking behaviors and career outcomes: Differences for men and women? *Journal of Organizational Behavior, 25*, 419–437. doi: 10.1002/job.253.

Frame, C. (2018). San Antonio named country's first military spouse economic empowerment zone. TPR News. Retrieved from http://tpr.org/post/san-antonio-named-countrys-first-military-spouse-economic-empowerment-zone.

Gajendran, R. S., & Harrison, D. A. (2007). The good, the bad, and the unknown about telecommuting: Meta-analysis of psychological mediators and individual consequences. *Journal of Applied Psychology, 92*(6), 1524–1541. doi: 10.1037/0021-9010.92.6.1524.

Garg, R., & Telang, R. (2017). To be or not to be linked: Online social networks and job search by unemployed workforce. *Management Science, Articles in Advance.* doi:10.1287/mnsc.2017.2784.

Glassdoor for Employers. (n.d.). Top HR statistics: The latest stats for HR and recruiting pros. Retrieved from https://www.glassdoor.com/employers/popular-topics/hr-stats.htm.

Global Workplace Analytics & FlexJobs. (2017). 2017 State of telecommuting in the U.S. employee workforce. Retrieved from https://globalworkplaceanalytics.com/whitepapers.

Granovetter, M. (2005). The impact of social structure on economic outcomes. *The Journal of Economic Perspectives, 19*(1), 33–50.

Grossman, A. S. (1981). The employment situation for military wives. *Monthly Labor Review, 104*(2), 60–64.

Jobs and Childcare for Military Families Act of 2018, S. 2457, 115th Cong. (2018).

Jones, G. (2013). The experience of obtaining employment for enlisted active duty service members' spouses: A phenomenological study (Dissertation). Retrieved from ProQuest Dissertations and Theses database. (UMI No. 3590107)

Lift the Relocation Burden from Military Spouses Act, H. R. 1796, 115th Cong. (2017).

Lim, N., & Schulker, D. (2010). *Measuring underemployment among military spouses.* Santa Monica, CA: RAND Corporation.

Little, R. D., & Hisnanick, J. J. (2007). The earnings of tied-migrant military husbands. *Armed Forces & Society, 33*(4), 547–570.

Lockhart-Durkee, K. (2014). *Social media and your job search: Maximizing your network for a successful transition.* Fairfax Station, VA: Competitive Edge Services, Inc.

Maurer, R. (2017, June 23). Employee referrals remain top source for hires. Retrieved from https://www.shrm.org/resourcesandtools/hr-topics/talent-acquisition/pages/employee-referrals-remains-top-source-hires.aspx.

Military Spouse Employment Act of 2018, S. 2379, 115th Cong. (2018).

Number of employers using social media to screen candidates at all-time high, finds latest CareerBuilder study. (2017, June 15). Retrieved from http://press.careerbuilder.com/2017-06-15-Number-of-Employers-Using-Social-Media-to-Screen-Candidates-at-All-Time-High-Finds-Latest-CareerBuilder-Study.

Ott, L. E., Morgan, J. K., & Akroyd, H. D. (2018). Impact of military lifestyle on military spouses' educational and career goals. *Journal of Research in Education, 28*(1), 30–61. Retrieved from https://docs.wixstatic.com/ugd/baaa29_b0abf1e82512461780393c22164edcfb.pdf.

Payne, D. M., Warner, J. T., & Little, R. D. (1992). Tied migration and returns to human capital: The case of military wives. *Social Science Quarterly, 73*(2), 324–339.

Philbrick, J. L., & Cleveland, A. D. (2015). Personal branding: Building your pathway to professional success. *Medical Reference Services Quarterly, 34*(2), 181–189. doi: 10.1080/02763869.2015.1019324.

Savitsky, L., Illingworth, M., & DuLaney, M. (2009). Civilian social work: Serving the military and veteran populations. *Social Work, 54*(4), 327–339.

Schiffer, C. O., Maury, R. V., Sonethavilay, H., Hurwitz, J. L., Lee, H. C., Linsner, R. K., & Mehta, M. S. (2017). Comprehensive report of the military family lifestyle survey. Blue Star Families. Retrieved from https://bluestarfam.org/survey/.

Trougakos, J. P., Bull, R. A., Green, S. G., MacDermid, S. M., & Weiss, H. M. (2007). Influences on the job search self-efficacy of spouses of enlisted military personnel. *Human Performance, 20*(4), 391–413. doi:10.1080/08959280701522114.

Wanberg, C. R., Kanfer, R., & Banas, J. T. (2000). Predictors and outcomes of networking intensity among unemployed job seekers. *Journal of Applied Psychology, 84*(4), 491–503.

Wolff, H., & Moser, K. (2009). Effects of networking on career success: A longitudinal study. *Journal of Applied Psychology, 94*(1), 196–206. doi:10.1037/a0013350.

Chapter Eleven

Military Spouses with Advanced Degrees

A Unique Subpopulation to Study for the Science of Motivation and Goal Pursuit

Jennifer N. Belding

You're probably reading this book because you either are a military spouse with an advanced degree or you're interested in learning more about what we endure, perhaps because you're considering joining our ranks. Some military spouses are motivated to get an advanced degree, while others are motivated by an idea of what they could do with that degree down the line. Regardless of the goals for obtaining the degree, it's fair to say that a great deal of work and commitment is required. Most students who pursue an advanced degree begin with a high school education, obtain an undergraduate education (perhaps starting with an Associate's Degree), apply to their graduate program, complete required coursework, write a thesis and/or dissertation, defend it, and ultimately get a job.

However, life is rarely that simple or direct. Many students take time to determine what degree they want to pursue, which may result in changing their undergraduate major one or more times (U.S. Department of Education, 2017). Some students take time off between their undergraduate and graduate education for a variety of reasons, including a desire to strengthen their application, earn income, or take a break from school, among other factors (e.g., Hamby, 2015). Once the degree has been attained, the mere goal of getting a job can feel like a herculean task. Although most graduate advisors are familiar with being employed at an institute of higher education, there are not nearly enough open positions for assistant professors compared to the number of graduate students attaining doctoral degrees, and there may be relatively little support for those considering work in lucrative industry or government settings in certain disciplines (McKenna, 2016).

In short, obtaining and using an advanced degree requires a remarkable amount of motivation, and there are a number of roadblocks that students may encounter on their path. Military spouses are a unique group that may be subject to even more of these roadblocks than their civilian counterparts. These barriers can test our motivation and perseverance, ultimately making it more challenging to obtain the goals we set for ourselves.

This chapter reviews the social psychological science of motivation and goal pursuit that is applicable to military spouses with advanced degrees and discusses how unique elements of our service to our service member and our country may force us to overcome obstructions along this path. The first part of this chapter reviews key constructs related to goals, such as goal setting, goal striving, and self-control. The second part of this chapter focuses on a unique element of personality, called grit, which is associated with motivation and goal pursuit over the lifetime. Throughout the chapter, I highlight how the unique elements of military service can serve as challenges to one's academic goal pursuit and may put military spouses at a unique disadvantage compared to our civilian counterparts. Finally, the chapter closes with my personal recommendations based on scientific literature and empirical research related to goal pursuit and my experiences as a military spouse.

GOALS

The term "goal" is ubiquitous, but it has a unique meaning in social psychology. Specifically, goals are the mental concept or idea of an end-state that people want to achieve. Everyone possesses and pursues them, but this process of pursuing one's goals can be quite challenging. As a result, a great deal of research has examined the activation of, pursuit of, and competition between goals (see Fishbach & Ferguson, 2007). This research has focused on a few key concepts including goal setting, goal striving, self-regulation, and self-control.

Before reviewing results from decades of research, it is important to define these terms as they have specific meanings that ought not be misconstrued. Goal setting involves the identification of goals that are important to a given person. When we set goals, we have either implicitly or explicitly acknowledged that this goal is personally relevant to us and that this end-state is something that we desire and wish to work toward (see Locke & Latham, 2002; Oettingen & Gollwitzer, 2007). Goal striving, on the other hand, focuses on the process by which we achieve those goals (Oettingen & Gollwitzer, 2007). In short, these two terms represent the life cycle of goals, from identification to completion or abandonment. Self-control, on the other hand, refers to direct competition between multiple goals that are mutually exclusive (see Mann, de Ridder, & Fujita, 2013; Fujita, 2011). People experience a self-control conflict when they experience two goals simultaneously in which a smaller, more proximal reward and a larger, more distal reward are in direct competition (see Fujita, 2011).

Although these terms refer to very different concepts, they are all related in that they can be leveraged to comprehend when, how, and why people are successful and unsuccessful at achieving their goals. Furthermore, these concepts can be readily applied to understanding the challenges and pitfalls military spouses with advanced degrees may face over time. By developing an appreciation of how a military spouse's experiences may introduce challenges during goal setting, goal striving, and self-control, we can begin to offer insights for how to best encourage military spouses to achieve the great tasks of which they are capable.

Goal Setting

Goal setting is an umbrella term that refers to the knowledge of how people identify goals that are personally relevant. A wealth of research on this topic abounds (e.g., see Locke & Latham, 2002). Many researchers argued that an understanding of goal setting can be readily applied to a variety of domains outside of psychology (for health behaviors, see Siegert & Taylor, 2004, and Mann et al., 2013; for consumer behavior, see Bagozzi & Dholakia, 1999).

In particular, goal setting interventions have been shown to be successful for students pursuing academic goals (e.g., Chase, Houmanfar, Hayes, Ward, Vilardaga, & Follette, 2013; Morisano, Hirsh, Peterson, Pihl, & Shore, 2010). For example, Morisano and colleagues (2010) demonstrated that students who were struggling (i.e., those on academic probation or with a grade point average [GPA] less than a 3.0) who completed a short (2.5 hour) guided goal setting intervention compared to those who completed a control task showed increased GPAs, increased likelihood of maintaining a full course load, and even reported less negative affect four months later. Additionally, Chase and colleagues (2013) showed that goal setting interventions, particularly when accompanied by a focus on values, can be successful at increasing GPAs and decreasing attrition among undergraduate students.

One of the most commonly shared ideas in goal setting interventions is that people should set SMART goals (e.g., Latham, 2003; Locke & Latham, 1990). Unfortunately, there has been some acronym shift over time where the letters have been interpreted in different ways in applied contexts (see Rubin, 2002). Nonetheless, the concept that goals should be SMART—that is, specific, measureable, attainable, relevant, and timely—has merit and can be applied to military spouses with advanced degrees in several ways.

Goal Setting for Military Spouses with Advanced Degrees

Specific

Students who set specific goals that are approach-oriented (e.g., improve my statistical understanding) rather than avoidance-oriented (e.g., avoid failing my statistics test) are more likely to be successful in their academic pursuits (Elliot & Sheldon, 1997). Similarly, students who set mastery goals (e.g., I will understand how to conduct a linear regression analysis) rather than performance goals (e.g., I will get an A on my linear regression test) are more likely to succeed (Elliot & Dweck, 1988). Taken together, this suggests that a military spouse who carefully considers and selects specific goals that focus on what he or she can do both at this duty station and over time is likely to be more successful than one whose goals are vague.

Measurable

In general, people experience positive affect when achieving their goals. An inability to see progress over time has even been associated with negative mental health outcomes, such as depression (Emmons, 1992). Therefore, it is important to set goals that are measurable in some way. When a goal is too broad or general (e.g., "be healthy"), it is challenging to see progress. For a military spouse who has relatively little certainty about what the future holds, they may be particularly susceptible to frustration at a lack of progress. By setting goals that are concrete and measurable in some way (e.g., "I will write the method section for this paper by the end of the week"), military spouses may be more likely to achieve their goals.

Attainable

For goal setting to be effective, the goal must also be attainable (Locke, 1982), both objectively and subjectively. Beliefs about one's abilities, often called self-efficacy, are particularly important in goal pursuit (e.g., Zimmerman, Bandura, & Martinez-Pons, 1992). Military spouses who carefully and selectively choose goals that are both objectively and subjectively attainable are more likely to succeed over time. For example, consider an academic military spouse whose goal is to obtain tenure in an academic setting. It is worth considering whether this spouse will be in a single place long enough or if he or she is willing to live apart from the service member for a period of time. If the answer to one or both of these questions is no, then a tenured position is likely out of reach during military service, and other goals ought to be pursued. As another example, consider a military spouse who wishes to write a paper or book chapter that is due two weeks after a Permanent Change of Station (PCS). Is it realistic to expect to write a manuscript over a move or before the house has been unpacked? If not, perhaps one's time and energy is best directed toward another goal or revising the goal so that it is more realistic under a given set of circumstances.

Relevant

One's goals and the tasks to achieve those goals ought to be relevant. Unsurprisingly, research has shown that people engage in behaviors that are more relevant to their self-identities (e.g., Fishbein, Triandis, Kanfer, Beeker, & Middlestadt, 2000). Therefore, goals and tasks that are more directly relevant to one's identity (regardless of one's status as a military spouse) are typically more successful. A military spouse whose goal is to be a researcher is more likely to be effective if she focuses on engaging in research-relevant behaviors in some way (e.g., serving as a reviewer for journals, collaborating with colleagues to the extent possible).

Timely

It may come as no surprise that people are more likely to complete tasks that have deadlines (Ariely & Wertenbroch, 2002). Unfortunately, people routinely underestimate the amount of time it will take to accomplish a given task, which has been labeled the planning fallacy (see Buehler, Griffin, & Ross, 1994; 2002). This effect often occurs because people think about the future when identifying how long a given task will take rather than relying on past experience and may thus underestimate the as yet unknown barriers that may hinder one's performance. For example, an author may expect it to take a month or so to write a chapter for an edited volume, when in reality it takes much longer because the author developed a cold, had several short-fuse timelines simultaneously arise, and forgot that finals week was nigh. A military spouse academic is well advised to set deadlines for himself or herself and allow ample time for the planning fallacy to throw everything off course.

Goal Striving

Once we set goals, we must continue to pursue them. Unfortunately, we don't pursue goals in a vacuum. People's lives are complex. We have an intricate system of goals constantly vying for our attention and motivation. I, for example, feel as if I am always juggling many goals. Right now, my focus includes (in no particular order) being successful at my paid position, writing and editing chapters for this book, volunteering my time and data analysis skills for a nonprofit organization that is dedicated to helping students from disadvantaged backgrounds be successful in college, volunteering within the military community, trying to be fit after several setbacks, fostering a healthy relationship with my husband, and raising my young son. Alas, there are only so many hours in a day (24, to be exact) and these goals are often at odds with one another. I cannot both cook a healthy dinner and spend time with my son. (I've tried—the spaghetti sauce stains all over my kitchen tell the story of how unsuccessful that was.) I can't both spend all of my time at work and play board games with my husband.

Self-Control

When goals are in direct competition with each other and are mutually exclusive, people experience self-control conflicts (also referred to as dual motive conflicts; see Fujita, 2011). In general, these conflicts involve a choice between a short-term temptation (i.e., something desirable in the near future, but less desirable in the distant future) and a long-term goal (i.e., something desirable in the distant future, but less desirable in the near future). When people choose to pursue the long-term goal over the short-term temptation, they have successfully exerted self-control. For example, imagine that I have a goal to lose those last 10 pounds of pregnancy weight, but I also need to eat a quick lunch before my next meeting. Panda Express is nearby, quick, and has delicious, but unhealthy, orange chicken. In this moment, there is a direct conflict between eating the orange chicken and losing weight, and I must choose. If I choose the orange chicken, I have failed to exert self-control. If I choose to forgo the orange chicken in favor of a healthier option (e.g., a salad from a just-as-quick grocery store), I have succeeded at exerting self-control.

Research on self-control has been of interest to social psychologists for decades, but has exploded in recent years. While some researchers cite early work with pigeons as the beginning of research on self-control (e.g., Rachlin & Green, 1972), its true origins can be traced back even further. A historical review is beyond the scope of this chapter, but several particularly well-known phenomena are useful to review as they are particularly relevant to military spouses with advanced degrees.

One of the most famous programs of research on self-control is Walter Mischel's Marshmallow Test (see Mischel, 2014). As Mischel entertainingly explains on an episode of the *Colbert Report*, in the Marshmallow Test paradigm, an adult experimenter offers a child the opportunity to eat either one marshmallow now or two marshmallows after a short delay. While different studies over several decades tweaked and adapted this general paradigm, the key concept was to assess how long children were able to delay gratification (see Mischel, 2011). Over the course of four decades or more, science has shown that children who can delay gratification are likely to be more successful. For example, they are likely to score higher on standardized tests of aptitude (e.g., the SAT; Mischel et al., 1988; Shoda et al., 1990), are more likely to achieve higher education and have higher self-worth (e.g., Ayduk et al., 2000), and are even less likely to be obese (Caleza, Yanez-Vico, Mendoza, & Iglesias-Linares, 2016).

Subsequent research attempted to identify strategies that promote delay of gratification. For example, early work by Mischel and colleagues examined what they labeled "hot" versus "cool" cognitive processing (e.g., Metcalfe & Mischel, 1999; Mischel & Ayduk, 2004). When edible temptations are directly in front of us, for example, we are subject to the emotional allure of the smell, look, and taste. This has been called "hot" processing because of the in-the-moment affective reaction to the stimulus. In contrast, "cool" processing is generally more cognitive and distant. When the temptation is not directly in front of us, for example, we are less tempted by it and are more able to think about the reasons to delay gratification. In fact, research with preschool-aged children demonstrated that when the temptations were visible and children could focus on them, they were less able to delay gratification than when the temptations were out of sight (Mischel & Ebbesen, 1970).

Strategies to Promote Self-Control

Unfortunately, people don't always have the option to remove temptations from our immediate environments. Instead, we must rely on other strategies to encourage self-control. One strategy that has been shown to be successful in a wide variety of domains draws on Construal Level Theory (CLT; e.g., Trope & Liberman, 2010). Construal Level Theory is a theory of psychological distance. As things get farther from us in some way (e.g., physical distance, time, likelihood of occurring), the way we think about these things changes. As distance increases, we lose specific or nuanced details of a given event, concept, or experience. Instead, we must rely on the gist or general idea to understand our environment. Thus, our mind-set shifts as psychological distance increases. When things are psychologically proximal, we engage in low-level construal, which involves paying attention to the nuanced and idiosyncratic details of the situation and focus on the ways in which a given situation may be unique. When things are psychologically distant, however, we do not have those concrete details on which to focus, so people engage in high-level construal, or engage in cognitive abstraction which allows us to consider the global and goal-relevant features that are likely common across similar situations. People are also able to engage in high- or low-level construal regardless of how proximal or distal the event may be (see Trope & Liberman, 2003; 2010; 2011).

Overall, research suggests that high-level construal is associated with self-control. When people experience a self-control conflict, those who engage in high-level construal are more likely to successfully exert self-control (e.g.,

Fujita & Han, 2009; Fujita, Trope, Liberman, & Levin-Sagi, 2006). Some of my own work articulates that this occurs in part because high-level construal allows us to weigh our long-term goals more heavily than the short-term temptations, thus enabling us to make better choices (Belding, Naufel, & Fujita, 2015).

For example, imagine someone who tans in tanning beds or at the beach. Unfortunately, this behavior is not healthy because it increases people's risk for skin cancer. When the person goes to the doctor, the physician may share negative information about their risk for skin cancer and a need to change their behavior (e.g., apply sunblock, stop tanning). When people receive this diagnostic, negative information, they experience a self-control conflict between short-term self-enhancement (the goal to feel good about oneself) and long-term self-improvement (the goal to get better over time). In essence, listening to their doctor may make them feel bad in the present or near future, but it can also help them become healthier in the distant future. When people were experimentally induced to engage in high-level construal (vs. low-level construal), they were more receptive to the information, actively sought out more information (that was consistent with the initial information rather than counterargumentative), and were ultimately more motivated to change their behavior. This occurred in part because high-level construal enabled them to recognize that the doctor was sharing that information because he or she was trying to help them, not be a jerk (Belding et al., 2015). Taken together, research on construal level and self-control suggests that people who engage in high-level construal are more likely to succeed. A military spouse interested in pursuing an advanced degree or finding an opportunity to use that degree in some employment setting would be wise to try to see "the bigger picture" and take a distanced perspective of his or her situation and goals.

Ego-Depletion

Further complicating matters, though, is research on ego-depletion, which suggests that people are limited in their ability to exert self-control over time. The theory of ego-depletion originated with the metaphor of self-control to a muscle. In a sense, our ability to exert self-control is like a muscle because it can be strong, but it can be taxed to the point where it can no longer perform. This theory suggests that when we exert self-control on a task, our resources to exert self-control on a subsequent task are diminished (Baumeister, Muraven & Tice, 2000; Muraven, Tice, & Baumeister, 1998). For example, participants who were told to suppress their thoughts (e.g., don't think about a white bear) on an initial task were less likely to persist on a subsequent task to solve unsolvable puzzles (Muraven et al., 1998). Similarly, forcing oneself to eat healthy radishes instead of chocolates led to less persistence on subsequent challenging tasks (Baumeister, Bratslavsky, Muraven, & Tice, 1998). Additional research has suggested that the mechanism for this effect is reduced motivation and attention for the subsequent tasks (e.g., Inzlicht & Schmeichel, 2012) as well as blood glucose levels (e.g., Baumeister, Vohs, & Tice, 2007).

Although large meta-analyses have shown ego-depletion to be reliable (e.g., Hagger, Wood, Stiff, & Chatzisarantis, 2010; but see Hagger et al., 2016, for a multilaboratory registered replication effort that may cast doubt on these results), ego-depletion is not inevitable. Some researchers have argued that individuals who are particularly motivated can overcome the effects of ego-depletion (Baumeister & Vohs, 2007). Additionally, it appears that ego-depletion is more likely to occur for those who believe it; that is, people who believe that self-control is limited are more likely to show poorer self-control over time than those who do not embrace this resource-based perspective of self-control (Job, Dweck, & Walton, 2010). Other strategies that have been shown to be effective at attenuating the effects of ego-depletion are implementation intentions (i.e., if-then statements that serve as memory cues for subsequent behavior; Webb & Sheeran, 2003; see Gollwitzer, 1999), self-affirmation (e.g., elaborating on why one's values, such as intelligence, is important; Schmeichel & Vohs, 2009), and positive affect (Tice, Baumeister, Shmueli, & Muraven, 2007).

Consider the perspective of a military spouse with an advanced degree around the time his or her partner deploys. In the weeks leading up to the deployment, there is chaos in the house. We often feel obligated to spend as much time as possible with our soon-to-depart partner, while also preparing to be on our own. We may strive to keep our routines normal, even when there is a need to go to Walmart at 2300 to ensure that one's partner has those last two to three items on the pack list. Right after one's partner leaves, military spouses may feel lonely, wishing to stay in bed for the day even knowing that the day may be easier if one has an activity planned. This is just one example of the daily experiences of military spouses that may predispose them to a near state of constant ego depletion, which makes the attainment of other goals even more challenging. When that military spouse has an advanced degree and lofty educational or career aspirations on top of all of these elements, it can feel like a perfect storm threatening one's goals.

Goal Striving for Military Spouses with Advanced Degrees

The science of motivation will likely continue for decades more, but the advances thus far are remarkable and can easily be conceptualized for military spouses with advanced degrees. While all people have complex goal systems,

I expect that military spouses—particularly military spouses with advanced degrees—are unique in the way they set and pursue their goals over time. Consider the many goals we set for ourselves. We have academic goals, employment goals, family goals, health goals, and more. Unfortunately, our relationship with someone who serves in the military can complicate goal setting and striving in a plethora of ways.

When someone is in a relationship with a member in the U.S. Armed Forces, it is reasonable to expect that the spouse's life will be influenced in a number of ways. For example, active-duty service members move on average every three years or so. Additionally, service members are often required to spend short to prolonged intervals away from home. These events can occur with a great deal of notice, none at all, or somewhere in between. Additionally, the uncertainty with which these events will occur is profound. As a result, the way military spouses with advanced degrees set and strive for their goals may be in constant flux.

I, for example, went to graduate school to become a social psychologist because I found research fascinating and wanted to dedicate a significant part of my life to it. (I also liked the idea of teaching college courses.) During my last year of graduate school, I was on the job market. We knew that my husband's first orders on active duty would land us in one of three places (San Diego, Bethesda, or Portsmouth), but we didn't know where or for how long. This presented a unique challenge for me in terms of goal setting. Where should I apply for work? What types of positions should I apply for? Was a tenure-track position feasible or even worth applying for if we couldn't guarantee my husband would be stationed somewhere long enough for me to earn tenure? If I had tenure, would I stay behind if my husband had orders to move? Given all of these unknowns, how could I set a SMART goal? Even if I did set a SMART goal, would I be able to successfully strive for it?

In addition to their academic- and employment-related goals, military spouses with advanced degrees also likely have goals commonly endorsed by many Americans: to have a family and be healthy.[1] By virtue of being a military spouse, we can presume that these incredible people have at least some level of commitment and concern for their families. They have a significant other serving in the U.S. Armed Forces. They may have children. They also may want to work out and/or eat healthy food. They likely want to have good mental health.

Unfortunately, a significant other's military service can present a number of threats to striving for these goals. For example, a military spouse who is the parent to two young children may now be a part-time single parent while the service member deploys for six months or more. Indeed, an upcoming departure may change the value we associate with certain goals. It can become that much more important to spend quality time together as a family before a prolonged absence, but it can be particularly hard to achieve that given pre-deployment requirements and workups. After departure, tasks that were (hopefully) split in some way between the two people (the service member and the spouse) now fall squarely on the shoulders of the spouse, who may have limited friends or family members to help due to a recent move. This may prompt military spouses to experience more self-control conflicts, such as a conflict between spending quality time with one's children and cooking a healthy dinner. These goals that were previously balanced with the assistance of one's spouse are now in direct competition because deployment does not come with more hours in the day to accomplish everyday tasks, even though it may feel like the days drag.

Military spouses, particularly those with advanced degrees, could benefit from several of the strategies identified by the science of motivation. First, thoughtfully considering one's system of goals can help identify which goals are truly important versus less important at certain times. For example, is keeping a clean house really that important when your service member is deployed? Perhaps it is if a messy house is a stressor for you, but perhaps it is not in other cases. By identifying valued goals, we can set ourselves up for success. Second, when goals compete, as they inevitably will, try to engage in high-level construal. Think about *why* the more distant goal is important to you. This should enable you to weigh the long-term goal over the short-term goal and ultimately exert self-control. Third, consider developing implementation intentions and healthy habits. Try to conceptualize the things you need to do as if/when-then statements, which can then help cue your behavior over time. For example, to remember to take out the trash, you may train yourself to think, "When I feed the dog and click the marker saying she's been fed on Thursday night, then I will take the trash out so the garbage crew can pick it up on Friday morning." Fourth, and perhaps most importantly, recognize that most goals are not easy to achieve and stumbles are common. Although you may struggle to strive for your goals, recognize that this is a normal part of life and treat yourself with a little bit of grace, but get back to it.

It is also worth pointing out that military service can also enhance goal pursuit in some ways. Although it may be counterintuitive, a service member's deployment can possibly induce extra time in one's day. Instead of spending time playing board games or watching television together, a military spouse may now have time to complete a great project (such as editing a book on being a military spouse with an advanced degree). Similarly, moving from place to place and adapting to changing employment may allow you to build a unique skillset and perspective that others do not possess. It is possible that this constellation of skills can make you more hirable upon the transition to civilian life. Furthermore, moving from place to place may force you to step outside of your comfort zone, make new friends, and ultimately grow as a family. All of these are valid goals to set for oneself, and thus military service can be beneficial despite the sacrifices it entails.

GRIT

In addition to the social or environmental features that may influence a military spouse's desire and ability to set the goal for and pursue an advanced degree, personal characteristics may also play a role in his or her success. Pursuing an advanced degree requires a tremendous amount of motivation and dedication. As a result, people who obtain these degrees are likely to have more grit than those who do not (Duckworth, Peterson, Matthews, & Kelly, 2007). Grit is a personality trait that may be most easily understood as the long-term stamina or endurance in pursuing one's goals over a lifetime. Central to the construct of grit is the idea that persevering toward long-term goal pursuit occurs with repeated effort and dedication (e.g., Duckworth, Kirby, Tsukayama, Berstein, & Ericsson, 2011), which is why grit is comprised of two subdimensions called perseverance and consistency (Von Culin, Tsukayama, & Duckworth, 2014, but see Credé, Tynan, & Harms, 2017, for results of a meta-analysis suggesting that many of the effects of grit are due to perseverance).

People with grit are more likely to complete challenging goals despite obstacles and setbacks (Duckworth & Gross, 2014). For example, grit is associated with happiness and satisfaction with life in general (e.g., Singh & Jha, 2008). The mechanism behind this effect has been attributed to the different means by which people pursue happiness. For example, Seligman (2002; 2011) has suggested that people can pursue happiness by fostering a sense of meaning, experiencing flow, and pursuing pleasure. When one derives happiness from a sense of meaning (e.g., volunteering, making others' lives better) and experiencing flow (i.e., a state of being fully subsumed into an activity where one barely seems to notice the passage of time; Csikszentmihalyi, 1988), those who score higher in grit are more likely to be happy (Von Culin et al., 2014). However, for those who derive happiness by pursuing pleasure from transient activities or experiences, those with less grit tend to be happier because they engage in more varied behavior over time (Von Culin et al., 2014).

More specifically, grit has also been associated with academic pursuits as well. In a study of 4,813 high school students from the Chicago Public School system, grit measured during junior year was positively associated with likelihood of graduating from high school (Eskries-Winkler, Shulman, Beal, & Duckworth, 2014, Study 3). This pattern of results held even when controlling for conscientiousness and motivation to do well in school, a variety of situational factors (e.g., perceived safety in school), standardized achievement test scores, and demographic variables (e.g., socioeconomic status). Furthermore, grit was also associated with higher GPAs and likelihood of graduating from college (Duckworth et al., 2007).

Similarly, several studies have shown grit to be positively associated with education and training among military samples. For example, students at the United States Military Academy, West Point, who scored higher (versus lower) in grit were less likely to drop out during the particularly strenuous first summer of training (Duckworth et al., 2007, Studies 4 & 5). These results were further replicated in other studies (Maddi, Matthews, Kelly, Villarreal, & White, 2012). Additionally, Eskreis-Winkler and colleagues (2014, Study 1) also demonstrated that grittier soldiers were more likely to complete an Army Special Operations Forces (ARSOF) course.

In addition to happiness, satisfaction with life, and academic pursuits, grit has also been positively associated with employment and relationship quality. For example, in a prospective longitudinal study of sales staff at a vacation ownership corporation, grittier sales staff were more likely to be working for the company six months later than their less gritty counterparts (Eskries-Winkler, et al., 2014, Study 2). Furthermore, grit may be positively associated with relationship quality over time. For example, grit was negatively associated with divorce among men (Eskries-Winkler et al., 2014, Study 4).[2] Taken together, grit may be more important for success than other personality characteristics (see Duckworth et al., 2007; Eskreis-Winkler et al., 2014; but see Maddi et al., 2012 for a contrasting view).

A very plausible conjecture is that military spouses with advanced degrees possess more grit than both their civilian counterparts and fellow military spouses. As I discussed in the beginning of this chapter, pursuing an advanced degree requires a tremendous amount of effort. Those who succeed likely do so in part because they have the perseverance and consistency required to continue exerting self-control and pursuing their goals over time. Additionally, I doubt a single military spouse would say that being married to someone in the U.S. Armed Forces is easy. It requires grit to constantly adapt to the ever-changing landscape of our service member's occupational obligations. Those who are considering a future as a military spouse with an advanced degree, whether they're already a military spouse and are considering pursuing a new degree or whether they have their degree and are considering a committed relationship with someone in the military, should have plenty of grit.

Although grit is considered a personality characteristic, some researchers argue that grit can be developed over time (see Hochanadel & Finamore, 2015). For example, grit increases with age (Duckworth & Eskries-Winkler, 2013). One postulated means by which grit can be developed draws on the idea of incremental mind-sets (see Dweck, 1999). Carol Dweck, one of the leading researchers in this field, argues that people can have one of two mind-sets when it comes to goals: an incremental theory or an entity theory. Those with incremental theories of intelligence fundamentally believe that they can continue to develop and increase their intelligence over time, while those with entity mind-sets believe that they have a set amount of intelligence and additional effort will yield minimal results (Dweck, 1999). When faced with setbacks in goal pursuit, those with incremental mind-sets are better able to adjust, continue exerting effort, and are more likely to achieve their goals (Hochanadel & Finamore, 2015). For this reason, military spouses with advanced degrees are encouraged to embrace an incremental theory and be grittier than their counterparts.

PERSONAL RECOMMENDATIONS

Throughout this chapter, I have reviewed a small selection of reasons why pursuing an advanced degree and career associated with it is challenging for military spouses. Nonetheless, it is important to recognize that although this path is nearly always difficult, there are many spouses who have made it work. With proper goal setting, goal striving, grit, and ultimately faith in oneself, I believe that any military spouse can achieve his/her goals. The following is a list of concepts and advice that I have found helpful in my time as a graduate student, researcher, and military spouse.

1. It's important to remember that life is tough. As a military spouse pursuing an advanced degree and career, you will encounter barriers. Struggling with and ultimately succumbing to these challenges is not the metric of your success as a person or as an academic. A better metric of success is how you respond to challenges.

    Consider a situation in which you are confronted with negative feedback, such as comments from an advisor on your dissertation. As previously articulated, this negative feedback can present you with a self-control conflict between short-term self-protection motivation in which you want to dismiss the feedback because it makes you feel bad about yourself and long-term self-improvement (Belding et al., 2015). So, when presented with challenges, think not that the challenge itself means you have failed, but rather that you have a unique opportunity to improve. Give yourself credit for having gotten as far as you have and then keep going. In short, be as gritty as sandpaper!

2. Prioritize your work in whatever form it may be. There are always opportunities to make use of your remarkable knowledge and skillsets if you make it a priority in your life. Through less than ideal duty stations, deployments in which everything seems to be going wrong, and the near-constant changing environments military spouses endure, treat each roadblock as an opportunity to grow and improve. These ideas are consistent with Carol Dweck's work on mind-sets (Dweck, 1999). In fact, research has shown that those with incremental mind-sets (vs. entity mind-sets) respond better to negative feedback (e.g., Yeager & Dweck, 2012).

As you encounter roadblocks, do your best to see opportunities to improve. Even if you must resign from one job as you prepare to move yet again, consider whether there are other opportunities in this new place. If you are in a remote location with relatively little hope of finding the type of job that you desire, can you find another way to hone your skills and add to your CV or résumé? For example, if your goal is an academic position, can you do some freelance work for a textbook publishing company, teach online classes, work toward developing new classes, or perhaps even use the time to craft new teaching materials for others? Can you perhaps volunteer for editorial positions or positions within a scholarly society relevant to your discipline? If your passion is research, can you work on finishing up some papers for data you've already collected or perhaps consider writing that literature review you thought the field needed? Furthermore, are there opportunities to volunteer that will help fill a gap on your résumé/CV?

3. Related to the idea of being open to new opportunities, be open to different ways to conceptualize your experiences as evidence of your skills. Just because the job you had for those two or three years in Twentynine Palms wasn't a position at a college or university doesn't mean it wasn't valuable! When you take advantage of what others may consider nontraditional work experience, it may be hard to create a résumé or CV that sells your skills. If you are committed to being a professor at a college or university but take time to work for a nonprofit for a couple years at a remote duty station, how can you conceptualize the skills you used at that nonprofit as relevant to academia? Did you engage in critical thinking, conduct literature reviews, identify knowledge gaps, etc.?

Although it may be difficult to flexibly construe your skills and activities this way, keep in mind that there are a wealth of resources for military spouses with regard to employment, including career counselors at key family support centers (e.g., Fleet and Family Support Center for Navy spouses) who can help you think through a variety of ways to portray your skills and experiences.

4. Do your best to keep your own expectations both realistic and optimistic. While military spouses often have very limited knowledge of what the future holds, we do know that everything will change and probably sooner than we'd like. The field of psychology has a wealth of information about the importance of our expectations on behavior that is beyond the scope of this chapter (see Olson, Roese, & Zanna, 1996). For example, decades of research on self-fulfilling prophecies suggest that our expectations may become reality in part because they change our behavior, which results in a change in behavior in those we deal with, which subsequently validates our expectations (e.g., Jussim, 1986). For example, if a military spouse believes that he will not be able to find a job at that next duty station, he may not put as much time into updating and polishing his résumé or applying for positions. As a result, he's unlikely to be hired at that duty station. On the other hand, someone who believes that he will find a job will continue dedicating time to sending in applications, convey a sense of confidence during interviews, and ultimately land a position. This is why it is essential to be both realistic and optimistic.

CONCLUSION

In this chapter, I have reviewed research from social psychology on goal pursuit and motivation and posited that military spouses are in a unique position when it comes to developing and utilizing their skillset. Although the path to a graduate degree is rarely straightforward and easy, military spouses may encounter even more roadblocks than our civilian counterparts. These obstructions may test a military spouse's commitment to or certainty in his or her goals. Nonetheless, military spouses are likely grittier than their civilian counterparts if for no other reason than to be a military spouse requires being married to someone in the Armed Forces, which is tough (see Karney & Crown, 2007). Military spouses may be particularly likely to abandoning unimportant goals while simultaneously discovering and prioritizing valued goals. Taken together, while military spouses with advanced degrees are likely to struggle as they pursue their academic and career goals, they can be successful in general and perhaps even more so than their civilian counterparts under the right circumstances.

NOTES

1. The proposition that Americans likely share a goal to be healthy may seem idealistic given our remarkable propensity to be obese. While this is true, my argument here is that very few, if any, of us say, "I want to be diseased" or "I want to be injured."
2. It is unclear why these results did not hold for women in this study. The researchers suggested that it could be due to the idea that men may find it harder to remain married to women than the opposite, but there is no data to date which supports this hypothesis.

REFERENCES

Ariely, D., & Wertenbroch, K. (2002). Procrastination, deadlines, and performance: Self-control by precommitment. *Psychological Science, 13*(3), 219–224. doi: 10.1111/1467-9280.00441.

Ayduk, O., Mendoza-Denton, R., Mischel, W., Downey, G., Peake, P. K., & Rodriguez, M. (2000). Regulating the interpersonal self: Strategic self-regulation for coping with rejection sensitivity. *Journal of Personality and Social Psychology, 79*(5), 776–792. doi:10.1037/0022-3514.79.5.776.

Bagozzi, R. P., & Dholakia, U. (1999). Goal setting and goal striving in consumer behavior. *Journal of Marketing, 63*, 19–32. doi:10.2307/1252098.

Baumeister, R. F., Bratslavsky, E., Muraven, M., & Tice, D. M. (1998). Ego depletion: Is the active self a limited resource? *Journal of Personality and Social Psychology, 74*(5), 1252–1265.

Baumeister, R. F., Muraven, M., & Tice, D. M. (2000). Ego depletion: A resource model of volition, self-regulation, and controlled processing. *Social Cognition, 18*(2), 130–150. doi:10.1521/soco.2000.18.2.130.

Baumeister, R. F., & Vohs, K. D. (2007). Self-regulation, ego depletion, and motivation. *Social and Personality Psychology Compass, 1*, 1–14. doi:10.1111/j.1751-9004.2007.00001.x.

Baumeister, R. F., Vohs, K. D., & Tice, D. M. (2007). The strength model of self-control. *Current Directions in Psychological Science, 16*(6), 351–355. doi:10.1111/j.1467-8721.2007.00534.x.

Belding, J. N., Naufel, K. Z., & Fujita, K. (2015). Using high-level construals and perceptions of changeability to promote self-change over self-protection motives in response to negative feedback. *Personality and Social Psychology Bulletin, 41*(6), 822–838. doi:10.1177/0146167215580776.

Buehler, R., Griffin, D., & Ross, M. (1994). Exploring the "planning fallacy": Why people underestimate their task completion times. *Journal of Personality and Social Psychology, 67*(3), 366–381.

Buehler, R., Griffin, D., & Ross, M. (2002). Inside the planning fallacy: The causes and consequences of optimistic time predictions. In T. Gilovich, D. Griffin, &

D. Kahneman (Eds.), *Heuristics and biases: The psychology of intuitive judgment* (pp. 250–270). New York, NY: Cambridge University Press. doi:10.1017/CBO9780511808098.016.

Caleza, C., Yanez-Vico, R. M., Mendoza, A., & Iglesias-Linares, A. (2016). Childhood obesity and delayed gratification behavior: A systematic review of experimental studies. *The Journal of Pediatrics, 169*, 201–207. doi:10.1016/j.jpeds.2015.10.008.

Chase, J. A., Houmanfar, R., Hayes, S. C., Ward, T. A., Vilardaga, J. P., & Follette, V. (2013). Values are not goals: Online ACT-based values training adds to goal setting in improving undergraduate college student performance. *Journal of Contextual Behavioral Science, 2*(3–4), 79–84. doi:10.1016/j.jcbs.2013.08.002.

Credé, M., Tynan, M. C., & Harms, P. D. (2017). Much ado about grit: A meta-analytic synthesis of the grit literature. *Journal of Personality and Social Psychology, 113*(3), 492–511. doi:10.1037/pspp0000102.

Csikszentmihalyi, M. (1988). The flow experience and its significance for human psychology. In M. Csikszentmihalyi & I. S. Csikszentmihalyi (Eds.), *Optimal experience: Psychological studies of flow in consciousness* (pp. 15–35). New York, NY: Cambridge University Press.

Duckworth, A., & Eskreis-Winkler, L. (2013). True grit. *Observer, 26*, 4.

Duckworth, A., & Gross, J. J. (2014). Self-control and grit: Related but separate determinants of success. *Current Directions in Psychological Science, 23*(5), 319–325. doi:10.1177/0963721414541462.

Duckworth, A. L., Kirby, T. A., Tsukayama, E., Berstein, H., & Ericsson, K. A. (2011). Deliberate practice spells success: Why grittier competitors triumph at the national spelling bee. *Social Psychology & Personality Science, 2*, 174–181. doi:10.1177/1948550610385872.

Duckworth, A. L., Peterson, C., Matthews, M. D., & Kelly, D. R. (2007). Grit: Perseverence and passion for long-term goals. *Journal of Personality and Social Psychology, 92*(6), 1087–1101. doi:10.1037/0022-3514.92.6.1087.

Dweck, C. S. (1999). *Self-theories: Their role in motivation, personality and development*. Philadelphia, PA: Taylor & Francis.

Elliott, E. S., & Dweck, C. S. (1988). Goals: An approach to motivation and achievement. *Journal of Personality and Social Psychology, 54*(1), 5–12.

Elliot, A. J., & Sheldon, K. M. (1997). Avoidance achievement motivation: A personal goals analysis. *Journal of Personality and Social Psychology, 73*(1), 171–185.

Emmons, R. A. (1992). Abstract versus concrete goals: Personal striving level, physical illness, and psychological well-being. *Journal of Personality and Social Psychology, 62*(2), 292–300. doi:10.1037/0022-3514.62.2.292.

Eskreis-Winkler, L., Shulman, E. P., Beal, S. A., & Duckworth, A. L. (2014). The grit effect: Predicting retention in the military, workplace, school, and marriage. *Frontiers in Psychology, 5*, 1–12. doi:10.3389/fpsyg.2014.00036.

Fishbach, A., & Ferguson, M. J. (2007). The goal construct in social psychology. In A. W. Kruglanski & E. T. Higgins (Eds.) *Social psychology: Handbook of basic principles* (pp. 490–515). New York, NY: Guilford Press.

Fishbein, M., Triandis, H. C., Kanfer, F. H., Becker, M., & Middlestadt, S. E. (2000). Factors influencing behavior change. In *Handbook of Health Psychology*, Baum, A. S., Revenson, T. A., & Singer, J. E. (Eds.). Mahwah, NJ: Lawrence Erlbaum.

Fujita, K. (2011). On conceptualizing self-control as more than effortful inhibition of impulses. *Personality and Social Psychology Review*, *15*(4), 352–366. doi:10.1177/1088868311411165.

Fujita, K., & Han, H. A. (2009). Moving beyond deliberative control of impulses: The effect of construal levels on evaluative associations in self-control conflicts. *Psychological Science*, *20*(7), 799–804. doi:10.1111/j.1467-9280.2009.02372.x.

Fujita, K., Trope, Y., Liberman, N., & Levin-Sagi, M. (2006). Construal levels and self-control. *Journal of Personality and Social Psychology*, *90*(3), 351–367. doi: 10.1037/0022-3514.90.3.351.

Gollwitzer, P. M. (1999). Implementation intentions: Strong effects of simple plans. *American Psychologist*, *54*(7), 493–503.

Hagger, M. S., Chatzisarantis, N. L. D., Alberts, H., Anggono, C. O., Batailler, C., Birt, A. R., . . . Zwienenberg, M. (2016). A multilab preregistered replication of the ego-depletion effect. *Perspectives on Psychological Science*, *11*, 546–573. doi: 10.1177/1745691616652873.

Hagger, M. S., Wood, C., Stiff, C., & Chatzisarantis, N. L. D. (2010). Ego depletion and the strength model of self-control: A meta-analysis. *Psychological Bulletin*, *136*(4), 495–525. doi:10.1037/a0019486.

Hamby, S. (2015, July 28). Should you take a gap year before grad school? [Blog post]. Retrieved from https://www.psychologytoday.com/us/blog/the-web-violence/201507/should-you-take-gap-year-grad-school.

Hochanadel, A., & Finamore, D. (2015). Fixed and growth mindsets in education and how grit helps students persist in the face of adversity. *Journal of International Education Research*, *11*(1), 47–50.

Inzlicht, M., & Schmeichel, B. J. (2012). What is ego depletion? Toward a mechanistic revision of the resource model of self-control. *Perspectives on Psychological Science*, *7*(5), 450–463. doi:10.1177/1745691612454134.

Job, V., Dweck, C. S., & Walton, G. M. (2010). Ego depletion—Is it all in your head? Implicit theories about willpower affect self-regulation. *Psychological Science*, *21*(11), 1686–1693. doi:10.1177/0956797610384745.

Jussim, L. (1986). Self-fulfilling prophecies: A theoretical and integrative review. *Psychological Review*, *93*(4), 429–445.

Karney, B. R., & Crown, J. S. (2007). Families under stress: An assessment of data, theory, and research on marriage and divorce in the military. Santa Monica, CA: RAND Corporation.

Latham, G. P. (2003). Goal setting: A five-step approach to behavior change. *Organizational Dynamics*, *32*(3), 309–318. doi:10.1016/S0090-2616(03)00028-7.

Locke, E. A. (1982). Relation of goal level to performance with a short work period and multiple goal levels. *Journal of Applied Psychology*, *67*(4), 512–514. doi:10.1037/0021-9010.67.4.512.

Locke, E. A., & Latham, G. P. (1990). *A theory of goal setting and task performance*. Englewood Cliffs, NJ: Prentice Hall.

Locke, E. A., & Latham, G. P. (2002). Building a practically useful theory of goal setting and task motivation. *American Psychologist*, *57*(9), 705–717. doi:10.1037/0003-066X.57.9.705.

Maddi, S. R., Matthews, M. D., Kelly, D. R., Villarreal, B., & White, M. (2012). The role of hardiness and grit in performance and retention of USMA cadets. *Military Psychology*, *24*(1), 19–28. doi:10.1080/08995605.2012.639672.

Mann, T., de Ridder, D., & Fujita, K. (2013). Self-regulation of health behavior: Social psychological approaches to goal setting and goal striving. *Health Psychology*, *32*(5), 487–498. doi:10.1037/a0028533.

McKenna, L. (2016, April 21). The ever-tightening job market for Ph.D.s: Why do so many people continue to pursue doctorates? *The Atlantic*. Retrieved from https://www.theatlantic.com/education/archive/2016/04/bad-job-market-phds/479205/.

Metcalfe, J., & Mischel, W. (1999). A hot/cool-system analysis of delay of gratification: Dynamics of willpower. *Psychological Review*, *106*(1), 3–19.

Mischel, W. (2011). Self-control theory. In P. A. M. Van Lange, A. W. Kruglanski, and E. T. Higgins (Eds.), *Handbook of Theories of Social Psychology*, Volume 1. Thousand Oaks, CA: Sage, 1–22.

Mischel, W. (2014). *The marshmallow test: Understanding self-control and how to master it.* New York, NY: Little, Brown, and Company.

Mischel, W., & Ayduk, O. (2004). Willpower in a cognitive-affective processing system: The dynamics of delay of gratification. In R. F. Baumeister & K. D. Vohs (Eds.), *Handbook of self-regulation: Research, theory, and applications* (pp. 99–129). New York, NY: Guilford Press.

Mischel, W., & Ebbesen, E. B. (1970). Attention in delay of gratification. *Journal of Personality and Social Psychology*, *16*(2), 329–337.

Mischel, W., Shoda, Y., & Peake, P. K. (1988). The nature of adolescent competencies predicted by preschool delay of gratification. *Journal of Personality and Social Psychology*, *54*(4), 687–696.

Morisano, D., Hirsh, J. B., Peterson, J. B., Pihl, R. O., & Shore, B. M. (2010). Setting, elaborating, and reflecting on personal goals improves academic performance. *Journal of Applied Psychology*, *95*(2), 255–264. doi:10.1037/a0018478.

Muraven, M., Tice, D. M., & Baumeister, R. F. (1998). Self-control as a limited resource: Regulatory depletion patterns. *Journal of Personality and Social Psychology*, *74*(3), 774–789.

Oettingen, G., & Gollwitzer, P. M. (2007). Goal setting and goal striving. In A. Tesser and N. Schwarz (Eds.), *Intraindividual processes, Volume 1 of the Blackwell Handbook in Social Psychology*. M. Hewstone and M. Brewer (Eds) (pp. 329–347). Oxford: Blackwell.

Olson, J. M., Roese, N. J., & Zanna, M. P. (1996). Expectancies. In E. T. Higgins & A. W. Kruglanski (Eds.), *Social psychology: Handbook of basic principles* (pp. 211–238). New York, NY: Guilford Press.

Rachlin, H., & Green, L. (1972). Commitment, choice, and self-control. *Journal of the Experimental Analysis of Behavior*, *17*(1), 15–22. doi:10.1901/jeab.1972.17-15.

Rubin, R. S. (2002). Will the real SMART goals please stand up? *The Industrial-Organizational Psychologist, 39*(4), 1–2.

Schmeichel, B. J., & Vohs, K. (2009). Self-affirmation and self-control: Affirming core values counteracts ego depletion. *Journal of Personality and Social Psychology, 96*(4), 770–782. doi: 10.1037/a0014635.

Seligman, M. E. (2002). *Authentic happiness.* New York, NY: Free Press.

Seligman, M. E. (2011). *Flourish.* New York, NY: Simon & Schuster.

Shoda, Y., Mischel, W., & Peake, P. K. (1990). Predicting adolescent cognitive and self-regulatory competencies from preschool delay of gratification: Identifying diagnostic conditions. *Developmental Psychology, 26*(6), 978–986. doi:10.1037/0012-1649.26.6.978.

Siegert, R. J., & Taylor, W. J. (2004). Theoretical aspects of goal-setting and motivation in rehabilitation. *Disability and Rehabilitation, 26*(1), 1–8. doi:10.1080/0963 8280410001644932.

Singh, K., & Jha, S. D. (2008). Positive and negative affect, and grit as predictors of happiness and life satisfaction. *Journal of the Indian Academy of Applied Psychology, 34,* 40–45.

Tice, D. M., Baumeister, R. F., Shmueli, D., & Muraven, M. (2007). Restoring the self: Positive affect helps improve self-regulation following ego depletion. *Journal of Experimental Social Psychology, 43*(3), 379–384. doi:10.1016/j.jesp.2006.05.007.

Trope, Y., & Liberman, N. (2010). Construal level theory of psychological distance. *Psychological Review, 117*(2), 440–463. doi:10.1037/a0018963.

Trope, Y., & Liberman, N. (2003). Temporal construal. *Psychological Review, 110*(3), 403–421. doi:10.1037/0033-295X.110.3.403.

Trope, Y., & Liberman, N. (2011). Construal level theory. In *Handbook of Theories of Social Psychology: Volume 1* (pp. 118–134). Thousand Oaks, CA: SAGE Publications Inc. doi: 10.4135/9781446249215.n7.

U.S. Department of Education (2017). Beginning college students who change their majors within 3 years of enrollment. *National Center for Education Statistics Data Point.*

Von Culin, K. R., Tsukayama, E., & Duckworth, A. L. (2014). Unpacking grit: Motivational correlates of perseverance and passion for long-term goals. *Journal of Positive Psychology, 9*(4), 306–312. doi:10.1080/17439760.2014.898320.

Webb, T. L., & Sheeran, P. (2003). Can implementation intentions help to overcome ego-depletion? *Journal of Experimental Social Psychology, 39,* 279–286. doi:10.1016/1031(02)00527-9.

Yeager, D. S., & Dweck, C. S. (2012). Mindsets that promote resilience: When students believe that personal characteristics can be developed. *Educational Psychologist, 47*(4), 302–314. doi:10.1080/00461520.2012.722805.

Zimmerman, B. J., Bandura, A., & Martinez-Pons, M. (1992). Self-motivation and academic attainment: The role of self-efficacy beliefs and personal goal striving. *American Educational Research Journal, 29*(3), 663–676. doi:10.3102/00028312029003663.

Chapter Twelve

"We Get It Done Because We Have To"

Military Spouses with Advanced Degrees, Career and Educational Experiences, and Grit amongst Uncertainty

Leandra Hinojosa Hernández

Over the past decade, my spouse and I have spent *at least* 48 months apart, totaling half of our time together: three years geobacheloring while I completed my doctoral degree, one five-month deployment that occurred immediately after our wedding, and one seven-month deployment that occurred while I wrote my first book (See Hernández & De Los Santos Upton, 2018). This 48-month time frame does not include short trips for educational and development trainings, data collection, and conferences on my end (completed on my dime as a result of my adjunct faculty member status) and countless pre-deployment and post-deployment underway periods on his end. Moreover, during the past decade, we have completed one cross-country permanent change of station (PCS; which is on the low end, compared to other spouses), and I have chosen to be an "unapologetic adjunct" for the foreseeable future because of the difficulties associated with attaining tenure while serving as a military spouse. In the meantime, I have worked on developing my research agenda and publications and also teaching military students and military spouses at National University and Trident University International with pride.

Of course, my experience as a military spouse is not unique, and my sacrifices pale in comparison to other spouses I have been lucky to know during my husband's time in the military. As the chapters in this volume have shown, military spouses with advanced degrees have made countless educational and career sacrifices, often as a result of their affiliation with the military. I am not saying this to victimize military spouses by any means, but rather to highlight how military spouses must constantly negotiate their educational and career choices in the midst of several factors: PCS moves; selecting in-person or online advanced degree programs; out-of-pocket payment for licensing and credentialing; uncertainty about employment in a new city; challenges associated with attaining childcare resources either off or on base;

serving as a single mother or father while a spouse deploys; lack of a support system; making the decision to geobachelor because it serves the interests of family life or career progression; and dropping everything to prepare for an unexpected underway mission period or deployment. Military spouses make these sacrifices and "hold down the fort," so to speak, with grit, pride, and support of their spouses' service.

Jenn and I decided to co-edit this volume together in late 2017 after a few conversations about our roles as FRG Vice President and Ombudsman for our spouses' commands as well as conversations with other military spouses with advanced degrees in certain Facebook groups about career joys and woes, educational experiences, and the process of starting over after a PCS. The echo of shared experiences rippled with each comment about academic perseverance, the delights and hardships associated with serving as a military spouse, and academic/research inquiries and tips, among other topics. As academics, she and I of course looked to scholarly research to find resources to share with other spouses (and also each other); however, we both lamented the lack of academic research on military spouses with advanced degrees and were inspired to contribute to larger academic, public, and government discourses on military spouses and career/educational experiences. As such, my chapter conjoins this volume's topics and chapters by qualitatively analyzing the experiences of 85 military spouses with advanced degrees in career and educational contexts shaped by challenges, barriers, and strategies used to thrive amidst uncertainty.

LITERATURE REVIEW

Although military spouses might comprise a small subset of the larger American population, military families encounter and respond to many of the same issues as civilian families, with added challenges from military-specific experiences (Drummet, Coleman, & Cable, 2003; Rothrauff, Cable, & Coleman, 2004). Overall, in 2018, there were 2.1 military personnel and nearly 2.8 million dependents, which includes spouses, children, and other family members (DMDC, 2018). Research suggests that a little over 50% of active-duty military service members are married (DOD, 2015): 41.3% of service members are married with no children, 34.9% are married with children, and overall, 41.2% of active-duty service members are parents. Of these spouses, 641,639 are spouses of active-duty service members, and 374,621 are spouses of those in the reserves and guard. From an age perspective, military spouses are equally distributed across age ranges, although research suggests that military spouses are more likely to be younger, racial/ethnic minorities, have graduated from high school or have at least some college experience, and have young children at home (Harrell, Lim, Castaneda, & Golinelli, 2004).

The communication and psychology disciplines, among others, have a rich, sustained trajectory of military communication research and scholarship that analyzes military family communication, the relationship between the media and the military, and rhetoric surrounding the military (Louie & Cromer, 2014; Maguire, 2015; Maguire, Heineman-LaFave, & Sahlstein, 2013; Maguire & Wilson, 2013; Parcell & Maguire, 2014a; Parcell & Maguire, 2014b; Parcell & Webb, 2015; Sahlstein, Maguire, & Timmerman, 2009). However, one of the main areas in this sub-field that lacks scholarly attention and inquiry is that of military spouses with advanced graduate degrees, who face unique challenges as they navigate academic and professional spaces while simultaneously experiencing military-related and life circumstances.

Employment

Being a military spouse and a career professional or academic are both challenging independently, but those challenges are magnified immensely when experienced simultaneously. As Harris (2009) has noted, it is a steep price to pay for military spouses to successfully pursue the dual roles of professional and family lives, especially considering that both the military system and family life are greedy institutions (Segal, 1986). By greedy institutions, as was discussed in Chapter 3, both military and professional career contexts require ultimate time and dedication sacrifices, which is amplified for spouses in academic contexts. From a relocation perspective, as Kohen (1984) illustrates, the military based its career structure on the system of service members being single males, due to the fact that World War II and some subsequent conflicts were fought by primarily single men. As a result of this acknowledgment, scholars and practitioners have begun to advocate for a more effective system that considers a balance between military career demands with family needs. Additionally, military life is accompanied by many joys, trials, and tribulations, which are all influenced by the unique constellations of circumstances affecting communication, psychological well-being, and family functioning throughout underway periods, deployment, and family relocation, (Knoblock, Theiss, & Wehrman, 2015; Maguire, 2015; Park, 2011). Each of these factors can complicate the already challenging tasks associated with academic life such as selecting a program (online, face-to-face, or hybrid, depending on one's circumstances); developing relationships with faculty members and crafting a research agenda, portfolio agenda, or selecting an internship or externship program; drafting and defending a thesis or dissertation; applying for academic and nonacademic jobs; obtaining tenure; and sustaining psychological well-being for all members of the family. Military spouses in non-academic professional contexts experience several pressures, associated with first obtaining a position, staying in a position long enough to establish tenure and access to a 401k or retirement plan, developing professional networks, and the ability to start the process again with a pending PCS move.

From an employment perspective, military spouses are less likely to be employed at all and more likely to be underemployed than average civilian spouses (Harrell, Lim, Castaneda, & Golinelli, 2004; Meadows, Griffin, Karney, & Pollak 2016), as is discussed in Chapter 10. They work as many hours as their civilian counterparts, but still earn significantly less for that work. Additionally, military spouses encounter several barriers pertaining to acquiring a position and benefitting from the tenure, networking, and job security advantages from being in a particular career location for more than a few years. Some employers might be hesitant to hire military spouses for fear of rapid mobility (Drummet, Coleman, & Cable, 2003) linked to tied migration (Hisnanick & Little, 2015), the following of one's spouse to different duty stations, as is discussed in Chapter 1. Another barrier experienced is the difficulty of balancing work with parenthood. One-third of the participants in Harrell, Lim, Castaneda, & Golinelli's (2004) study were "reluctantly" out of the workforce because they experienced issues locating a day care; full-time parenting was not their preferred first choice. Two-thirds of the participants in this study felt that being a military spouse negatively affected their work opportunities because of frequent moves, service member absence, and perceptions of "the inflexibility of the military workplace to satisfy family demands and an unwillingness on the part of the military to help accommodate the needs of military parents," with the spouse's military rank playing an important role: "The more senior the service member, the more likely the spouse is to perceive a negative impact, ranging from slightly fewer than half of those married to junior enlisted personnel to more than three quarters of senior officer spouses" (Harrell, Lim, Castaneda, & Golinelli, 2004, p. xxiv).

Education

The U.S. Chamber of Commerce Foundation (2017) notes that more than 34% of military spouses have earned a college degree, and 15% go on to pursue a post-graduate degree. However, research illustrates that similar challenges impact military spouses' career experiences *and* educational experiences, and most of the research focuses on military spouses attaining associate's degrees or bachelor's degrees. Harrell, Lim, Castaneda, & Golinelli's study (2004) shows that military spouses who *do* persevere and complete their degree generally take longer than civilian spouses to complete their bachelor's. Moreover, of over 1,000 military spouses, only one-tenth of the participants felt they benefitted from their military spouse status; 45% felt that their educational experiences suffered negatively as a result of their military spouse status, and 45% perceived no effect on their education (Harrell, Lim, Castaneda, & Golinelli, 2004). While positive educational factors included the perceived financial stability of military life and academic programs available either on or near base, negative educational impacts included the following:

> "Service member absence and military work schedules were the most commonly cited negative factors affecting spouses' educational opportunities, with frequent moves also mentioned as detrimental. The frequent moves delayed completion of degree programs, as spouses struggled to transfer credits and satisfy multiple programs' degree criteria. Further, spouses often faced the choice of either paying higher out-of-state tuition rates or further delaying their studies while they waited for residency status." (Harrell, Lim, Castaneda, & Golinelli, 2004, p. xxv)

Other challenges associated with military spouses and education, in addition to cost and work hours, included family responsibilities, transportation problems, and inconvenient school hours (Friedman, Miller, & Evans, 2015). At the associate's degree, occupational certificate, and licensing level, the MyCAA program has been cited as an educational benefit, as it is an educational financial assistance program that provides up to $4,000 in tuition and examination assistance to qualified military spouses. It also provides employment readiness counseling and other career services. However, its limitations include the following: 1) only spouses of service members on active duty in pay grades E-1 to E-5, W-1 to W-2, and O-1 to O-2 are eligible; 2) only 18% of eligible spouses used the MyCAA program at the time this study was conducted, and 54% of spouses mentioned they were unaware of the program; and 3) spouses who were aware of the program reported not using it because of time constraints (Friedman, Miller, & Evans, 2015).

Thus, given these career and educational challenges faced by military spouses, this chapter was guided by the following questions:

1. What barriers or issues do military spouses with advanced degrees face in educational contexts?
2. What barriers or issues do military spouses with advanced degrees face with advanced degrees in career contexts?
3. What strategies or factors facilitate the successful experiences of military spouses with advanced degrees in educational and career contexts?

To answer these research questions, a qualitative analysis was conducted of 85 interviews with military spouses.

Method

Qualitative methods allow researchers to explore human understanding and lived experience. As such, it is a particularly useful method to understand the nuances and negotiations that spouses experience in their everyday lives as they navigate military, academic, and career contexts. Qualitative methods can also help unpack the processes contextualizing military spouse experiences and explore what "really" is going on when military spouses with advanced degrees try to make sense of their career and educational aspirations alongside military spouse employment requirements (Britten, 2011). Moreover, qualitative research is a useful tool for understanding societal issues that arise from cultural contexts (Covarrubias, 2002; Kreuter & McClure, 2004; Tracy, 2013), "cultural" contexts in this case referring particularly to the intersection of academic, military, and occupational cultures for military spouses with advanced degrees. In order to understand the participants' emergent and collaborative social realities, after receiving IRB approval, I conducted semi-structured, in-depth interviews with 85 military spouses who have at least one advanced degree *or* who are in the process of completing an advanced degree. In-depth interviews allowed me the ability to explore participants' views of reality (Reinharz, 1992), elicit the language used by participants to describe their experiences, garner their stories and explanations, and perhaps lead to new phenomena that were not previously considered (Lindlof & Taylor, 2010). Interviews lasted 45 minutes to an hour on average and asked general questions about educational experiences, career experiences, and work-life balance. As an insider in the research study—a military spouse and academic—I was able to relate to several of the participants' experiences, which contributed positively to rapport and the interviewer-interviewee relationship.

Participants were recruited through two Facebook groups (with administrator approval) designed for military spouses with advanced degrees. I posted my recruitment message on the discussion board for both groups and was joyed to see the overwhelming military spouse support of and response to this study and the overall book project. The breakdown of military spouse demographics and educational levels is located on the next page.

I conducted a thematic analysis to explore the various themes, categories, and codes that emerged from the data and from my participants' experiences (Lindlof & Taylor, 2010). According to Boyatzis (1998), thematic analysis is, in its most basic sense, a way of seeing. More specifically, Braun and Clarke (2006) claim it is "a method for identifying, analyzing and reporting patterns (themes) within data" (p. 79). Thus, I created categories and a coding scheme based on patterns, similarities, and notable exceptions in the data (Lindlof & Taylor, 2010). I first identified categories pertaining to educational experi-

Table 12.1. Participant Demographic Information

Age	Ages 20–25: 2
	Ages 26–30: 15
	Ages 31–35: 30
	Ages 36–40: 15
	Ages 41–45: 8
	Ages 51–55: 2
	Ages 56+: 1
Gender	Women: 81
	Men: 4
Racial/Ethnic Identification	White: 62
	Hispanic/Latino: 7
	Black/African-American: 10
	Asian-American: 2
	Mixed: 4
Education	Master's degree: 38
	Doctorate: 36
	Doctoral Candidate: 8
	Graduate student: 3
Number of Children	No children: 29
	1–2 children: 36
	3+ children: 20
Military Spouse Branch Affiliation	Army: 30
	Navy: 26
	Coast Guard: 5
	Air Force: 6
	Army National Guard: 3
	Air National Guard: 1

ences, career experiences, and work-life balance, focusing on the words, phrases, and sentences pertaining to categories such as "educational attainment" or "military disadvantages," for example; once the initial categories were created, they were later collapsed into more refined codes. Data analysis revealed four main themes and their associated codes: educational barriers, educational positive outcomes, career barriers, and career positive outcomes. I also engaged in member checking and reflecting (Tracy, 2010) with a smaller subset of participants where participants and I discussed the study's findings. Participants were able to reflect upon the themes and collaborate in the research process by exploring how the findings lined up with their experiences. All participant experiences and quotations utilized in the next section are referred to with pseudonyms to protect participants' identities.

THE ADVANTAGES AND DISADVANTAGES OF MILITARY LIFE

Educational Barriers and Positive Outcomes: "A Double-Edged Sword"

The first two themes, educational barriers and positive outcomes, highlights the negative and positive educational experiences military spouses faced while pursuing their advanced degrees and navigating the terrain of military spousehood including PCSs, deployments, and un/supportive thesis and dissertation committee members. This theme can be summarized best by Stephanie's comment expressed during her recounting of her master's degree trajectory: "What seemed very linear was redefined by marrying into the service. Here's my path, here's a road block, here's a curve, and you just have to be flexible."

Relocation Barriers

The first major barrier to timely educational attainment was the extension of a degree due to service members' job demands like deployments and relocation to live with one's spouse.

Elizabeth, a spouse with a master's degree in human resources, described the pressures she felt to complete her master's degree in one year (instead of two) so that she could PCS with her spouse to another state so they could live together. Michelle, a spouse who has a Ph.D. in English, mentioned that the completion of her doctorate degree "took much longer than expected" because she moved to live with her spouse when he relocated out of the country. She attributes this to the fact that she had to look for work in a new country and accustom herself to a new country's culture and norms while completing her dissertation from afar. However, she credits the successful completion of her degree to her graduate director who "helped keep [her] connected" and support from her writing groups. Similarly, Amanda, who has a doctorate in audiology, had to prolong her thesis for a year—as well as her externship and graduation dates—because she and her husband were relocated overseas. Stephanie's educational goals were also postponed because of military relocation. She wanted to pursue a master's degree in psychology but could not locate any programs near where she and her family were first stationed: "Then we PCSd, deadlines for another degree program passed, and I had my first child." She eventually earned a master's degree in health-care leadership at her husband's next duty station. In a doctoral context, Rebecca, a doctoral student, said the military impacted her education "severely": "I had to wait to first start my PhD because we were never in a place long enough for me to get a PhD, and I wasn't willing to separate my family." Elizabeth, who has a doctorate in communication, expressed the same issues when trying to select a doctoral program, noting that being a military spouse was an "extreme hindrance" for her Ph.D. Rachel, who has a doctor of nurse practitioner degree, mentioned that the military base locations provided limited options for school choices. As the examples illustrate, the experiences for this particular subset of participants became more daunting as the degrees progressed, indicating that perhaps working toward a doctorate is more challenging than working toward a master's degree amidst military relocation requirements.

Sarah, a spouse with a master's degree in social work, was one of many participants to describe her education as a "double-edged" sword. She stated that her education experiences were challenging and less than ideal: "It was disruptive and directive. Where I started my degree wasn't where I wanted. [The military] directed my degree, and I had to adjust accordingly. However, every time we moved, we developed new communities and support groups." Susan, a doctoral candidate in Francophone studies, discussed the "double-edged sword" of military spouse life when she said, "Being in a military family has freed me from the stresses of being an academic and a breadwinner, but PCSing away from my school and program has taken away from my school resources." Erica, a doctoral candidate in a traditional face-to-face communication doctoral program, also discussed the "double-edged sword" of being a military spouse pursuing a Ph.D.: on the one hand, she was able to work on her dissertation both in the United States and in Japan while she PCSd with her spouse; however, after discussing the intersection of her career goals with her advisers' wishes in the interview, she stated that the military "limits options, affects family life, and it's hard because it makes me feel like I'm not in control of my own path or future."

As a result of being transferred overseas, Leslie, a spouse with a doctorate in teacher leadership, had to leave in the middle of her doctorate program. Discussing military life relocations and work-life balance amidst deployments, she said, "I went through my whole PhD knowing I might not finish, and I had to be okay with that. Living overseas made getting my dissertation topic approved difficult, and I had to jump through several extra hoops for my data collection." Conversations about her doctoral program with her husband resulted in the overarching conclusion, "I can walk away from everything as a military spouse and I'll walk away from my PhD if I have to. Geobaching was non-negotiable; it was never an option." Similarly, Steven, who has a doctorate in psychology, stated that being a military spouse left him few options: "I was very locked in when choosing my program. I had to go to a particular university because we didn't want to geobach. We had to plan everything based upon where she would get stationed."

Work-Life Balance Barriers

For other spouses, similar to Leslie's experience, the educational barriers pertained to balancing work expectations, school expectations, and home life. Alondra, a spouse with a master's degree in conflict training, mentioned that she "couldn't keep up" with her online bachelor's and master's degrees because work-life balance proved to be a challenge: "My relationships suffered, managing time was difficult, and I neglected my family and friends. I had to be the single mom running the home while my husband was deployed, and I couldn't keep going. There was no more gas in the tank." She later stated that she realized she needed to ask for help, which was both a blessing and a curse: "I realized I couldn't do it all, and it hurt my pride." Elizabeth, who has a doctorate in communication, expressed similar sentiments:

> "Once I was in my PhD program, it was all me. I was Mom and Dad, and I had to experience and do everything. I had to believe my husband's butt was on the line for some kind of greater good to really keep me going. If it wasn't for me being committed to my program, I would've quit because the realities of being a military spouse set in at that point. It was incredibly difficult."

Positive Outcomes

From a positive standpoint, some spouses credited their decision to pursue a master's degree, a change in degree field, or even a change in their research agenda directly to the military. First, some spouses noted that they are thankful for the military because it gave their education new directions and new goals. Renee, a spouse with a doctorate in communication, reflected upon her educational experiences fondly and credited being a military spouse with her goal of obtaining her doctorate: "If it wasn't for following him, I would've gone down a different road. I would've stopped after my BA. The rest of my life changed from that point on." Similarly, Diana, a spouse with a master's degree in communication, said, "The military changed what I'm doing today. It gave me the chance to be in a location where I could get my master's, and I love teaching college students. It stripped me from prior goals, but it also gave me new ones." Leslie, a spouse with a doctorate in teacher leadership, originally could not find a job when she and her spouse were transferred overseas. She decided to change from education to an international relations program on base, which was a "true parallel to what [my husband] was doing," bringing them together. She later researched military children's education for her doctorate, crediting the military with her new research agenda. As she noted, "[Being a military spouse] changed my focus, my conversation."

In addition to valuing new directions afforded and inspired by the military, other spouses credited the military with introducing them to new support avenues and groups. Lisa, a spouse with a doctorate in health sciences, credited the military as helping her travel to new locations and providing a network with a large research consortium. Melissa, a spouse with a doctorate in sociology, said she was thankful to be a military spouse because her military support community she connected with after moving to live with her husband provided a level of connection she did not feel with her graduate colleagues: "I went from the isolation of grad school to the close friends and camaraderie in the military. I socialized, I researched, I moved to a city with more diversity, and made new connections I didn't have before. The military wasn't detrimental at all. The way I see it, the next adventure is always just around the corner." Thus, participants described the educational benefits and disadvantages of being a military spouse, including opening new doors, locating to more promising or hindering locations, and the stresses of selecting a program amidst potential relocations and deployments. Several of these benefits and disadvantages characterized the next theme, which is career barriers and positive outcomes.

Career Barriers and Positive Outcomes: "Pressing the Reset Button Every Few Years"

Similar to the aforementioned theme, almost all of the participants discussed barriers to attaining and fulfilling their career goals based upon the military lifestyle: PCSing, relocation, licensing and credentialing issues upon moving to a new state, inability to earn tenure or spend sufficient time in a position to earn long-term benefits, and the perception of military spouses as "temporary" employees. According to the Blue Star Families (2016) Military Family Lifestyle Survey, the majority of active-duty military families earns a single income, and military spouse unemployment is still a challenge, despite a desire for employment. Out of the participants in this survey—over 8,300 respondents—48% of military spouses were employed, 29% were not in the labor force, and 21% were unemployed. Moreover, two in three military spouses were unemployed, even though they wanted to work, and mentioned that family commitments, service member job demands, and family childcare were the top reasons for unemployment. These unemployment reasons were among the top reasons mentioned by participants in this study, in addition to being overqualified for positions. As Arlene, a spouse with an MBA, stated, "The military had total control over my career progression. His career superseded mine, so I had to adopt the motto, 'I just have to get in and fit in.'

His career is linear, and mine is like the stock market—up and down, up and down."

Relocation, Job Regression, and Underemployment

First, several spouses discussed their dissatisfaction with job regression and underemployment resulting from frequent relocations and employer perceptions, with several spouses referring to this as "starting at the bottom of the totem pole." Amy, a small business owner, reflected upon earlier milestones in her career and said, "It's a lot of getting a job, quitting, getting a job, and then quitting. It's all about the moving and the uncertainty." Cynthia, a spouse with a master's degree in physical education, said, "Every time we move, we have to cut our connections and rebuild every time we're in a new place. I don't blame employers for being hesitant to hire us. They probably think, 'We won't have you long enough to invest in you.'" Similarly, Renee, a spouse with a doctorate in communication, said, "Employers have so many perceptions of us as military spouses. It puts us in a different position: 'Are you going to be around, or are you going to move again? Should I hire you at that point?' I mean, I should technically be earning 30% more at this point but I work as an adjunct and bop around the country instead of staying in one place." Lindsey, a pharmacist, took several lower-paying positions "just to get a job" and was working part-time at the time the interview was conducted because she was unable to get a full-time pharmacy position in the city of their new duty station: "I was taken out of my management position when we moved, my salary decreased, and then my licensing costs increased. I was very discouraged." Bernadette, a practicing lawyer, expressed similar sentiments when she said:

> "It's just disheartening. I regret going to law school. With my salary, I'm always starting at the bottom every time, especially with my licensing. It's hard to find a job at all, and most of us just take whatever is available. I've had to put my interests and goals to the wayside. I even took a $20,000 pay cut when we moved just so I could have some kind of a job."

Donna, a spouse with a master's in forensic psychology, noted during her interview that she experienced "unbelievable difficulty when I followed my husband around," and after a few years she "still hasn't been able to make it work." She expressed similar sentiments as Bernadette when she said, "Starting over is soul-crushing. Why did I even get an advanced degree in the first place if I can't find work when we move?"

Academic Underemployment

For military spouses who are academics in pursuit of tenure-track jobs, the relationship between relocations and lack of tenure was particularly salient and demotivating. Rebecca, a doctoral candidate and educator, said, "I take thousands and thousands in pay cuts every time we move. If it wasn't for the military, I would've never left my initial position. Every time we move, I lose out on FMLA, sick time, and everything else." Similarly, Amanda, who has a doctorate in audiology, discussed her struggles in attaining a position when she and her spouse moved overseas: "The military rhetoric for military spouse employment doesn't really equal to follow through. I always have to start at the bottom of the totem pole, and there's no sick leave or protections because we're temporary. Is it worth it to do licensing and fees when I'll only be here for a short time?" After completing her doctorate, Michelle could not attain a tenure-track academic position due to several relocations and is adjuncting at a few different online programs "just to make my ends meet." Elizabeth, who has a doctorate in communication, also discussed the stressors of attaining tenure, stating, "Being a military spouse negatively impacted my ability to get a tenure-track job. I was stuck in adjunct hell for so long. I have to pay for everything out of pocket because there's no adjunct support for conferences and research, and it's demotivating." Eileen, a spouse with a doctorate in industrial and organizational psychology, mentioned, "Being a military spouse has affected my career in every single way. I work four part-time jobs, none of which have anything to do with each other. I am still regularly applying for jobs." Reflecting upon how she has moved four times in two years, Jennifer, who has a master's degree in public administration and criminal justice, said "The military stopped my career progression." Heidi, a doctoral candidate in biological sciences, also said, "Moving so much will damage my earning potential with a significant pay cut. It has harmed my career progress as a scientist because I might never be able to have my own lab." Finally, Shantel, a doctoral candidate in administrative leadership, said, "It's been a long and exhausting journey. We have so much experience but can't move up. The military has impacted my momentum upward. It's up, down, up, down. It's a strain because you get tired of it."

Dissatisfaction with Military Career Services

Second, several spouses noted that there is a discrepancy between military career services offered and military spouses with advanced degrees as a target population. Jennifer, who has a master's degree in public administration and criminal justice, utilized career services offered on base and said they are better suited for entry-level spouses: "It's as if we don't exist. The hiring office took too long to offer jobs, but then my position was an entry-level position and told me I was too advanced for the job. There was nothing specifically for us who have at least a bachelor's degree." Dawn, a finance executive, said, "The preferred placement program is absolute garbage. Also, resume services on base weren't great either. They aren't certified and not suitable for military spouses with advanced degrees." Estella, a spouse with a doctorate in health-care administration, was dissatisfied with services offered by different military non-profit organizations because they were "only geared toward entry-level spouses"; she was also dissatisfied with base services for similar reasons: "They looked at my CV and didn't know what to do with me. They told me I was over-qualified for everything they had to offer." Gloria, a spouse with a master's degree in social work, said, "The organizations on base don't know how to deal with someone whose experience exceeds their own. It was awkward because they didn't really know how to help me." Thus, in terms of career experiences, participants identified a web of factors impacting their goals and hireability, including relocation, inability to earn tenure, starting over in a new location, and perceptions of military spouses as employees. However, some spouses reframed these barriers positively to locate new career opportunities and, in certain cases, create their own opportunities.

Positive Career Outcomes

Several participants used their experiences as military spouses to work with military-affiliated organizations or create their own small businesses for more job security. Leanne, a spouse with an MBA, works in higher education with faculty members and students. She attributed her passion to working with military students and hiring military spouses to her experiences as a spouse herself: "It has made me advocate to hire more military spouses in our department." Ramona, a spouse with a master's degree in teaching, and Esther, a spouse with a master's in counseling psychology, both now work in a military research setting and use their experiences to research and advocate for families transitioning out of the military. Gloria, a spouse with a master's degree in social work, works with military family therapy: "Here, being a military spouse has worked in my favor, and I'm really passionate about working with military families." Arlene, a spouse with an MBA, bridges both of these contexts because she started her own business and also advocates for military spouses in her human resources position: "You've got to reinvent yourself and diversify yourself to be more employable. I started my own business, and I also advocate for military spouses in human resources." Caroline, a spouse with a doctorate in political science, initially planned to pursue a tenure-track career in academia. However, upon realizing that this might be a challenging endeavor, she decided to create a business that coaches graduate students: "I needed a job that keeps going, despite the uncertainty. What kind of portable career could I do to take with me? I needed something that could handle all of the transitions." Amy, a board-certified behavior analyst, started an educational advocate business to work with students and ensure they get the educational services they need. Melissa, a spouse with a doctorate in sociology, utilized her research experience and skills to start her own research consulting company: "I might have never started a business if I wasn't a military spouse. I created a business, my own business, and I created my stability, even if it's not always going to be stable." Thus, similar to the educational experiences theme, several military spouses positively reframed their positionality as military spouses to positively influence their career decisions and experiences, even if their current positions do not alight with their original career goals.

DISCUSSION: MILITARY SPOUSES AND GRIT AMONG UNCERTAINTY

Military families are assets to national defense, local communities, and employers. As Blue Star Families (2016) illustrates, military families are "central to the health and capability of the All-Volunteer Force and are good neighbors actively engaged in making their civilian communities great places to live. Service members may be employed by their respective services, but they work for all Americans—and so do their families" (p. 6). With this recognition of the importance of military families, researchers and organizations have started to interrogate factors affecting military spouse satisfaction, as this is one of the key factors in shaping service member retention rates. The Blue Star Families (2016) Military Family Lifestyle Survey found that "extended family separations, frequent moves, and outdated expectations that military spouses sublimate their personal, professional, and familial priorities to support their service member's military service are the most prevalent topics identified as substantially reducing the quality of life and attractiveness of martial service" (p. 6). The sublimation of professional priorities in educational and career contexts served as the focus of this chapter, and the findings support earlier research on military spouse dis/satisfaction with their educational and career pursuits.

Along with the other chapters in this volume, this is one of the first studies to explore the factors shaping military spouses' pursuit of advanced degrees and the barriers they face when pursuing employment. Perhaps unsurprisingly, military spouses with advanced degrees face several of the same barriers that military spouses without advanced degrees face in educational and career contexts. As research illustrates, frequent relocation might be the single greatest contributing factor to spouses' in/ability to maintain a career (Castaneda & Harrell, 2008; Cooke & Speirs, 2005; Hosek, Asch, Fair, Martin, & Mattock, 2002; Lim & Golinelli, 2006; Lim, Golinelli, & Cho, 2007; Lim & Schulker, 2010), and the same is true in this chapter. Relocating to live with one's spouse impacted spouses' institutional selection, program selection (both discipline and method of program offered [face-to-face, online, or hybrid]), and ability to complete degree programs. Moreover, frequent relocation impacted spousal licensing and certification, with several spouses airing grievances about the personal cost of licensing with no assistance from the government. Frequent relocation also impacted spouses' employment, unemployment, and underemployment; employers' perceptions of spouses' hireability; and tenure and promotion. However, alongside these barriers, spouses showed their resilience by employing one principal strategy: positively reframing their experiences and contexts to work in their favor. For example, participants utilized their experiences as military spouses to inspire new research agendas, inspire new employment opportunities with military family advocacy at the heart of their efforts, and even use career barriers to inspire their entrepreneurial spirits and skills. This is indicative of what Belding refers to in Chapter 11 as grit, or the unique personality component associated with motivation and goal pursuits. As she discusses, grit is long-term stamina or endurance in pursuing one's goals; as such, individuals with grit are more likely to complete goals in spite of obstacles, and grit is positively associated with successful academic pursuits and employment and relationship quality.

For this particular group of participants, grit was an unspoken outcome of being a military spouse; some participants even mentioned that spouses "need to have the determination" in order to succeed in their relationships, educational goals, and careers because "being a military spouse isn't for the faint at heart." When asked about work-life balance, several spouses responded with a variation of "We get it done because we have no other option." Describing relocation, deployments, being single parents when spouses are away, and "holding down the fort" amidst separation and schedules constantly in flux, participants stated that they "get everything done because [we] have to." Alondra said, "We get it done because it's just what we do." Alyssa, a spouse with a master's in public health, said, "The military makes me more mindful of my dedication to my goals and of how I need to carry on. Self-sufficiency is so important for us, and it helps me do everything I need to in order to get things done." When reflecting upon completing her doctorate, working, and taking care of her family amidst several PCSs, Alexandra said:

It's hard, of course, but we make it work because we have to. We'll figure out a way to make it work. We always do. I just want people to understand the new generation of military families. The military can be a bit antiquated. Academic military spouses can be determined and make it happen.

Thus, the unique aspect of the phrase "holding down the fort" in this context is that it is double-sided: it refers to the way in which the homefront is simultaneously framed as a battlefront, one where military spouses fight internal and external educational and career battles against the absence of spouses who are deployed and fighting their own internal and external battles while serving our country.[1] However, inspired by their grit and tenacity, military spouses with advanced degrees utilize different strategies to cope in such contexts, such as positively reframing their experiences and utilizing the military to build new social support groups, resources, and connections.

Limitations & Future Directions

Utilizing qualitative research methods, this chapter has investigated the career and education experiences of 85 military spouses with advanced degrees and identified both positive and negative outcomes in career and higher education contexts. In spite of the large population sample size (85 spouses in a qualitative study), there are still limitations that should be addressed. First, this chapter (and the volume as a whole) lacks male spouse perspectives *and* dual military spouse perspectives. While this chapter fulfills this gap in a small manner—with four male spouses and four dual military couples—it is necessary to understand the experiences, challenges, and needs of male spouses with advanced degrees and also dual military couples. In this chapter, the four male spouses' experiences were similar to those of the women spouses, but more research needs to be conducted to identify the needs of this particular population. Second, while this chapter identified themes pertaining to underemployment, unemployment, and underdeveloped resources for military spouses with advanced degrees, further research is needed to understand the economic impact of military spousehood on underemployment, licensing, and credentialing, particularly for spouses in legal, health, medical, and education contexts who need to pay out of pocket for state credentialing and licensing with each PCS move.

As this chapter has explicated, military spouses with advanced degrees experience several joys and challenges in career and education contexts as a result of frequent relocation, deployments, and other military career requirements. A combination of positively reframing perceived military lifestyle constraints with grit and tenacity serve as strategies to help military spouses thrive within and cope amidst the uncertainties of military life. In the volume's conclusion, the volume's contributors will share their advice, support, and encouragement for current and future military spouses who have advanced degree and career goals and aspirations with the main theme: there are challenges, but there are also benefits. Resiliency, perseverance, and creativity is the mantra for success.

NOTE

1. The author would like to thank Dr. Jennifer Belding for her comments on this sentiment.

REFERENCES

Blue Star Families. (2016). Military Family Lifestyle Survey. Retrieved from https://bluestarfam.org/wp-content/uploads/2017/03/ComprehensiveReport-33.pdf.

Boyatzis, R. E. (1998). *Transforming qualitative information: Thematic analysis and code development.* Thousand Oaks, CA: Sage.

Braun, V., & Clarke, V. (2006). Using thematic analysis in psychology. *Qualitative Research in Psychology*, *3*, 77–101.

Britten, N. (2011). Qualitative research on health communication: What can it contribute? *Patient Education and Counseling*, *82*, 384–388.

Castaneda, L. W., & Harrell, M. C. (2008). Military spouse employment: A grounded theory approach to experiences and perceptions. *Armed Forces & Society*, *34*(3), 389–412.

Cooke, T. J., & Speirs, K. (2005). Migration and employment among the civilian spouses of military personnel. *Social Science Quarterly*, *86*(2), 343–355.

Covarrubias, P. O. (2002). *Culture, communication, and cooperation: Interpersonal relations and pronominal address in a Mexican organization.* Lanham, MD: Rowman & Littlefield.

Defense Manpower Data Center (DMDC) (2018). DoD personnel, workforce reports & publications. Retrieved from https://www.dmdc.osd.mil/appj/dwp/dwp_reports.jsp

Department of Defense (DOD) (2015). 2015 demographics: Profile of the military community (Special Report).

Drummet, A. R., Coleman, M., & Cable, S. (2003). Military families under stress: Implications for family life education. *Family relations*, *52*(3), 279–287.

Friedman, E. M., Miller, L. L., & Evans, S. E. (2015). Advancing the Careers of Military Spouses. RAND Corporation.

Harrell, M. C., Lim, N., Castaneda, L. W., & Golinelli, D. (2004). *Working around the military: Challenges to military spouse employment and education.* Santa Monica, CA: RAND National Defense Research Institute.

Harris, G. L. A. (2009). Women, the military, and academe: Navigating the family track in an up or out system. *Administration & Society*, *41*(4), 391–422.

Hernández, L. H., & Upton, S. D. L. S. (2018). *Challenging Reproductive Control and Gendered Violence in the Américas: Intersectionality, Power, and Struggles for Rights*. Lanham: Lexington Books.

Hisnanick, J. J., & Little, R. D. (2015). Honey I love you, but. . . . Investigating the causes of the earnings penalty of being a tied-migrant military spouse. *Armed Forces & Society*, *41*(3), 413–439.

Hosek, J., Asch, B. J., Fair, C. C., Martin, C., & Mattock, M. (2002). *Married to the military: The employment and earnings of military wives compared with those of civilian wives*. RAND Corporation.

Kohen, J. A. (1984). The military career is a family affair. *Journal of Family Issues*, *5*(3), 401–418.

Knoblock, L. K., Theiss J. A., & Wehrman, E. C. (2015). Communication of military couples during deployment: Topic avoidance and relational uncertainty. In E. S. Parcell & L. M. Webb (Eds.), *A communication perspective on the military: Interactions, messages, and discourses* (pp. 39–58). New York: Peter Lang.

Kreuter, M. W., & McClure, S. M. (2004). The role of culture in health communication. *Annual Review of Public Health*, *25*, 439–455.

Lim, N., & Golinelli, D. (2006). *Monitoring employment conditions of military spouses* (Vol. 324). RAND Corporation.

Lim, N., Golinelli, D., & Cho, M. (2007). *"Working Around the Military" Revisited: Spouse Employment in the 2000 Census Data* (Vol. 566). RAND Corporation.

Lim, N., & Schulker, D. (2010). *Measuring underemployment among military spouses*. RAND Corporation.

Lindlof, T. R., & Taylor, B. C. (2010). *Qualitative communication research methods*. Thousand Oaks, CA: Sage Publications, Inc.

Louie, A. D., & Cromer, L. D. (2014). Parent–child attachment during the deployment cycle: Impact on reintegration parenting stress. *Professional Psychology: Research and Practice*, *45*(6), 496.

Maguire, K. C. (2015). Military family communication: A review and synthesis of the research related to wartime deployment. In E. S. Parcell & L. M. Webb (Eds.), *A communication perspective on the military: Interactions, messages, and discourses* (pp. 19–38). New York: Peter Lang.

Maguire, K. C., Heinemann-LaFave, D., & Sahlstein, E. (2013). "To be so connected, yet not at all": Relational presence, absence, and maintenance in the context of a wartime deployment. *Western Journal of Communication*, *77*(3), 249–271.

Maguire, K. C., & Wilson, S. R. (2013). Introduction to the special section on communication and wartime deployment. *Health communication*, *28*(8), 749–753.

Meadows, S. O., Griffin, B. A., Karney, B. R., & Pollak, J. (2016). Employment gaps between military spouses and matched civilians. *Armed Forces & Society*, *42*(3), 542–561.

Parcell, E. S., & Maguire, K. C. (2014a). Turning points and trajectories in military deployment. *Journal of Family Communication*, *14*(2), 129–148.

Parcell, E. S., & Maguire, K. C. (2014b). Comfort, cliques, and clashes: Family readiness groups as dilemmatic sites of relating during wartime. *Journal of Social and Personal Relationships*, *31*(4), 497–515.

Parcell, E. S., & Webb, L. M. (2015). *A communication perspective on the military: Interactions, messages, and discourses* (Eds.). New York: Peter Lang.

Park, N. (2011). Military children and families: strengths and challenges during peace and war. *American Psychologist, 66*(1), 65.

Reinharz, S. (1992). *Feminist methods in social research.* New York, NY: Oxford University Press.

Rothrauff, T., Cable, S. M., & Coleman, M. (2004). All that you can be: Negotiating work and family demands in the military. *Journal of Teaching in Marriage & Family, 4*(1), 1–25.

Sahlstein, E., Maguire, K. C., & Timmerman, L. (2009). Contradictions and praxis contextualized by wartime deployment: Wives' perspectives revealed through relational dialectics. *Communication Monographs, 76*(4), 421–442.

Segal, M. W. (1986). The military and the family as greedy institutions. *Armed Forces & Society, 13*(1), 9–38.

Tracy, S. J. (2010). Qualitative quality: Eight "big-tent" criteria for excellent qualitative research. *Qualitative Inquiry, 16*(10), 837–851.

Tracy, S. J. (2013) *Qualitative research methods: Collecting evidence, crafting analysis, communicating impact.* West Sussex, UK: Wiley-Blackwell.

U.S. Chamber of Commerce Foundation. (2017). *Military spouses in the workplace: Understanding the impact of military spouse employment on military recruitment, retention, and readiness* [Hire our Heroes series]. Retrieved from U.S. Chamber of Commerce Foundation website: www.uschamberfoundation.org/sites.

Conclusion
Advice from the Trenches
Jennifer N. Belding and
Leandra Hinojosa Hernández

Throughout this volume, a collection of military spouses with advanced training and education have presented their thoughts and knowledge on the unique situation and experiences that they have as a function of being highly educated military spouses. The chapters in this volume have articulated the choices that these individuals have made on 1) becoming military spouses, 2) earning an advanced degree, and 3) attaining careers, as well as the challenges they have faced and the strategies they have used to thrive. We hope that this volume shines light on the ways in which military service affects families and serves as a source of support and reassurance for those with lofty educational and career aspirations.

The contributors to this volume are quite diverse. In addition to representing a variety of branches of service, the authors represent a variety of service components, including active duty, reservists, and retirees. While several authors identify as heterosexual, others identify as lesbian, bisexual, and pansexual. The majority of the contributors are American by birth, but several also maintain citizenship in other countries. Three authors are current graduate students, while the remainder have all earned a terminal degree. Furthermore, the authors represent a wide variety of disciplines including communication, psychology, creative writing, law, and others. While some contributors fell in love with their service member prior to dedicating themselves to their chosen fields, others fell in love with their fields first. Several contributors have children, several do not currently have children but hope for them in the future, and several do not desire children at all.

Despite this tremendous diversity, one take home message is clear: being a military spouse with an advanced degree is hard. To be fair, being a military spouse (regardless of educational attainment) is tough. However, it can be uniquely challenging when you have an advanced degree or desire one, as this volume articulates. From the decision to pursue a graduate degree or marry a service member to the transition to civilian life, there are a number of roadblocks and challenges that military spouses have faced. This life is not for everyone. Nonetheless, one of our contributors said it best when she explained, "It is always exciting, and you get to see places around the world and have unique experiences. It's an interesting life to live on the outskirts of two all-encompassing cultures, but you have to make your own little world with your spouse to make it worth it."

KEY THEMES

There Are a Variety of Challenges

While nearly all military spouses understand the struggles that come with employment given permanent changes of station, deployment, and the unpredictability of military life, some elements of service are harder for military spouses with advanced degrees. The struggles to find and maintain meaningful employment and be compensated appropriately are noteworthy, as several of our contributors discussed at great length. Most resources that exist are targeted for entry-level positions and/or obtaining an undergraduate degree and are less helpful for those with advanced degrees.

Beyond employment, there are unique challenges involving the perception of one's own identity as a military spouse. As several of our contributors noted, military spouses with advanced degrees (particularly those working in academia) may be in a position to constantly defend or justify their spouse's occupation to colleagues who are less than supportive. Similarly, it is easy to feel out of place at military family events when you know that you are in the minority. Indeed, military spouses with advanced degrees may often feel unfairly stereotyped in their different social circles. Some of us have felt targeted by stereotypes of being too aloof because we have full-time jobs; others have expressed their concerns that our fellow military spouses judge us because they think we'll look down on them as an unemployed or less formally educated spouse. It can be hard to resolve one's sense of self-identity with that of our service as a military spouse, which can take a toll over time. It can be tough to feel always out of place or feeling like the military always wins and your turn (as the spouse) will never come.

But There Are also Benefits

While being a military spouse comes with a unique number of challenges, it also provides a wealth of benefits that many of our contributors appreciate tremendously. For example, the opportunity to serve one's country, see the world, and experience other cultures (whether they pertain to different regions of the United States or other countries entirely) provides a unique perspective on life that could otherwise be hard to come by. Additionally, military service often comes with benefits, including scholarships (e.g., the GI Bill) and having a stable paycheck for your family. In fact, several of our contributors have described how they were only able to pursue an advanced degree in part because of the financial security offered by their spouse's military service.

Beyond these relatively straightforward and expected benefits, there are other less tangible positive outcomes as well. For example, those of us teaching at institutes of higher education may find it easier to relate and connect with students. There is a natural tendency to build rapport more easily with our veteran or military spouse students, as well as with civilian students from areas of the country that we may have experienced in our time as military spouses. Several of us who are researchers also have articulated how being a military spouse can influence the way we pursue research or other forms of academic investigation. Additionally, those of us who have managed to find gainful employment across duty stations have also amassed a more varied set of knowledge and skills than we would have if we stayed in one place and with one employer throughout our lives.

Unfortunately, Many of Us Are Not Fully Satisfied

While many of our contributors acknowledge that they are happy with their lives and their marriages, we experience cognitive dissonance, which is defined as conflicting thoughts. We are all loved and are in relationships with people we care about very deeply, which is excellent. However, many of us have felt like we've experienced more challenges than we should simply because we fell in love with someone who is or has served in the military. Sometimes, we question whether obtaining an advanced degree was or is worth it. At other times, we question whether being in a relationship with a service member is worth it.

RECOMMENDATIONS

We believe that the experiences and lives of military spouses with advanced degrees can be easier in a few ways. While it is clear that much more research is needed, after consultation with all of our contributors and participants, we offer the following suggestions for the service member (i.e., our spouses), military leaders and support specialists, faculty and staff at higher education institutions, and policy makers. We close with a collection of direct quotations from our contributors to other military spouses who either have or are considering an advanced degree.

Recommendations for Our Spouses

We offer two fundamental suggestions for the service member husbands and wives: provide support and respect. The first suggestion, to provide support, is a suggestion that applies to all service members. Your military service requires us to make sacrifices, so do your best to consider our desires as much as the military allows you to do so. Ask us what we want—in terms of our careers, our lifestyles, and our futures. When possible, include us in the decision to rank upcoming duty stations or to re-enlist versus separate from service. Be open to the possibility of geobaching so that we can finish our degrees and/ or work at a job that we love. But, perhaps more importantly, help us find our support group. It can be very hard to find like-minded spouses, so when you know of one, introduce us! Finally, help us keep the bigger picture in mind. It is easy to be so frustrated by an upcoming move or deployment and forget to remember that our families are tremendously important and easy to undervalue in the world of academia.

The second suggestion, to have respect, is also crucial and involves respecting both our work and us as people. Value feminist ideals and recognize that there should be equality regardless of sex or gender. Many people fail to use appropriate titles for female academics in particular. Several of our contributors have commented throughout this volume how much it means to them when they are appropriately referred to as "Dr. So-and-so" at military events. You are referred to by your rank and you have worked hard to achieve that rank, but so have we. When you introduce us, call us your spouse but also by our appropriate title. Please believe that our careers are just as important as yours, because they are. Similarly, acknowledge the work we do (even when we're unemployed) and attend events with us. We attend the various family events on base, so you should attend events with us on campus when invited. Show interest in the things we know, study, and teach. Learn our terminology, just as we have learned what PCS, CAC, Cover, DEERS, OPSEC, PERSEC, and more mean.

Recommendations for Military Leaders and Support Specialists

Many words are often said about the value (both moral and economic) of two incomes for families and the importance of a service member's life at home affecting his or her military career; it is a point worth raising when considering recommendations for military leaders and those who work directly with military families. Although it is easy to understand why military spouses may have limited free time during the evenings due to childcare responsibilities, it is just as understandable that military spouses may have limited time to attend events during the day due to work, particularly if they have an advanced degree. We encourage military communities, under the guidance of military leadership, to build and foster connections with local universities and colleges to facilitate both military spouses' opportunity to earn their degrees as well as achieve gainful employment. Additionally, while there are scholarship opportunities specifically geared toward military spouses, these should be extended above and beyond what may appear as primarily stereotypically feminine careers (e.g., nursing). While portable careers for military spouses are ideal, not all careers and disciplines have this option, yet military spouses should still be able to take advantage of scholarships to earn these degrees if that is their passion.

We also encourage the various Family Support Centers (e.g., the Navy's Fleet and Family Support Center) to continue assessing and improving their current services. While we salute and appreciate the preexisting resources for military families as a whole, it is necessary to recognize that military families are changing and that requires adapting your services. An unfortunately remarkable number of military spouses with advanced degrees have commented that some phrases used in typical seminars or workshops feel exclusionary; cultural awareness and sensitivity training is important. For example, please stay away from phrases such as "keeping busy" when talking about employment as it implies that the spouse is working not out of a genuine desire to do so, but rather to simply pass the time as if they have nothing better to do. While the services provided are often excellent, we encourage you to empirically assess the effectiveness of such resources. Specifically, regarding military spouse employment, we implore you to recognize that military spouses do not only seek entry-level positions. There is a need to expand your services beyond such limitations. Similarly, recognize that the wonderful diversity we have in military spouses requires a plethora of different resources and recommendations. For example, hiring fairs often do not help military spouses with advanced degrees, so don't try to suggest that one as an opportunity unless you know that someone at that event is looking for that specific role. While we highlight these suggestions for improvement, we also implore you to realize that you are the first and most meaningful step in helping military spouses.

Recommendations for Faculty and Staff at Colleges and Universities

Military spouses with advanced degrees only achieve this status by, well, earning an advanced degree at a college or university. When asked to provide feedback for this chapter on recommendations for faculty and staff at institutions of higher education, one of our contributors said the following statement, which could not be truer:

> "If I may address them directly: Take us seriously. Spouses spend a lot of time feeling sidelined and are often conditioned to believe their interests and passions are worth pursuing only when/if it is convenient to the military.... Make space for us. We have much to offer. We have stamina, resiliency, world experience. We have stories; we are teachers and mentors; we are community activists. The single best thing you can do for military spouses is to be flexible and understanding. If a military spouse is preparing to welcome a service member home from deployment and asks to be excused from class, please don't be a curmudgeon and let them! If you recognize that military spouses often have so little control over their lives, you will be able to see how they can overcome any barrier set before them."

There are also several policies that will help. First, create policies that facilitate the transfer of both undergraduate and graduate coursework. While most universities have policies to this end, military spouses may often be unintentionally penalized by harsher requirements. Second, allow courses to be taken out of sequence or simultaneously; doing so may allow a military spouse to complete a degree before a permanent change of station. Third, support and facilitate the development of military-friendly networks for service members, spouses, and veterans. These policy suggestions do not mean that you should hold military spouses to a lower standard than civilian students, but rather that you merely take the time to more fully consider the situation a military spouse faces. Armed with these policies, you can help build a remarkable force of highly educated military spouses who can provide a service to this country more than you know.

Recommendations for Policy Makers

Policy makers are frequently asked to solve the world's problems, and it must be a tough job. While the suggestions we offer here are not new, we wish to communicate once again their importance. As a policy maker, you are in a position to highlight issues that are important to you. We ask you, respectfully, to be a voice on behalf of military spouses. Many policy makers speak to the importance of the military, but the role of a military family is infrequently mentioned. When military families are discussed, it is often with an air of respect and importance, but is ultimately fluff. Instead, we ask you to put your time and energy into truly understanding our plight because by doing so, you will be able to better convey the challenges we face and help change the culture of our country into one of support and acceptance.

Licensing portability is one of the most commonly requested policies lawmakers can enact. Military spouses move with their service members from state to state (and even country to country) at the order of someone they have never met. In many cases, this means that they cannot perform the job that they spent several years learning, preparing, and ultimately getting paid for. The mere process of applying for a license for license-requiring professions (e.g., law, medical care) nearly prohibits a military spouse's opportunities for employment unless luck is involved and the family stays in one place for more than two years at a time. There needs to be better options for military spouses, including fast-tracking licensure applications, waivers for fees, and opportunities to maintain licenses over time even when a non-resident of a given domicile.

Of course, not all military spouses with advanced degrees require licenses and yet they still face employment challenges. We urge you to help facilitate the hiring of military spouses by prohibiting discriminatory hiring processes. We ought to be hired and paid according to our education and experience, even if we have gaps on our résumés. If you can also facilitate telework opportunities, flexible work schedules, and increased childcare, that would be a boon. In short, please solve all of our problems.

FINAL THOUGHTS

As this book prepared to go to print, we asked all of our contributors if they had any final thoughts or words of encouragement they wished to pass along to those who follow us. Rather than paraphrase what our contributors said, we provide a list of direct quotations. We hope these ideas give you courage, faith, and reassurance that you can be successful in this life and that you are not alone. When in doubt, rely on us as your support group.

"Your work is valuable, necessary, and just as important as your spouse's!"

"Breathe and remember it's not you vs. your spouse; it's you vs the military most of the time. My way of coping is workaholism and it seems to work pretty well, so I highly recommend that and working out. You can never publish too much or run too far, right? I would also recommend always working to gain more skills. I always think that the more skills you have, the more useful you can be to a future employer and it feels good to keep learning."

"Do not forget your self-worth and the time you invested in your education. Don't feel guilty for taking the time to go to conferences or other events that will further your career when the opportunities are presented to you. We do so much to help further our spouse's military career that it is more than okay to do the same for our own career."

"The same persistence needed to successfully earn an advanced degree will be needed (and possibly more so) to craft a satisfying career while following your spouse in the military. The degree is just the beginning, not the end. Make the most of your multiple relocations by building a robust professional network everywhere you go—you most assuredly will need to rely on them at future points in your career."

"Network, network, network! You don't know where the next opportunity is."

"If possible, find and regularly network with other military spouses in your degree area. It is relieving to speak with someone that is familiar with your educational background and employment experiences because they have lived it too and completely understand."

"Give your spouse your class schedule, even if they do not ask for it. It will help them navigate your schedule a bit better. Share details of your academic life; they will appreciate how hard you are working. If they understand your academic life, they can celebrate your accomplishments with you, even if they cannot be physically there with you. Show interest in their work life as well, with the understanding that they may not be able to share all of the details of their work. Celebrate their accomplishments and promotions too."

"Know what resources are out and know who to turn to for support; have a relationship agreement with your partner and come up with strategies together to maintain passion in your relationship."

"Each situation is unique; what works for your neighbor may not be the best fit for you."

"Consider your priorities. As a military spouse, I accepted that his career came before mine and my focus would be our family. I admired his service to our country and know he values my contributions. This balance worked well for us. In time, and I knew it would be a lengthy journey, I have been able to begin my career outside of our home."

"Organize according to your goal and stay committed while being flexible."

"I also absolutely recommend being a mentor to another spouse in your advanced degree area, and also obtaining a mentor yourself—no matter how long you've been in your career field."

"Share your story."

"Resiliency, perseverance, and creativity is the mantra for success."

"Don't give up!"

"Thank you for your service."

Index

academic advisors, 8, 23, 45, 132, 134, 139–40, 189, 217, 230
academic community, 3, 7–9, 59, 64–73, 109–24, 134, 154–58
academic culture, 7, 59, 64–70, 94, 99–100, 101–102, 260, 262
adjunct professor, 30–31, 34, 71–72, 122, 239, 250–51
administrators, 8, 22, 120, 139–40
Afghanistan, 25, 47, 88, 90, 91, 92, 94–102, 146, 150, 151
Air Force, 25, 32, 41, 46–47, 50, 59, 130, *245*
ambivalence, 122
anti-colonialism, 88, 93, 104
Army, 3, 4, 5, 15–18, 23, 27–29, 31, 33, 40, 49, 50, 59, 62, 63, 111, 115, 130, 134, 136, 160, 172, 211, 229, *245*
Army Spouse Employment Partnership, 27
autoethnography, 8, 15, 33, 42, *43*, 55, 56, 98, 180–82, 190–91

career barriers, 5, 9, 164–65, 203, 245, 254
career paths, 8, 66, 261
children, 2, 19, 20, 23, 34, 45–48, 52, 113–17, 133, 138, 140, 158, 160, 172, 226–27, 240–41, *245*, 248, 259

civil rights movement, 89
Coast Guard, 59, 130, *245*
communication, 5–8, 59, 70, 73–76, 87–90, 92, 93, 94, 96, 98, 101–104, 121, 126–29, 143, 145, 149, 183–85, 241, 247–48, 250, 251, 259; during deployment, 6, 184; social media, 184
conflict, 70, 73–76, 120, 159, 161, 241
conservative ideology, 60–61, 114
cross-cultural communication, 7–8, 70, 76

deployment, 1–3, 7–8, 38–40, 45, 47, 52–53, 55, 70–71, 76, 88, 91, 92–99, 115, 117, 125, 127, 128, 129, 139, 145–46, 150, 151, 155, 158–59, 167, 170, 172, 179–80, 183–84, 187, 197, 210, 225, 227, 231, 239–41, 246, 247, 249, 254–55, 260, 262, 264
depression, 6, 95, 184, 220
discrimination against LGBT service members, 186–88
dissertation, 17, 26–35, 50, 132, 154, 189, 217, 230, 246–47
dissonance, 115, 126, 261
diversity, 51, 65–67, 87, 92, 118, 191, 208–9, 249, 259, 263

269

employer, 4, 16, 27, 45–47, 72, 132, 166, 170–72, 190, 198, 205–12, 242, 250, 253–54, 261, 265
employment, 1–9, 16, 18, 19, 24, 26–35, 37, 39, 47–55, 72, 115, 125, 136, 160, 163–73, 189–90, 197–213, 224, 226, 229, 232, 239, 241–44, 249–56, 260–66
employment strategies for military spouses, 203–12

faculty, 9, 22, 31, 65–72, 96, 132, 139, 157–58, 239, 241, 252, 262, 264
Family Readiness Group, 23, 29, 73–74, 115, 146
Family Readiness Officer, 113
feminism, 116, 262
financial challenges, 39, 47, 55

gay, lesbian, bisexual, trans, 9, 15, 62, 66, 68, 69, 110, 111, 115–16, 180, 182, 185–88, 191, 259
gender, 4, 8, 15, 63, 70, 73–75, 109, 113–15, 117–18, 179, 181–82, 188–89, 262
gender norms, 60, 62, 64, 68, 74
gender performativity and expression, 73, 117–18, 188
GI Bill, 40, 136, 198, 261
goals, 218–28
greedy institutions, 16, 17, 70, 73, 75–76, 241
grit, 9, 218, 228–32, 239–40, 253–55

hegemony, 65, 120, 191n1
heteronormativity, 109, 112, 115, 120
hippie culture, 89

identity, 7, 9, 17, 62, 87–104, 109–10, 111, 118, 122, 145, 147, 160, 181, 182, 187–89, 203, 221, 260
Ideological State Apparatus, 111–12, 120
information seeking, 125–42

instructors, 8, 65, 68, 122, 128, 134, 138–40, 145
internment camps, 87–104
Interpersonal Process Model of Intimacy, 88, 98–102
intersectionality, 9, 87–88, 104, 111–12, 119, 180, 188, 189
intimacy, 87–104, 180–81, 184–85
isolationism, 60–61
ivory tower, 65, 66, 67

job satisfaction, 5, 27–28, 33–34

keeping busy, 8, 50, 143–61, 263

law, 19, 51, 72, 77, 163–73, 213, 250, 259, 265
licensure, 72, 134, 163–72, 209, 239, 243, 249, 250–51, 254, 255, 265
loneliness, 97, 114–15, 225, 265
love, 9, 44, 95–96, 143–48, 180–81, 184–85, 191, 248, 259, 261–62

Marine Corps, 32, 59, 63, 87, 88, 90–91, 92, 94–96, 109–23 123n2, 130, 164, 186
Marine Corps Ball, 94, 101, 113
marital communication, 7, 59, 95, 121
marriage, 17, 43–49, 50–53, 56, 74–76, 94–95, 111–12, 118, 127, 144, 153, 187–91, 261
military culture, 3, 7, 59–64, 73–76, 94, 95, 191, 260
military leaders, 9, 32, 51, 55, 116, 236–64
military spouse attorneys advice for, 170–73; Bar examination, 166–67; barriers to employment, 163–65; licensing accommodations, 167–70; professional organizations, 166; promotion, 163
military spouse blogs, 159–60
Military Spouse Employment Partnership, 32, 211

military spouse employment support organizations, 199, 210–11
Minority Stress Theory, 180–81, 187
Morale, Welfare, and Recreation, 28
motivation, 5–9, 26, 38–56, 67, 126, 181, 203, 217–33, 239–56
motivation-hygiene theory, 39
multiculturalism, 87, 98

naturalization, 93
Navy, 32, 50, 59, 62, 63, 130, 164, 179, 183, 190, 211, 232, *245*, 263
networking, 17, 24, 29, 121, 129, 134–37, 166, 171–73, 182, 184, 189, 198, 204–9, 213, 242, 249, 264–66

otherness, 89
Outside of the continental United States (OCONUS), 18, 19, 21, 24, 46, 50

patriotism, 60, 87–104
perseverance, 9, 28, 34, 52, 54, 217–33, 240, 256, 267
poetry, 8, 143–61
policy makers, 9, 262, 264
portable fields, 40
post-traumatic stress disorder (PTSD), 3, 89, 95, 96, 151, 160, 179, 184
program logistics, 131–33
Puerto Rico, 46

queer romantic relationships: 179–80, 182, 186–87

racism, 66–67, 109, 120, 158
recruiting, 41, 61–62, 67, 91, 109–23, 205–6
regulations, 8
relationship satisfaction, 3, 59, 75
relocation, 1–4, 7–8, 15–16, 22, 24, 37–41, 47, 55, 70–72, 95, 120, 125, 127, 132–33, 165–69, 198–203, 208–10, 241, 246–54, 260, 266
repressive state apparatus, 111, 120

resilience, 7, 9, 189, 254
respect 29, 41, 51, 60, 64, 67, 87, 94–95, 104, 110, 117, 163, 183, 187, 203, 253, 262, 264–65
résumé, 24, 27, 166, 167, 170, 171, 172, 204, 206, 208, 209, 211, 231–32, 252, 265
retention, 5, 66–67, 198, 253
retirement, 23, 31, 46, 50, 54, 154, 242, 259
role conflict, 16–18, 33, 38, 110

school applications, 18, 20, 146, 154, 165, 217
separations, 1–3, 17, 39, 52, 71, 76, 92, 98, 198, 253–54
September 11, 2001, 90, 92
sexism, 109, 112, 120, 158
sexual assault, 63–64, 68–69
sexual harassment, 62–63, 69, 109
social ostracism (search shame), 62, 69, 89, 117
social psychology, 9, 179–80, 218, 222, 226, 232
social support, 3, 6, 16, 25, 74, 129, 187, 189, 255
stress, 2–3, 6, 9, 17, 76, 95–97, 100, 113, 125–28, 132–36, 146, 151, 179–81, 184, 187–89, 203, 227, 247–51, 260
survey, 1, 6, 9, 27–29, 125, 130, 164, 170, 200–201, 205, 249, 253

teaching, 21–23, 31, 34, 44, 48, 50–51, 71–72, 92, 96, 101, 114, 145, 147, 150, 154, 158, 159, 165, 226, 231, 239, 247, 248, 252, 261, 262, 264
tenure-track, 71–72, 88, 95, 119, 226, 251
theory of human motivation, 39
therapy, 134, 165, 252
thesis, 21–23, 132, 217, 246
tied migration, 4, 7, 8, 16, 17, 19, 26–27, 31, 33–34, 198, 242
Title IX, 68–69

tradition, 15, 22, 64–65, 73, 88, 91, 94, 111, 147, 159–60
transfer credit, 55, 71, 243
transgender individuals, 68, 116, 122, 191
triangular theory of love, 180, 184

uncertainty, 7–8, 68, 76, 125–42, 179, 183, 226, 239–40, 250, 253, 260
Uncertainty Management Theory, 8, 126–27
Uncertainty Reduction Theory (URT), 126
underemployment, 4, 16, 53, 164, 199–202, 250–51, 254–55, 260
unemployment, 4, 16, 19, 40, 47, 72, 125, 164, 198–204, 209, 213, 249, 254–55, 260

Uniform Code of Military Justice, 60–61
United States Military Academy, 20, 229

value of education, 52–53
Vietnam War era, 89–90, 92–93, 104
violence, 59, 60, 63–65, 68–69, 75, 89, 109, 111–12, 146, 153, 159–60
volunteering, 15, 17–19, 23–26, 31, 34, 59, 72, 74, 114, 145, 197, 207, 209, 221, 228, 231

War College, 21, 153
West Point, 26, 30, 229
working with service members, 158–59

About the Editors

Dr. Leandra Hinojosa Hernández (Ph.D., Texas A&M University) is a lecturer in the Jack J. Valenti School of Communication and Center for Mexican-American Studies at the University of Houston and an adjunct faculty member in communication at National University and Trident University International. She utilizes Chicana feminist and qualitative approaches to study Latina/o cultural health experiences, Latina/o journalism/media representations, and Latina/o cultural identities in reproductive justice and gendered violence contexts. Dr. Hernández is the co-author of *Challenging Reproductive Control and Gendered Violence in the Américas: Intersectionality, Power, and Struggles for Rights* (2018, co-authored with Dr. Sarah De Los Santos Upton of UT El Paso) which was the recipient of the 2018 NCA Feminist and Women's Studies Bonnie Ritter Book award. She is also the co-editor of the forthcoming books *This Bridge We Call Communication: Anzaldúan Approaches to Theory, Method, and Praxis* and *Latino/a Communication Studies: Theories, Methods, and Practice,* both forthcoming with Lexington Press. As the co-editor for Lexington Press' book series *Lexington Studies in Health Communication* and Peter Lang's *Cultural Media Studies* book series, she enjoys collaborating with scholars on new and innovative communication research projects. Furthermore, as the Chair for the National Communication Association La Raza Caucus and Latina/o Communication Studies Division, she works to foster the study of Latina/o Communication for students and scholars alike. As a USN spouse, she enjoys working with military families both in and out of the classroom, serving as the USS Comstock FRG Vice President (2016–2018) and also teaching military service members and spouses at the higher-education level.

Dr. Jennifer N. Belding, Ph.D., is an independent scholar who earned her doctorate in social psychology from Ohio State University. While in traditional academic settings, Dr. Belding scientifically studied the interplay of attitudes, persuasion, motivation, and goals. Drawing on her unique perspective that people can be persuaded to achieve their goals, she studied when and how people are receptive to negative feedback, how people are persuaded by themselves or others to achieve goals, and how the strength of one's goals influences their behavior. In nontraditional academic settings, such as being a contractor at a military research command, Dr. Belding has studied issues directly relevant to the health and well-being of our service members, including epidemiological investigations related to blast injury and traumatic brain injury, as well as developing and evaluating interventions to improve leadership, team communication, and clinical practice. Dr. Belding also enjoys teaching when afforded the opportunity to do so and has taught courses on introductory psychology, social psychology, research methodology, social cognition, stereotyping, prejudice, and discrimination, teaching of psychology, and a post-baccalaureate class on the psychological, sociological, and biological foundations of behavior for premedical students.

About the Contributors

Dr. Marcia M. Bouchard holds a Bachelor of Science in Business Management from the University of Maryland University College (UMUC), a Master of Arts in Liberal Studies from Georgetown University and a Doctor of Management from UMUC. In addition to having a 15-year career in banking, Marcia enjoyed many opportunities as a trailing spouse (Army wife), which included teaching and numerous positions as a volunteer community leader. She currently teaches in the Doctor of Management program at UMUC and is a planning commissioner in the Town of Herndon, Virginia, where she resides with her husband Brigadier General Ronald Bouchard (U.S. Army retired).

Catherine "Katie" Cole (M.A., Texas A&M University–Corpus Christi, 2017) is a research associate for the Office of the President & Division of Academic Affairs at Texas A&M University–Corpus Christi. She is a Naval Aviator military spouse and has volunteered in numerous military support organizations. Her research primarily focuses on military family support organizations with an emphasis in military spouse communication. She has previously been published in *Communication Education*.

Henrì Cooper is a skilled and professional educator. Specializing in teaching elementary education, she has been passionate about teaching children from the beginning of her career. She received her Bachelor of Science in Elementary Education from Hampton University and a Master of Arts in Initiatives in Educational Transformation from George Mason University. Currently, Henrì is an educational facilitator at a District of Columbia Public School—Maury Elementary School where she has taught first grade through adult education courses for more than 20 years. Of her 30+ years of teaching, she says: "I love the times when my students get that 'I got it' look in their eyes—the times they have those 'aha!' moments, and then put those realizations into practice. It's a wonderful feeling! Growing up I had some amazing people who nurtured me. Those people ranged from family members to members of my community. A great many of these people were educators, and I so wanted to be 'like' them, but I didn't think I wanted to be a teacher. But I sort of fell into teaching because it was a natural thing to do; it wasn't something forced . . . it just seemed to be what I was called to do. Watching children grow and develop has been a blessing to me." Henrì had a similar experience as a Basic Skills Educational Program instructor (BSEP) in one of her first jobs as a military spouse at Fort Campbell, Kentucky. In assisting Soldiers to obtain that "aha" moment, she used her educational skills to prepare Soldiers to take the ASVAB test and advance their careers. While her family departed active military service after 13 years, she continued supporting in a volunteer capacity. She holds a leadership role with the Washington Teacher's Union and remains an active member of Delta Sigma Theta, Inc., a not-for-profit organization dedicated to public service.

Elise Dixon is a fourth-year doctoral candidate in Writing, Rhetoric and American Cultures at Michigan State University. Constellating queer, feminist, multimodal, and cultural rhetorics as foundations in her scholarship, Elise has focused her inquiries on the composing practices of queer writers, military wives, and writing center consultants and clients. She currently works as an interim assistant director at the Writing Center at MSU, teaches professional writing, and is an InsideTeaching MSU fellow. Elise's husband is a staff sergeant in the United States Marine Corps and has been enlisted for 13 years. They have lived in Washington, Ohio, and Michigan, where Elise's husband has been involved in five different reserve and active-duty units.

Katherine Lee Goyette is an associate attorney at Fendley & Etson, Attorneys at Law, in Clarksville, Tennessee, primarily practicing in the areas of criminal defense, family law, juvenile law, and personal injury. She is a graduate of the University of Kansas School of Law (LL.M. in Elder Law) and Washburn University School of Law (J.D.). Katherine is the president of the Military Spouse JD Network, a military spouse bar association that advocates for military spouse law licensing accommodations nationwide, educates the public about challenges faced by military spouse attorneys and their families, and encourages the hiring and professional development of military spouse attorneys. For more information, please visit www.msjdn.org.

Alissa E. Harrison is the senior vice president for Muse Technologies, an innovative small business that provides client support through change management, capacity building, coaching, and leadership training. With over 30 years of IT and Program Management experience, her expertise includes providing strategic leadership and oversight planning, managing enterprise-wide IT programs, and delivering complex business system solutions in the private and public sectors. Dr. Harrison is an adjunct faculty member in the Graduate School at University of Maryland University College (UMUC) and the School of Business at George Mason University. As an adjunct professor in the UMUC MBA Program, she supported students pursuing graduate degrees with disabilities. She is an author and published researcher and consultant in millennial leadership development. She has published articles on building leadership competencies and the influence of best practices in developing millennial leaders. Her study, "Exploring millennial leadership development: An evidence assessment of information communication technology and reverse mentoring competencies," is published in the *Case Studies in Business and Management*. As a military spouse of a retired senior service member, she is aware of the challenges and continues to volunteer her time by supporting Soldier and Family activities, community programs, and non-profit organizations. She is a lifetime member of the Military Child Education Coalition (MCEC). Dr. Harrison holds a Doctor of Management from the University of Maryland University College, Master of Arts Degree in Administrative Science from the George Washington University, and a Bachelor of Science in Chemistry from Howard University. She also maintains PMP, ITILv3, and coaching certifications.

Georgia K. Jones is an experienced training facilitator, presenter, and online instructor. For nearly a decade, she has been providing training and informational lectures in a wide variety of settings, including: military installations, school districts, government contractor offices, and online as a university adjunct. Georgia has provided training to a variety of audiences in both government and private sector organizations. She has developed and facilitated new-hire onboarding training in her previous role at Military OneSource, and as a contractor for the Air Force Wounded Warrior Program. She has provided program and policy training to U.S. Air Force and Department of Defense senior leaders, commanders, and unit personnel, traveling frequently to various military installations, and tailoring her presentations to specific audiences. In her most recent role as training specialist with the non-profit Military Child Education Coalition, she has facilitated training to educators, counselors, and military personnel in various communities. In addition, Georgia is a certified resilience training assistant, and provides resilience training to Air

Force squadrons and Key Spouse volunteers as requested. In her role as adjunct faculty at the University of Phoenix, she provides online instruction of Organizational Psychology curriculum, and fosters student learning by engaging in meaningful discussion and dialogue.

Lindsey Lee is an independent management consultant, specializing in employee management through indicated evidence-based solutions including employee education and training programs, organizational development strategies, and corporate investigation. Dr. Lee acts as a consulting project manager and curriculum developer, supporting K. Parks Consulting's organizational development services. She also provides expert consultation to the Lynch Service Company, provider of third-party workplace investigation services. For over three years, Dr. Lee was a member of the Department of Labor Employment Workshop Facilitation Team as a career transition trainer. In that role, she trained more than 1,500 transitioning service members in all aspects of conducting a successful job search including job search strategies, networking, résumé preparation, and interviewing skills. Dr. Lee also teaches undergraduate psychology courses and has been published in multiple scholarly journals including the *International Journal of Management and Decision Making* and *The Industrial-Organizational Psychologist*. Dr. Lee earned her Doctor of Philosophy and Master of Science degrees in Industrial/Organizational Psychology from Florida Institute of Technology Melbourne, Florida, and a Master of Arts in Forensic Psychology from University of Denver. She maintains membership in the Society of Industrial Organizational Psychology and the Association of Talent Development.

Annette Maldonado is a leading expert in higher education and workforce development with emphasis in curriculum design. Currently, she distributes her schedule between teaching as an adjunct instructor at George Mason University and consulting in professional development training. In the last 12 years, Mrs. Maldonado has held a variety of positions ranging from financial manager for the Department of Defense to program coordinator in Higher Education. As a volunteer, she is the Chapter Lead for the In Gear Career Networking Group in Washington D.C., Board Member at The Other Side of Service, and previously an active member of the U.S. Special Operations Command Force & Family Readiness Council in Tampa. In January 2017, she became a graduate of V-WISE Phoenix, an entrepreneurship program from Syracuse University. Her formal education includes a Bachelor of Science in Biology from the University of Puerto Rico and a Master's Degree in Business Administration from Wright State University in Dayton, Ohio. Her special interest in curriculum design for the workforce anchors the discrepancies she has witnessed as a military spouse, between higher education and the workforce, which was similar in pattern nationwide. She engages with military spouses and veteran advocacy groups to create guidelines and policies to create jobs and educational opportunities, primarily for the Post-9/11 Veteran Workforce. Annette has been a military spouse for more than 14 years, including six state-side relocations, four deployments, and many changes in careers. Currently stationed in the Washington, D.C., area, Annette lives with her husband, an Active Duty AF Civil Engineer Officer, and their daughter, a very active six-year old with a big imagination.

Amy May is an assistant professor at the University of Alaska, Fairbanks in the Department of Communication and Journalism. She serves as the executive director of the Public Speaking Center and Graduate Student Coordinator. Her research interests are focused primarily on the social construction of parenthood and the motherhood narrative, including the experiences of women who choose alternative paths to parenthood, such as surrogacy. Additionally, she studies academic contrapower harassment, focusing on students who bully professors. In addition to her academic pursuits, Dr. May is a military spouse, proudly serving with her partner of 20 years. Her experiences as the "trailing spouse" have shaped and framed her experiences in the academy, often creating opportunity and conflict.

Victoria McDermott is second-year graduate teaching assistant at the University of Alaska, Fairbanks in the Department of Communication and Journalism. She serves as an instructor of record for the Basic Course, Managing Director of the Public Speaking Center, and Social Media and Marketing Director for the department. She has an interest in gender communication, contrapower harassment within gender dynamics, and family communication, such as eloping. Her research interests also include the communication dynamics impacted by remote locations. Tori is a military spouse of an infantry NCO, who recently relocated from North Carolina to Alaska. She appreciates the challenges and opportunities that arise through her experiences as a military spouse, from eloping to geobatching to living in Alaska. She looks forward to many more years as a supportive military spouse.

Abby E. Murray is a poet, writing instructor, and the editor of *Collateral*, a literary journal publishing work concerned with the impact of violent conflict and military service beyond the combat zone. Her recent poems have appeared in *Prairie Schooner, New Ohio Review, Wrath-Bearing Tree, Rhino*, and other magazines. Her third chapbook, *How to Be Married after Iraq*, was released in 2018. She lives with her daughter and husband (when he isn't deployed or in the field) in Washington State, where she teaches free poetry workshops on post and off, in coffee shops, classrooms, and detention centers.

Michael Sollitto (Ph.D., West Virginia University, 2014) is an assistant professor in the Department of Communication & Media at Texas A&M University–Corpus Christi. His research primarily focuses on organizational assimilation, particularly about the role of workplace relationships in organizational members' entry, metamorphosis, and exit from the organization. He also explores student-student communication in the college classroom. He has published articles in *Communication Education, The International Journal of Business Communication, Communication Reports, Communication Research Reports,* and *Qualitative Research Reports in Communication.*

Karen Tannenbaum is a Ph.D. student and research scientist. She is a project coordinator for several ongoing research studies on interpersonal challenges among active-duty service members and improving team communication on shipboard teams. Her program of research focuses on women's experiences in the military and LGBT issues, including gender expression, identity-behavior discordance, and health outcomes. Her specific interests include clarifying protective and risk factors for suicide behaviors among transgender and gender diverse people with a military history, and understanding current service member perceptions of working alongside women in the military. She has given multiple invited talks on LGBT topics in the military, including issues related to sexual assault, and has experience teaching human sexuality courses to undergraduate audiences.

Beth van Kan is an advocate for student education. She is a certified K–12 library media specialist and is currently the Graham Park Middle School Librarian Media Specialist. Having joined the GPMS staff in 2015, she is delighted to be settled in Virginia. She divides her time by collaborating with colleagues to create cross-curricular lessons to ensure successful student learning of state and county student academic standards, maintain a virtual library web site, and publicizing library events to keep the student community actively engaged. Beth loves serving the students, staff, and parents of the Graham Park Community. Beth hails from the state of Ohio and was married there in 1990. As a military spouse, Beth has had the unique experience of traversing norms for both the enlisted and officer ranks. She and her family have lived in over 13 locations throughout the United States, Europe, and Asia. Like most military spouses, she continues to be an active member of her new community. Beth is an avid volunteer and continues this path since separating from the military in 2008. For example, she is the 2017 president elect of the Prince William County School Librarians' Association and former president of the Zama Community Spouse Association. Her most recent endeavor and position, committee chair for 6th Grade Parent Camp, is a project that she initiated and leads that occupies a majority of her free time. Beth holds a Bachelor of Arts in Political Science and a Masters of Science in School Library Media from McDaniel College. Additionally, she is an active member of the Prince William School Library Association, VA Association of School Librarians, American Association of School Libraries, and the America Library Association.

Precious Yamaguchi is an associate professor in the Communication Department Southern Oregon University. She graduated with her doctorate in Communication Studies from Bowling Green State University's School of Media and Communication Studies with research emphases in critical studies, international communication, intercultural communication, and digital media. Her academic research is interdisciplinary, focusing broadly on issues of culture, identity, generation, social media, technology, and international textile markets. She has received the National Communication Association Top Paper Award for a single-authored paper entitled, "The intergenerational communication of Japanese American female World War II internment camp survivors" in 2008, the Winifred O. Stone Graduate Fund Award for Outstanding Graduate Student in 2009, and was selected for the Top Dissertation Fellowship Research Award at Bowling Green State University for the 2009–2010 academic year. Her recent research, publications, and conference presentations have been focused on cybercultures, social media, electronic music, and hackathons. She has co-authored chapters published in the book *Cyberculture and the Subaltern: Weavings of the Virtual and Real* (edited by Radhika Gajjala, Ph.D.) and in the textbook *Uncensored Relationships and Stories to Build Them By (or not)* (edited by Nicholas Zofell, Ph.D.). Dr. Yamaguchi's single-authored book entitled *The Journeys and Strength of Japanese American Women: Stories and Life Experiences During and After World War II* was published by Rowman and Littlefield/Lexington Books in 2015. Her book focuses on the narratives of Japanese American women who were in World War II internment camps and how they have communicated their life experiences to their future generations.